REACHING YOUR

POWER
POTENTIAL

AUTHORITY ON EARTH AS IT IS IN HEAVEN

GARY & MARIE WIENS

Other books by Gary Wiens:

- *BRIDAL INTERCESSION: Authority in Prayer Through Intimacy with Jesus*
- *SONGS OF A BURNING HEART: Text, Poetry, Music & Art*
- *COME TO PAPA: Encountering the Father Jesus Knew*

REACHING YOUR POWER POTENTIAL: Authority on Earth as It Is in Heaven
Copyright © 2006
BHM Publishing
P.O. Box 481843
Kansas City, Missouri 64148
www.burningheartministries.com

All Scripture quotations are from the New King James Version of the Bible. Copyright © 1979, 1980, 1982, Thomas Nelson Inc., Publisher. Used by permission.

Printed in the United States of America
International Standard Book Number: 0-9786201-2-7

TABLE OF CONTENTS

INTRODUCTION:

A PATHWAY TO POWER

The book you are holding in your hands is about power and authority on earth as it is in heaven. You may wonder, "What in the world does that have to do with me?" We want to tell you that it has everything to do with you—you have a powerful destiny available to you, a future waiting for you of unimaginable proportions. It is an eternal future that will be experienced here on this earth, and it is within your grasp if you will commit yourself to the principles that Jesus gives in the Beatitudes found in Matthew 5:3-12, which are the focus of this book.

Perhaps you have wondered at times what the point of your life is. Sometimes you may think there isn't one, whether you're an executive in a large corporation or a stay-at-home mom trying to figure out if you'll ever again have a meaningful adult conversation. But deep down inside your heart, something tells you that there ought to be more to your life than you're currently experiencing. For some reason, you can't get away from the thought that you should be somebody important, that your influence should matter, and that people should pay attention to what you think and say.

You have these thoughts because God *has* created you for greatness and *has* determined that you should walk in a level of power and authority that is beyond any dream you have had. The yearning you have for a significant destiny is the wooing of God's Spirit; He wants *you* to pursue *Him* and discover the life He desires for you.

That is the focus of this book. We believe that God wants you to reach your power potential, to exercise His authority on earth as it is in heaven, and to learn how to live that way now, in this life. It's a grand theme, an epic story involving a journey with many dangers and pitfalls, and you are one of the main characters. The hero of this story, a man named Jesus Christ, has made the transformation of human beings His main focus in the drama of life. He has chosen you personally as the target of His affection, and He has big dreams for you.

Jesus, in cooperation with His Father, the God of the universe, has determined to share His place of power and authority with human beings who love Him and respond to His initiative in their lives. You are one of those people, and you are as important to Him as any person who has ever lived. Jesus' story is not complete without your complete participation, and He is determined to draw you in.

My wife Marie and I enjoy going to the movies once in a while. We are always on the lookout for a movie that has all the components to touch our hearts in a deep and lasting way. We want to see the underdog win. We want to see redemption for the character who is down and out. We want to see genuine romance, not the lust-filled temporary flings that contemporary entertainment so often portrays. We want to see the unlikely character come to his or her place of destiny, triumph over the odds, and capture the moment. We want to see the good guy get the girl, and we want her to be worthy of his affections. We want to see self-sacrifice and generosity of spirit, qualities of love and truth that draw us to become better people.

These components make up the formula for all the great stories of life. We are captivated by such stories because, down inside, we want to be the kind of people we see in them. If we focus on the feminine side of our personalities, we discover the longing to be beautiful and desirable, to have influence and authority alongside a regal partner, to order life in such a way that people around us are blessed and content. We desire to be worth fighting for, to have the sense of being valued above common things. These longings drive us, and unless we have been severely wounded—or maybe precisely because of various desperate circumstances in our lives—we find in ourselves a deep internal passion to experience them as a reality.

If we focus on the masculine side of our personalities, we discover the desire to be heroic, to be strong and wise, to save the day with some act of valor. We may want the authority to rule and to have the wisdom to rule effectively. We may long to be associated with a compelling leader, one whose bravery and integrity commands our loyalty and commitment. We want to be adventuresome and courageous, encountering danger and yet knowing that at the end of the day all will be well.

It is our firm belief that these longings reside deep within us because God created us to have them. He wants us to fulfill our desires in the context of an intimate relationship with Him as our Father and with His Son, Jesus, as our Bridegroom. God made us for a purpose, and the most amazing reality of life—what Scripture calls the "great mystery"[1]—is that He has determined for human beings to be conformed to the nature and character of Jesus Christ so that they may share in His authority and power for all eternity. In fact, He has even provided the path of spiritual development for us so that we can attain this power. This path is Jesus' Sermon on the Mount, the first and most important section of which is called the Beatitudes. Think of it! God created us for power and greatness, and He revealed the way for us to get there! The truth of what God has in store for those who love Him is outside the realm of intellectual comprehension and can only be accessed by revelation from the Holy Spirit through the Word of God.[2]

Those who believe in Jesus receive the promise of living eternally in an intimate relationship with Him. We will be made fully into His image[3] and will share in His divine nature.[4] We will have the same power and authority that Jesus had as a man walking on the earth[5] and now has as a man living in heaven in the Father's presence and that He will again have on earth when He physically returns to the planet to set up a literal kingdom under the authority of God, His Father.[6] The promises

1 See Ephesians 1:9-10; also 5:32
2 The foundational assumption here is that the Word of God—the Bible—is wholly true and accurate and that by the power of the Holy Spirit we can bring the truth of God's Word into our own experience. To discuss this extensively is beyond the scope of this book, but the trustworthiness of the Bible is the foundation upon which our argument is based.
3 See 1 John 3:1-3
4 See 2 Peter 1:2-4
5 See John 14:12
6 See Matthew 26:64

of God are astonishing, and what boggles our minds even more than *hearing* the promises is to begin to *believe* that they might actually be true. And they are true, because the man Christ Jesus, who rose from the dead, has guaranteed these things. All His promises are good![7]

The purpose of this book is primarily to describe the kind of people that we must become in order to receive these wonderful promises. A certain quality of life, a conformity of character, is essential for us to embrace, because the level of authority that God intends to give us can only be wielded by those whose character matches that of Jesus. Without having the character of Jesus formed in us by cooperating with the Holy Spirit, the weight of the glory and power that God created us to have would crush us. Only Jesus was found worthy to have all the authority in heaven and on earth,[8] and the wonder of His plan is that He intends to share that authority with human beings who agree to be made like Him and who will endure the process of change.[9]

The issue that makes all this seem difficult, if not impossible, is that we must become like Jesus in order to live in His authority. It's a little like telling a 36-handicap golfer that he has to play like Tiger Woods in order to get into heaven. If we have to play like Tiger or else be consigned to hell, then we're in deep trouble! We have no hope of ever playing with that kind of skill and power. If that's the requirement for life in the kingdom of God, we are hopeless.

But let's suppose that a miraculous thing could happen. Let's imagine that a miracle could happen, and Tiger Woods could come by some incomprehensible means to live inside my body. At that moment I would have his strength, his youthfulness, his coordination, his mental capacity, his God-given skill. Suddenly I would have everything it takes to play like Tiger because Tiger was inside me. What a day that would be! The practice range would be fun, because I would have the confidence to work on my game and to play at the highest level possible. Tiger Woods in me, the hope of glory!

That is precisely the reality for those who have given their lives to Jesus Christ. When we acknowledge His Lordship and recognize His right to rule our lives as King of all things, He does an amazing thing.

---

7   See 2 Corinthians 1:20
8   See Revelation 5:8-10
9   See 2 Timothy 2:12

He sends His own Spirit, the Spirit of Truth, the Holy Spirit who is called "the Helper," to live inside of us and give us the very power and authority that Jesus had on earth and still has.[10] We are filled with His strength in what the Scripture calls our "inner man" so that we can experience the deep love that God has for us.[11] Through the Holy Spirit we are given everything we need for life and godliness and are made participants in the divine nature.

We must cooperate with the process, making choices to agree with and to obey the will of God. And when we cooperate, the Holy Spirit releases the power to actually do what God requires of us! That's the reality of God's grace. He gives us the power of the Holy Spirit, which is to have the same depth of relationship with and the same ability Jesus had to obey the Father. Through His power in us, we have what it takes to be like Him, and to the degree that we cooperate with that process, His power and authority will be given to us.

No other way exists to inherit the power and authority you know should be yours. No other pathway exists to reach your power potential. There isn't one way for believers in Jesus and another way for those who choose not to believe in Him. *All* power is His, and His alone, and ultimately only those who follow Him will have any authority. The rest will be under severe and eternal judgment because they refused the One who gave Himself for their redemption and glory.[12]

The attainment of this power comes through a journey into the character of Jesus. This journey is beautifully outlined for us in Jesus' teachings called the Sermon on the Mount, and specifically in the Beatitudes. Although the principles given in the Beatitudes can be found throughout the Scriptures, the Beatitudes, recorded in Matthew 5:3-12, present these principles in the most concise and beautiful fashion. This book leads you down the pathway to power through a study of the Beatitudes, set in the context of the stories of our lives as God has led us.

The beauty of the gospel is that God has fallen in love with us as weak, broken people. It is the most compelling of all love stories, and the wonder is that it is true! The King of heaven and earth is in love with you! No matter where you have come from, no matter how deeply

---

10   See John 14:26; John 16:7-15
11   See Ephesians 3:14-21
12   See Hebrews 12:18-29

broken you have been, Jesus has set His gaze upon you from before the creation of the world, and He knows who you truly are. If you will only trust His love and His ways, He will lead you in the glorious existence that deep inside your heart you know should be yours.

In the next section of this book, Marie will tell you her story, for it is the perfect backdrop to show what Jesus' love can do, if we let it. Our testimony is this: if God will bring Marie and me to a place of authority and power, He will do it for *anyone* who trusts in Him.

After Marie's story, you will be taken into the journey that she and I have both begun and are still on, a journey into the character of Jesus by way of the Beatitudes. At the end of each chapter, we have provided Power Points, questions for discussion and reflection that you may work through individually, or with a study group.

May the Holy Spirit be your guide as you read, and may your heart be strengthened in the knowledge that a glorious future awaits you, a future filled with significance and meaning. You will reach your power potential. God Himself guarantees it.

MARIE'S STORY

The truths we present here were not worked out in the ivory tower of a safe religious setting, but in the cold and stark reality of life. The gift of the Beatitudes was a lifesaver for me, and our prayer is that you will find strength and encouragement through my story. – Marie Wiens

As near as I can remember, my first experience of terror was when I was about four years old. My father began creeping into my bedroom in the early hours of the morning before he left for work. This was my father, who I'd thought I could trust, the one that should have protected and loved me. But I had become terrified of him. This was the beginning of a deep secret I couldn't tell anyone, because I didn't even understand it myself. But even at a very young age, I instinctively knew it was wrong. I remember thinking at this tender age of ways to make my dad go away. I made a judgment that no one could be trusted, and this had a great impact on most of my relationships through life.

My father had opened a world that should not have been opened until adulthood and not until I married. At six years old, though, I did not understand all the feelings that I was experiencing, but I felt they were something to be ashamed of. This was confirmed when my first-grade teacher called my mom to report that I was having great difficulty in class. I didn't understand why I was such a bad child, or why I always seemed to cause trouble, or why there was so much whispering going on in my home.

I thought that I could solve the problem by running away. So at the age of seven I ran away to the plum tree in the backyard. I felt truly alone then, and I never wanted to go back into the house that was full of pain, loneliness, and perversity. Now I know that God knew the plans He had for me, not to harm me but to protect me, and that He had a destiny for my life. It was God who gave me the ability to know intuitively that a father should not be touching his child the way my father was touching me.

When I was nine years old, I couldn't keep this huge secret any longer. My mom, who was pregnant at the time with my sister, was sitting on the sofa in the living room. I walked up to her and said, "Mom, Dad has been coming into my bedroom every morning before he goes to work. He touches me where I don't think he should, and I'm scared." My mom's face turned ashen, and she began to faint, which caused me to be even more frightened.

The next day I was put briskly into the car to go somewhere with my mom and dad. No one told me where we were going, but I knew that something awful was happening. My mom was very sad and upset. All of a sudden, I realized we were pulling into the parking lot of our church, Christ the King Catholic Church, and my parents whisked me into the office of one of the priests. I knew this was very serious, because we had never had a meeting with the senior priest before.

I sat with my mom and dad, and the whole story unraveled. My mother told the priest what I had told her the previous morning. It seemed like we were there for many hours. The priest told me that I had to keep this a secret. He then told my parents that we could not risk a scandal in the church. From that day onward, the secret was buried. The anger and fear in our family grew, and my mother released her anger on me by giving me tongue-lashings and physical beatings.

I began to bury the pain of shame and a root of low self-esteem, which would take years to heal, began to grow in me. Later in my life, God led me to the Beatitudes and took me through His divine transformation that resulted in a new life of freedom. As you read my story you will see how God, through the Beatitudes, revealed to me an eight-step healing program which set me on a path to righteousness and a release of power in my life.

Out On My Own

It was a gloomy, cold day in Minnesota in the fall of 1957, and once again, at the age of fifteen, I decided to run away. I had already made such an attempt at seven and again when I was twelve, that time taking my ten-year-old sister with me. I hated my mom and dad and no longer wanted to live with their mental, emotional, and physical abuse. Because I was the oldest and ran away at such a early age I had witnessed only a few episodes of abuse with my four younger sisters. My sisters have since shared the pain they feel in their hearts of being abandoned by our mother while she was out partying with men and the agonizing destruction of their self-esteem as she screamed at them and called them names. I remember one day very clearly, though, when we came home from school to find that mom had thrown our clothes out the second-story window. They were strewn over the lawn. To this day none of us has a relationship with our mother other than being cordial.

My sisters all have serious medical problems, and two have suffered with depression and anger issues. I am convinced these problems were birthed out of buried inner pain resulting from abuse inflicted by our mother and father. It has only been recently that three out of five sisters have reconciled their differences. Throughout our lives mom and dad kept turmoil going between us girls by telling each of us negative things about the others.

I remember the day I saw one of my sisters run after my mom with a knife because mom was screaming and yelling, making an outrageous demand of her. My sister was acting out the same behavior at a young age as had been modeled to us children. The only way she knew how to express her pain was through angry outbursts. She was a young girl who learned she could control her environment with yelling and demanding her way. This behavior continues today, and she has great difficulty cultivating long-term friendships. As adults, while I was visiting in her home, we were having a discussion in which she and I disagreed. When I did not come around to her way of thinking, she lunged at me and grabbed my arm with such force that it begin to bleed. I have visible scars from that encounter to this day.

During my teenage years my mom was becoming more volatile. I decided to leave home for good, no matter what. At what I thought was the very mature age of fifteen, I went to my girlfriend Sharon's home and told her mom what had been going on in our house for years. Shocked and angry, she invited me to live with them. I accepted the invitation to stay. I discovered that I could go to school, enroll in the work program and graduate in two years.

And so began my new life filled with emptiness and loneliness—but at least I was free from the fear of my mom and dad. The next problem, however, was how to get back into my parents' house to get my clothes which I had left. Fortunately Sharon's mom protected me. She called to tell my mom that I was not coming home and asked her to pack my clothes so that we could drive over and pick them up.

My mom refused to let me have my clothes and said that I was never to come back home. My friends helped me out with a few items of clothing, and the rest I borrowed or purchased with the tiny check I received from my part-time job working in the printing department of a major grocery store corporate headquarters. Each time that I went shopping for clothes I had gone up another size because I was medicating my inner pain with food. As the weight scales went higher and higher, my self-esteem sunk even lower.

With high school graduation just around the corner, everyone was excitedly planning graduation parties and college careers or dreaming of marriage. I had to save every penny so that I could rent my cap and gown. I didn't have to worry about purchasing graduation invitations or announcements though, because there would be no one attending my graduation. My parents had made it clear that they would not be there. I went quietly to the graduation ceremony by myself and came home alone, blanketed in pain. My hard, defensive walls were beginning to build.

I felt that it was time to tell my maternal grandparents about the abuse that had been a family secret for so many years. For most of my childhood years I rarely saw my grandparents. My father's mother had died when I was a baby, and my paternal grandfather was forbidden by my mom to come around because of his inappropriate behavior. My maternal grandparents disliked my father for many reasons, so they disassociated themselves from our family. At the same time, my father isolated us so none of the secrets could be disclosed. For years I felt very sad that my sisters and I never had a relationship with any of our cousins and aunts and uncles. I now realize that in families with secrets, the predator and his or her codependents need to isolate their victims so that nobody finds out the truth and exposes them.

When I graduated from high school and contacted my grandparents, I was hoping that I could live with them. I thought I would find love, peace, and happiness there. I told them everything that had been going on in our family for years. They had never liked my father, and now they had grounds for it. This was just another reason to hate him.

Even though I moved in with my grandparents, I still felt very detached from everyone. Inside I was broken and lost and plotted to run away again in search of peace and happiness. This time I found a coworker I barely knew with whom to escape to San Francisco.

I had an old 1954 Chevrolet that I had purchased, so we packed up the car with everything we owned and set off across the United States with a couple hundred dollars. I soon discovered that the young girl I was traveling with wanted to earn cash for our trip by sleeping with strangers and charging them money. Even though I was a runaway, I was very innocent and naive. I knew that this behavior was wrong and told her if she continued this pursuit I would leave immediately. Looking back now, I can see that God had His hand on me, protecting and guiding me.

When we arrived in San Francisco, we stayed with her brother while we searched for jobs. It was not long before I ran out of money, so my friend and I had no other option but to head back to Minnesota. I was scared to death, because I had no place to go and no job. Approximately two hundred miles short of Reno, my car broke down. A car full of sailors came by and stopped to see if they could help us. Again, God was watching over us. It was very dangerous, even in those days, for two young girls traveling alone to break down in the desert. But the sailors turned out to be nice, and treated us kindly.

They drove us to Reno to a tow company. I was shocked and in despair when I realized that it was going to cost me hundreds of dollars to tow my car all the way from the desert into Reno. I consequently lost everything I had, because I traded my car, along with all my possessions, to the towing company as payment. Since I had no friends that I could turn to for help, my options were now severely limited: I could either beg my parents to help me, or I could live on the streets or in a shelter. It was simply too frightening to do the latter, so I made a collect call to my parents. I dreaded making that call, because I knew I was putting myself at risk again.

As I was speaking to my mom on the phone from Reno, my dad told her to leave me where I was because I was "no damn good anyway." My mom, of course, repeated this statement to me and I believed it because I had heard this from them all my life. She wired me just enough money, however, to take a bus home. Once again, I found myself on my way back to the familiar life of horror and pain.

Now eighteen, I had lost in a short time all the material items that I had accumulated, including my brave confidence that I could make it on my own. Back at home, I slid a dresser in front of my bedroom door every night, fearing that my father would start stalking my bedroom when I was fast asleep. In order not to feel depressed and hopeless, I began to fantasize about a man who would love me and take me away from all of this. I daydreamed of having a baby someday to love me. *Then,* I thought, I would be happy and everything would be okay.

I soon found a job and had to walk a mile to the bus stop every day in below zero temperatures because my parents refused to drive me. Sitting on the bus every day, I began to think more about my fantasy man who would love me and rescue me. We would have a baby, making us a family in every sense of the word. The day arrived when I met the man I had visualized on the bus, although he looked somewhat older.

We had only known each other six months when he married me, and I quickly became pregnant. It was only a couple of months later when my husband, Don, first hit me, breaking my eardrum as he pounded my head. That was the beginning of his abusive pattern of getting drunk, then threatening to kill me. His parents were quite wealthy and owned their own businesses. I thought that because they were affluent and successful they would surely help give me security. However, I had married my husband so quickly and was so naive that I had not asked questions concerning his prior life. I began to make inquiries after we were married. For the first couple of months of our marriage we lived with his brother and his wife. My new sister-in-law began to unravel the life story of the abusive man I had just married. I soon found out that my husband had been married four times previously and had other children from those marriages. He had abandoned them all. His parents had enough of him, and they were not going to take on another daughter-in-law.

In my dysfunctional way, I set about planning to have children whom I could love and who would love me. This, I thought, would bring me happiness and peace, even though I was living with an alcoholic who beat and threatened me. I believed that being a mom would be the answer to finding the love for which I was yearning. I got my wish, doubly so: I found out that I was pregnant with twins.

Early one evening, my husband dropped me off to do some shopping in downtown Minneapolis. He told me that he would pick me up on a specific corner when the stores closed. As it grew dark, I stood on that corner for two hours crying, because I knew that when Don eventually did show up, he would be drunk and violent. I had no money to call anyone, and in any case, I didn't know whom to call or whom to trust because I had no friends. It never occurred to me to call the police or to take refuge somewhere. In fact, it is typical of most victims and people with low self-esteem to rarely call the police or reveal their shameful secrets to others.

When my husband finally showed up, I could tell that he had been drinking for hours, but I felt I had no other choice but to get into the car. I was intimidated by him, I had nowhere else to go, and I was convinced that no one loved me anyway and that this was better than having no one at all. When I protested against his drunkenness, he hit me hard across the face and sped off with me in our new car, slamming into a city bus and smashing the length of the car on my side. He then ran three red lights at high speed, outrunning anyone who attempted to stop us. I was terrified. I thought if I made a fuss I would be thrown out or worse, killed.

It is difficult to comprehend the fear one feels when being controlled by a man who threatens to kill you if you make the wrong move. Abusers become masters at controlling the mind of the victim they have chosen. My low self-esteem fed right into my husband's victimization. He controlled who I saw, the little money I had, where I went, and he questioned everything I did. At twenty-one I never knew whether I would live from one day to another.

As I got closer to giving birth to my twins, my husband for some reason decreased his drinking. I stayed as quiet and docile as I could so as not to irritate him. It was about this time that I contacted his parents to corroborate more and more the shocking information I was finding out about my husband. They said that it was all true; his behavior had never changed, and therefore they wanted nothing to do with helping me or him. They told me that they had no contact with the other grandchildren or estranged wives and had no intention of helping me either. After giving birth I called my sister-in-law, who was married to an executive of a greeting card company, hoping they would help me financially to escape. She said I could come with the twin babies to stay with them in the Midwest for a couple of days. I was terrified, because it was the first time I had flown, and I was alone trying to get three-month-old twins on a plane by myself.

His sister picked me up at the airport and dropped me off at her home. Most of the time I was left alone in their home as they went on with their busy lives. They didn't offer to help me escape and didn't offer to help me financially. My situation seemed completely hopeless as I realized no one was going to help me.

Finally, after another visit to my husband's parents to plead for help, they changed their minds and offered a small amount of cash to help my husband start a cabinet building business at home. I realized I must try to make this marriage work, because if I didn't, the babies and I could end up on the streets and I could lose my children. Moving back home, I made a conscious decision to stay very quiet and unseen as much as possible. I believed that if I behaved a certain way, I could control my circumstances.

My husband was a custom cabinetmaker. He would work for a while and then go on three- or four-day drinking binges. On many of these evenings, I would get a call at approximately 3:00 am from a bar named Mousey's—a strip bar. The folks from Mousey's would tell me that if I didn't come and fetch my husband, they would call the paddy wagon. I would then either call my dad or load the babies in the car and travel miles to the worst area of downtown to pick him up. He would be reeking of alcohol, barely able to walk. Most of the time he could not remember where he had parked his car. All the way home, unless he passed out, he would call me vile names and threaten to kill me. It never occurred to me to leave him at Mousey's. I believed my only option was to get him home so we wouldn't get into trouble.

It may seem strange that during this time I would call on my father of whom I had been frightened all my life. Looking back it is easy to explain. My mom and dad got a divorce when I was twenty. It was a horrible court battle because no-fault divorce did not exist then, and the details of our childhood came out in court. Two of my sisters were involved in the testimony, but I removed myself from that whole process physically and emotionally. After the divorce, in my twisted way of thinking, I began to think that my father was now okay, so I called him on occasion. I had a love-hate relationship with him. I hated him when he used foul language and made crude remarks. On occasion I would visit him at his apartment if I needed something, and I would see pornography everywhere. But I still yearned to have a relationship with my father and to have him love me.

My life came to a major crisis when my husband disappeared for two weeks on a drinking binge. The babies and I had hardly any food in the house, and when I went to the bank to cash a check, I discovered that he had withdrawn everything. A few weeks later I received a phone call from Alcoholics Anonymous in California. They had picked him up on the street, where he had passed out and was mumbling something about having been mugged. He had lost all our money. He had even lost money that the bank had loaned on our receivables. AA said they were sending him home on an airline.

I picked him up at the airport, almost dying of humiliation when I saw him. He was filthy and smelled of alcohol and vomit. I had arranged for him to go to a rehabilitation center before he came home. We only had to get him to walk voluntarily through the door, and then the staff would put him in a strait jacket and lock him behind bars until he dried out. Thankfully, this worked.

After he came out of rehab, we joined a wonderful AA couples group in an upscale part of town. At last I felt we had a chance of turning things around. I hoped that the influence of these people would have some effect on him, because he had grown up in a wealthy home environment.

Six months into the program the president approached me and said that he had been observing my husband's behavior, which showed all the signs that he was soon going to drink again. I was devastated. And sure enough, two weeks later he was drinking again. Only this time he was even more violent when he returned. I was convinced that I was going to die at his hands some day, and indeed I came very close.

Only a few days later I received a call from one of our friends in the middle of the night, saying that I should get out of the house with the babies as soon as I could. Don was on his way home with an ex-convict who had murdered someone and was now on parole. This man was very dangerous. Just as I was getting the babies ready, I heard them come in through the front door. I had no time to call the police. In fact, I had never called the police in my life, because I was afraid of the consequences. The thinking process of a victim of abuse is often nonrational; one simply goes into a reactionary mode, and I had been effectively trained as a child not to tell the secrets for fear of severe punishment.

My husband and this man were both blind drunk. I could clearly hear their slurred words of profanity as they came in. I had no time to leave by the back door, so I lowered the babies out the window and jumped down after them. I ran for our lives, carrying a baby under each arm. I knew I would never again return to that home to gamble with my life and the lives of my children.

That event was so traumatic for me that to this day I cannot remember how I got transportation, money, or food to make my next move into an apartment with the babies. However, one of my sisters reminded me recently that I had called her to care for the twins for a few days while I found a home that would be safe for us. All I can remember is that I found a job at the Pillsbury Company, and they helped me in many ways.

The next few months of my life were a living hell as I tried to hide from my husband. Though I had moved, he found me, and shot at me through the door and stalked me. After being thrown into jail and then let out, he broke into my apartment and stole all my furniture. I felt unimaginable pain when I came home to an empty apartment, with two babies in my arms, wondering how I would ever be able to survive. My life began to spiral further downward from there. My self-esteem was at its lowest, and messages of shame raged in my head. All I could think was, "Who will ever love me? Who will rescue me? Who can I ever trust to not hurt me?"

I knew that I had to find a home in the country where my husband could not find us by an ordinary street address. I hired a lawyer to help me get my furniture back, and at the same time I filed for divorce. I paid the lawyer by giving up my wedding rings in barter for the billing. I moved to the country with my sister and the twins. I felt safe for a while, but soon my estranged husband was calling me at work, making verbal threats. So I determined I must get married again for protection or else we would soon die. I was struggling financially. One day I came home in the middle of the winter and the heat had been turned off. There sat my nanny and the twins, at two years old, on her lap with all of them in winters coats, hats, and mittens. I had to make a change, and fast.

After only a six-month window during which I met a man at work, I married again. I did not love this man, but I desperately needed him in order to stay alive. This time I married a professional man who was an alcoholic and who dabbled in drugs, and I had my third son with this man. After our son was born this man began to verbally abuse my twins. I saw the abuse escalating and knew that I must leave. After only four years of marriage I got another divorce. My destructive pattern was beginning to emerge.

I took my three boys and found an apartment and a new job. My mental condition was deteriorating, and I was desperate to find out what was wrong with me. I was so broken that I was losing my stamina to keep going, though I had to for the sake of my children. At my new job as a payroll manager, I met a very kind man in an executive role and set my goal to marry him. I reasoned that he would never hurt me because he was a gentle man. Without any kind of counseling or rehab, I entered this relationship, and we married a year and a half later. He took me out of a desperate financial situation and was very generous and kind to my three sons. We moved into a beautiful home in an affluent neighborhood, and I thought we would all live happily ever after. My twins were ten at the time, and my youngest son was five. It was soon that I was to realize the negative emotional impact this string of relationships was having on my sons. One of my sons was crying himself to sleep every night, not wanting to live any longer. This caused my guilt to go even deeper, but at least we had the resources to seek counseling for him.

Initial Tastes of Power

My success, as the world defines it, all began in 1980, after a friend and I started a cookie company called Flour Pot Cookies. We each invested seventy-five dollars to start our business out of our homes, baking chocolate chip cookies on a Popsicle stick. We inserted the Popsicle sticks into flower pots to create the effect of cookies blooming from the pots. We sold complete sets to restaurants and delis, who displayed them at their cash registers for sale. The media loved it! We drew the attention of the public and had many subsequent sales.

I lived in Minneapolis at the time, and my big break came when I called on Kemps Marigold Ice Cream Company with six cookie sandwiches in a freezer bag and no appointment. It was a Friday afternoon, and apparently the executives had nothing else to do, so they invited me in to taste our product. It was a God-appointed moment, because they enjoyed the product enough to invite me back. A few weeks later they ordered three million cookies! This infused much-needed capital into the company and gave us recognition with the Minneapolis Star & Tribune. A neighbor introduced me to the local Arby's franchise owner, who asked if we could ship him frozen dough so that the cookies could be baked on site in his stores. Two years later we acquired the national Arby's account, which increased sales by over a million dollars.

After my twins graduated from high school, my husband, my youngest son, and I moved to Iowa. I was traveling almost constantly for my business, and now my youngest son was beginning to unravel. His pain was so deep because of my dysfunction and the move to another state that he began to slip into a depression. Because he was a gifted child, always achieving top-of-his-class status, I became very alarmed when his grades began to slip and he was visibly unhappy. I knew that I had to get help soon.

One day I took a long walk because I was depressed and needed to be alone to figure out what I should do next. As I walked up the hill from my home I remembered that a neighbor I had just recently met had called and asked me to return her call. I decided to stop by Rosemary's home. This beautiful woman answered the door, and I remember thinking that she looked so peaceful and full of joy. Within a very short time of entering her home, something came over me and all the secrets of my life, which I had hidden so carefully, began to come out as Rosemary listened to me. She looked at me with such kind and loving eyes. As I was crying and describing my life, she said, "Honey, there is someone who can help you." I asked who she meant, and she said, "Jesus." She told me how much He loved me and wanted to come into my life and help me. She promised that I would never be alone again if I would give my life to Him. She took me into her bedroom, decorated in a light-blue velvet, and sat me down in front of her fireplace. She gently led me through a prayer of asking the Lord Jesus to forgive me of my sins. I cried like never before, and then something began to happen inside me. I felt a peace come over me and an unexplainable "knowing" that things were about to change in my life.

Rosemary took me to church on Sundays, and for the first time in my life I began to read the Bible. She was a great Bible teacher, and I began to understand what I was reading. A new world was opening up to me as I read the things that God says about me. They were all contrary to what my parents had said. But even as faith began to grow inside my heart, my marriage began to unravel once again.

My life at this time was such a drastic contradiction. On the inside of my home, disaster was looming, while on the outside I was building retail stores around the country and trying to understand the ways of a Christian.

I had a wholesale national distribution division which was growing by leaps and bounds. I began to do food shows around the United States as well as the largest food show in the world in Paris, France. I was putting together franchising agreements with the Arby's Corporation, and selling to many national food chains. My company caught the attention of *Inc. Magazine,* who did an article on its growth.

Within a couple of years we moved from baking cookies on a stick to a frozen cookie and dough manufacturing company generating about 1.5 million dollars in sales. Our manufacturing headquarters were in Minnesota, and my corporate offices were in Iowa. I had it all: a large home on the Country Club, jewelry, travel, and a corporate jet at my disposal to visit the best hotels in the United States. I felt the addictive taste of power and recognition.

Flour Pot Cookies began to double in sales, and in 1984 I became partners with a powerful and wealthy businessman who infused one million dollars of capital into development of the business. This man introduced me to the life of the jet setters and to a world I had never dreamed I would experience. I began a repetitive cycle of compromising my relationship with God, then becoming convicted about not reading the Bible and going to church, then being pulled back into the world of fame and money.

I met President George Bush Sr. on a number of occasions because my business partner was a heavy contributor to the Republican Party. As a result of a connection I made on a business trip, my company began to furnish the Senate and House of Representatives with designer cookie tins whenever they went on recess.

Soon doors opened for me to travel to Europe, Japan, Korea, the Philippines, and many other countries. Money became plentiful. I was really beginning to taste the essence of power and money in greater measure, and I liked the feeling because I could ignore the pain inside. But a conflict was growing inside me. I wanted deeply to be a godly Christian woman, but I was conflicted with the power I felt and how I used it. People came to me and said that I was aggressive, pushy, and materialistic. I sensed that something was wrong, but I didn't know how to change. I did not trust people, and I had made that vow long before to allow no one to hurt me again. That meant not letting people get close me for fear they would see my pain and cause more anguish for me. My secrets went even deeper inside so that no one would ever know the truth about my past. My props of clothing, jewelry, and fast cars served me well, at least for a time.

My husband and I began to fight about the lack of intimacy in our marriage and about my Christianity. He wanted no part of either. My perfectionism and controlling behavior would again rear its ugly head as I tried to keep everything in order. My husband also had very serious issues, which began to surface. We were fighting constantly and moved into a passive-aggressive mode where we never discussed the subjects again. We now had status, a large home, money to travel, and a thriving business; what was I to blame my pain on now? It was becoming more and more evident that I desperately needed help because inside I knew something was very wrong with me. I could produce power through striving, but only if I was aggressive and controlled outward circumstances. My relationships with people were all superficial, and I was desperately lonely.

Steps Toward Healing

One morning I asked myself what was the use of carrying on. I had no inner peace or happiness and nothing to hope for, even though I was financially well off. What was more, I could hardly remember a time when it had ever been different.

✗ My marriage was finally coming to an end. My husband asked for a divorce, telling me that God was my "thing." This was yet another rejection that brought up all the old pain, and I began to realize that God was trying to tell me something that I continually kept anesthetized with recognition and money. Desperate for relief from the additional pain and rejection of my impending divorce, I went to a therapist.

Every week I would open my wounds up for an hour and then leave bleeding, only to live with the pain for another week. I wanted to finally deal with all the pain and abuse from my childhood, so one day I asked my therapist if there was a treatment center to which I could go for a period of time.

A few days later I received a call from her, saying that she had found a place called the Halterman Center in London, Ohio. I was convinced that this was the answer for me, so I arranged to leave for the center two weeks later. At one thousand dollars a day, I thought I was going to a resort of some kind. I packed all kinds of reading material, boarded our company's Citation One airplane, and the pilot set course for London, Ohio. Prior to this, I had notified my three sons of my decision, and by a miracle the Navy allowed my son, Dan, emergency leave. His twin brother Dave left college for a week to join us, and my youngest son flew in from school with my business partner. My mother showed up, as did two of my four sisters. It seemed at last that I would have the support of my family as I began this period of treatment.

I was in for a shock, as God certainly had a plan for my life. In the admitting room of the facility, I suddenly realized that this was not a resort—not even close! I was in a residential wing of a hospital, and the first thing they required of me was to open my suitcase to show them the contents. They confiscated my magazines, books, mouthwash, aspirin, and just about everything else except my Bible and clothing. They then informed me that I had no telephone privileges for ten days (and even after that by permission only), and no TV or radio privileges for my entire thirty-day stay.

The other guests I found myself among in this strange place turned out to be the kinds of people I had always tried to avoid because of my lack of compassion and my capacity for fear. I was among people who were dying of AIDS, or were addicted to drugs and alcohol, or who had turned to the gay lifestyle.

I had previously prayed for a change in my life, and the Lord was beginning to take me very seriously! Romans 8:27-28 says, "Now He who searches the hearts knows what the mind of the Spirit is, because He makes intercession for the saints according to the will of God. And we know that all things work together for good to those who love God, to those who are called according to his purpose."

At this point I felt that God was taking things a little too seriously in working out His purposes! That first evening at the treatment center, I tried to find a way to escape, or so I thought. Scared, I waited for the staff to take me to my room so I could plan my escape. I later realized that I was not locked in, and could have walked out at any time. The Lord Jesus had blinded me to this obvious fact.

Even as the evening wore on and I was introduced to a woman with AIDS, victims of abuse, alcoholics, and drug addicts, it did not occur to me to demand to leave. A force stronger than I was orchestrating this event, right down to that evening when I decided to sneak down the hallway and out into the hospital to make a rule-breaking phone call to my closest friend, Madeline, asking her to send her plane to fetch me. This was the scariest place I had ever known, and I was behaving like I was a child locked in her room!

Madeline answered the phone and asked me to think things over. She said if I still felt the same in the morning, she would come get me. I then called my business partner and asked him to come back with the airplane and pick me up. He said, "Marie, you have never quit anything. Are you going to quit now?" I hung up the phone and committed myself to seeing this thing through.

So I stayed, and my life was turned inside out, never to be the same again. Acts 16:26 applies perfectly to me and my sons: "Suddenly there was a great earthquake, so that the foundations of the prison were shaken [my life]; and immediately all the doors were opened and everyone's chains were loosed." Soon I would realize that the Lord was about to have me live out Matthew 5:3-4: "Blessed are the poor in Spirit, for theirs is the Kingdom of God. Blessed are those who mourn for they shall be comforted."

The first week that I was there I mostly listened to the others in the group and thought, *Wow, they are really messed up because I do not have their problems.* I decided that my issues were really not a big deal and I would just stay quiet and listen and perhaps learn from their experiences.

During the second week the counselors asked me if I had something to say, and I said no. But they cleverly asked me questions that began to reveal my secrets. Before I knew what was happening, I broke down crying and screaming with the pain that I had kept hidden for thirty five years. The Lord took me into *"Blessed are those who mourn for they shall be comforted."*

The following week my children, two of my sisters, and my mother came for the family week, and their pain was revealed to me. We expressed much forgiveness, and my mother and sisters were able to reveal their feelings for the first time in a safe place. It was such a comforting place to have my feelings validated. My mother and I will never be close. I have come to realize that I will never be able to change her response to me and others. However, with the power and authority of the Lord, I was able to accept that my mom is not a stable person, who deals with anger outbursts over which I have no control.

During this time, my sisters and I confronted our mom on her lack of expressing affection and love to us. Her reply was in some ways not shocking. She looked us each in the face and said, "I never liked you and I never wanted you." This should have been dreadfully painful to us, but it wasn't. We had felt this most of our lives by her violent outbursts and her inability to hold us, kiss us, and tell us we were loved. It was a relief to finally hear the truth that we had felt in our hearts.

The counselors were thrilled that this information had been disclosed by our mother, because now they could begin the process of healing from the wounds and our discovery of who God says we are. The Lord had something great in mind and a purpose for our lives when he created us.

(Many years later, my mother and I have an amicable and respectable relationship. I have set clear boundaries and have forgiven her. Jesus now defines me, and my head is no longer bent in the direction of man's definition of who I am. What a place of freedom!)

In the fourth week of treatment, the Lord took me to a place of utter weakness and peace. *"Blessed are the meek for they shall inherit the earth."* I knew that I did not have to fight the battle by myself anymore. The secrets were out, and I was on the road to recovery. My anger had been released, and in its place was put a new realization of who God says I am and how much He loves me. I also realized God is tender and cares about me. God says in Zechariah 2:8 that I am the apple of His eye.

In 1988 I decided to sell my 51 percent of the company to my business partner, and I signed a contract to run the company as president until 1993. The business continued to grow, and so did I—spiritually. God was casting blessings on me from all sides. I discovered that I had the gift of teaching, and God instilled in me a great desire to share with others about His grace and mercies. I was the first in my extended family to become a Christian, and then one of my sisters, seeing such a big change in me, also accepted Christ. Then my sons began to change, and now my grandchildren, a couple of my sisters, and dad are all saved. The Lord was being faithful in bringing my family to Himself, in answer to the prayers I had so often prayed.

A few years later, I was nominated for a national entrepreneur award called Women of Enterprise, sponsored by the Avon Corporation and the Small Business Administration in Washington, D.C. To my surprise, out of hundreds of women nominated, I was chosen. The award was prestigious, and it was presented to me in New York. I appeared as a guest on *Good Morning America* as well as on *The Sally Jesse Raphael Show*. I was also featured in *USA Today, Good Housekeeping,* and many newspapers across the country. During this time I could not stop thinking about how great God is, wondering why I had not discovered His abundance of blessings a long time ago. I had not realized that if I did things God's way, I could have so much fun! In all of this I began to yearn to know the Lord deeper. I was thirsting and hungering for righteousness, although I did not have words for what I was feeling.

During this time I began to recognize the voice of the Lord more clearly through a very painful yet powerful experience, one that would help train me and confirm the voice of God to me. I had been dating my business partner for about a year and a half when we became engaged. In prayer one day, I asked the Lord if this was the man He wanted me to marry. I promised the Lord that if He showed me anything negative and harmful, I would end the relationship within minutes. A couple of days later he was over at my home having dinner. Prior to settling down to watch TV, he took his wallet out of his pocket, and put it on the table beside his chair. He left the room, and I heard a very quiet voice say, "You will find what you need inside his wallet."

I had never searched anyone's purse or wallet without their permission before! Within seconds, however, I was doing exactly that, and I discovered a business card from a woman in Portland, Oregon. It turned out he was having an affair.

I kept my promise to the Lord and ended the engagement within thirty minutes. The following day my assistant called me to tell me not to come to work because my business partner had taken the door off my beautiful office. Bedlam broke out in the office from that day forward.

The new owner of my company informed me that they no longer needed me as president. They offered to pay out my contract until 1993, but they were going to promote someone else to my position. My old business partner's wrath and vengeance was showing, and I know now that God was provoking him in order for me to reach the purpose for which God had created me. God was definitely testing whether my identity was truly in Him and whether I would remain faithful and joyful in spite of the circumstances.

In the fall of 1990, I made the decision to move as far away as I could without falling into the ocean. I had three failed marriages and one failed engagement behind me—all to men who did not know the Lord. I needed to start a new life, because my old one had completely fallen apart. What I needed was a fresh start with the Lord and with new friends—I needed a change of location.

Another Taste of God's Faithfulness

In 1990 I moved from the Midwest to Seattle, Washington, to begin a new life. It was at this point that I took two years off and went to live in the home of a pastor and his wife. They discipled me for seven months, and I grew closer to the Lord in an intimacy that I had never known before. *"Blessed are those who thirst and hunger after righteousness, for they will be filled."*

Two years after moving to Seattle, as I prayed for a new career and possibly another great success, the idea for a bagel bakery/restaurant began to form. I spoke to others about this idea and a prominent quarterback for the Seahawks football team asked to invest in the business. So now I had a business partner with a known name. Then I asked two friends if they would also like to become part of the partnership. We all then began to pray that if God's hand and blessing were on this business, everything would fall into place. I prayed that the lease, the building permit and the Small Business Administration loan would come together at the same time if this business was the Lord's will.

One day, as I sat at home, the phone rang, and it was the bank letting us know that the loan had gone through without a hitch. After I hung up, the contractor called to tell me that the building permit had gone through, and immediately after that the realtor phoned to tell me that the lease had been signed. The Lord answered all our prayers in an orderly, peaceful fashion—a clear sign to me that we should go ahead.

In September 1993, our first bagel restaurant, The Bagel and Chocolate Soup Company, opened in Seattle. It was a huge success, bringing in sales the first year of one million dollars. We had lines going out the door with people waiting to come in for chocolate soup and bagels. We dedicated the business to the Lord and played Christian music throughout the day. It was known as the "Christian hangout." Pastors came and studied and wrote their sermons there, and people learned about Jesus there, including some members of my staff. We had many prayer meetings on the premises and even witnessed a miracle from God when the neighboring landlord and ours got into a dispute over land boundaries. We, too, were dragged into the dispute. If the neighboring landlord won the judgment, we would not be allowed to have any deliveries, and we would no longer have an emergency exit. We would have had to shut the doors because the city would not have allowed us to operate without an emergency exit.

I called a prayer meeting at the restaurant in the evening. I asked my Bible study group as well as two of the elders from our church to come. A friend and I walked around the restaurant seven times, praying, while the others were praying the Scriptures and promises of God inside.

The next day I went to court, and the judge asked us if we could first go into a conference room, to see if we could settle the dispute out of court. I thought, *We have been trying to settle this for weeks already!* But the Lord was faithful in answering our prayers, and that day an agreement was reached that would benefit all the parties.

According to our business plan and because of the persuasion of a mayor from a neighboring city, I started searching out a property for our second bagel restaurant two years after the first one opened. The plan was to build five or six stores, then sell them for a profit. After we had found a suitable location for the second store, we began to pray that if this was God's will then the SBA loan, lease and building permit would come through in orderly fashion, just as with the first restaurant. We updated the business plan, making projections for financial prosperity. Then the first of many horrible events began to play out.

God's Fires of Refinement

The bank submitted the loan application to the SBA, and it was turned down because our debt-to-asset ratio was too high. I convinced the bank, through my own power of persuasion, not God's, that we could carry this much debt-load based on our projections. The bank gave us a loan of $350,000, collateralized by both my partner's home and mine.

The next sign of trouble that came was with the building permit. The building was a new construction and three stories high, so it was a challenge installing ventilation systems on the roof. Our permit was delayed by many weeks and cost thousands of dollars. It was another warning from the Lord that we did not heed!

Then, there came the most vocal of warnings. Our future landlord was being very difficult about the negotiations, to which he had already agreed, and was taking back parking spots he had originally committed to the restaurant. How much more obvious did the Lord have to be in His warnings to me that we were headed for disaster?

Then I discovered that my contractor, who was also an elder at my church, was illegally billing me and also my landlord. In addition, I discovered from another source that he, as project manager for our new thirty-two million dollar church, was diverting funds into his personal account. This delayed the opening of my restaurant by another few weeks, eating up our working capital. I did a full investigation and exposed him to the church and the general contractor. We were in the middle of construction and now had to look for a new contractor.

This was all just the beginning of the violent storms coming my way. I found my accountant was stealing from us. Around that same time I loaned my general manager $8,500 because he had a family crisis. Two months later he disappeared, never to be seen again, and the loan went unpaid. A driver for our wholesale division had a head-on collision in which a young man in the other car was killed and our van was totaled. I was working so many hours that I was exhausted. Then the landlord of our new restaurant was sued because he had a car towed that belonged to a customer who was eating in the restaurant at the time and was legally parked. This customer decided to lead a campaign to boycott my restaurant, even though I had nothing to do with the incident. Then the northwest was battered by one winter storm after the other, and we experienced numerous days of power outages, resulting in loss of revenue and spoiled food at both stores.

No amount of prayer seemed to make any difference, because God wanted to change *me*, not the business! He wanted to teach me intimacy with Him, trusting Him in spite of my circumstances. He was about to test everything He had taught me.

Here is the Scripture that seemed to jump off the page at me during this time: "Although the Lord gives you the bread of adversity and the water of affliction, your teachers will be hidden no more; with your own eyes you will see them. Whether you turn to the right or to the left, your ears will hear a voice behind you saying, "'This is the way, walk in it.'" (Isaiah 30:20)

In verse 26 of the same chapter, the Lord gives this promise: "The moon will shine like the sun, and the sunlight will be seven times brighter, like the light of seven full days, when the Lord binds up the bruises of his people and heals the wounds He inflicted."

Nothing was working. I was liquidating my stocks and life savings, trying to save the restaurants. My business partner would not help me and kept reminding me that he was a "silent partner." I tried hiring a consultant but could not afford one. Every month I would look at my financial statements and see huge losses. Finally a buyer materialized for the first restaurant, and we sold it. I then made the decision to close the second and newest restaurant, so as not to go further into debt. I was devastated the day we backed up the truck to begin emptying out all the furnishings.

I was financially ruined and had to file bankruptcy. But the worst was yet to come. My business partner decided to pay off the loan on the restaurant without notifying me. The bank handed over to him the note on my home that I had used for collateral. He called a few days later to say, "Either you sell your home and hand over your equity, or I will foreclose."

All of my pleadings fell on deaf ears, so I sold my home and handed $100,000 over to him. He left me $10,000 to move into the home of a friend. I sold over half my furniture and put the remainder in storage for what I thought would be only six months. It turned into three long years. I slipped into a major depression, all the time wondering what I had done wrong. I found myself out of a job and unable to collect unemployment because I had always owned my businesses. I did not even know how to begin looking for a new career. I had never put a resume together; I had always been a homemaker or entrepreneur.

But God was faithful. My best friend's husband called one day and asked, "How much do you need to live on?" He sent me that amount every month for eight months and also paid all my attorney bills. I will always be eternally grateful for the kindness of this man. What a merciful God we have!

God reminded me over and over not to moan and groan like the Israelites in the Old Testament of the Bible but instead to have peace and faith that He would work matters out. God told me that if I would remember this, I would not be shaken by the storm. He reminded me of John 14:27: "Peace I leave with you; My peace I give unto you. Do not let your heart be troubled, nor let it be fearful."

I sought medical help for the depression I was suffering from and therapy to deal with the shame. I know that the Lord provided these professional people to help me heal. As a result of my faith in God and my trust in Him, I have experienced joy that goes beyond my understanding.

A Foretaste of Spiritual Power

In the middle of this trial, I received a phone call from a woman who was a leader of a women's ministry, telling me that she knew that God was leading her to ask me to be the keynote speaker at their women's retreat. She knew nothing about me or about my financial situation. I knew that this had to be from the Lord, because she also told me that the other women's ministry leaders wanted another, well-known woman to be their speaker. I accepted the invitation on impulse just because for a minute or two it gave me something to look forward to.

As I got closer to the date and also closer to financial ruin, I thought to myself, *I am a failure. Who am I to teach anything?* But God said to me, "In your weakness you will find My strength. Teach them the Sermon on the Mount with the emphasis on the Beatitudes." Had I not obeyed, I would have missed the greatest blessing of my life. The Lord was about to take me to His next step in my healing: *"Blessed are the pure in heart for they shall see God."*

I knew at this retreat I had to be honest and open about all the things that I had gone through in my life. In Psalm 51, King David declares that God desires truth in the inner parts of an individual. The Lord was very clear that I needed to stand for truth in the inner parts and *then* I would see God. So I began to teach on the Beatitudes, one by one, telling my story and what the Lord had done and was doing to restore His power in my life.

As I was speaking, I saw a young, pregnant woman sobbing uncontrollably. I stopped my message because she was so disruptive, and asked her how I could help her. She replied, "No one can help me, I am probably going to die."

She was HIV positive, and there was a strong possibility that her baby would also be born infected. I gathered the women around her, and we believed God for a healing. She was healed, and her baby was later born healthy. That was in 1997. Today this woman has another child and is still HIV free. Other women, too, were healed and set free that day, through the teaching of the Beatitudes.

The Lord Jesus taught me the greatest lesson of my life through all of this. It is important for us to recognize that, in order for us to know the peace of God, we must believe in what the Bible tells us and, by faith, walk in those ways. This means a willingness to say to the Lord, "I will trust You and believe that You love me." The Lord had a destiny and plan for my life that He could not accomplish unless I cried out for His help. His main goal in creating us was to have a close, loving, and intimate relationship with Him. Unfortunately, we usually do not respond to Him in that way unless a financial, medical, or emotional crisis hits us. God is a tender and loving Father, and He is yearning to show us that.

The Lord showed me through my crisis that I was the "apple of His eye," (Zechariah 2:8) and that He had so much for me that I could not even imagine. After being unemployed many months I began to get fearful when a man approached me at a luncheon and said he had been trying to reach me. He introduced himself as a development officer (fund-raiser) for Northwest Medical Teams, a Christian international crisis relief organization. He asked me if I would like to work with him in Seattle to build the new office and raise money for the organization. Little did I know that my life was going to take a major new direction.

A few weeks later, after many interviews with the board and president, I was hired. Months later I was on my way to Romania and a life-changing experience visiting the orphanages in that country. I had never seen such poverty and so many children abandoned with no one to love them. God changed my heart, and I began to understand things that grieved Him. My heart was in anguish when I saw the children in prison-like stone quarters, void of toys, color, and pictures. Most of the orphanages were dark and dingy. Some had terribly bad odors. But what really broke my heart were the children that would come running out for a hug and would never leave my side, afraid I would leave them.

My next adventure with Northwest Medical Teams took me deep into Mexico, where I saw children and adults that lived in the dumps. After that, I co-led a team to Moldova to a children's hospital. I saw horrible atrocities in the burn unit because of a lack of money. Because they had no pain medication for the children, they gave them hallucinogens. Between isolation units there was broken and jagged glass that the staff did not bother to remove. The children were at risk to infect others as well as be severely cut.

On my return flight I was crying out to the Lord, "What would you have me to do? Why have you taken me out of my comfort zone and into this world of poverty-stricken humanity?" The Lord spoke to me and said clearly, "Teach my people about poverty." What a startling word!

The Lord gave me a vision of a multisensory museum that would display in real life the misery and pain in the world, including the war in Kosovo, the dumps of Mexico, the orphanages in Romania, and the hospital in Moldova. I organized and led a team in a fund-raising event to develop this vision. It was a rousing success and brought tears to the eyes of our guests. The event included a dinner auction that raised a large amount of money for the organization.

Three years later I started yet another consulting business for non-profit organizations on fundraising. A major consulting contract was with Youth With A Mission (YWAM). I raised money for the University of the Nations in Kona, Hawaii, where I met Gary, my husband.

What a journey I have been on! What power and peace I have received from the Lord with my healing through the Beatitudes. Now would you like to go on that journey with us and experience significance and power?

Where God Wants to Take You

In this book you will see the process of transformation that God has taken me through for me to know His love and to tap into His divine purpose for my life. In the same way, He craves and longs for a relationship with you. Once you have begun the process of healing and once God starts speaking to you about His unconditional love, He will put strategic people in your life and give you revelations about how much He cares for and loves you.

In this book you will read many stories of people God used to facilitate this process of transformation in my life. You will come to see and recognize events in your own life that are the work of God guiding you toward His purpose for your life and a relationship with your heavenly Father. You will learn how to rid yourself of the ugly messages in your head that are lies from Satan. You will learn how to interact with Jesus' power just as He has promised through the teaching on the Beatitudes. My prayer is that you will come to know your power potential as you give yourself to God's principles outlined in this book.

CHAPTER ONE:

THE MOST POWERFUL PEOPLE IN THE UNIVERSE

The Spirit Himself bears witness with our spirit that we are children of God, and if children, then heirs—heirs of God and joint heirs with Christ, if indeed we suffer with Him, that we may also be glorified together. (Romans 8:16-17)

Blessed and holy is he who has part in the first resurrection. Over such the second death has no power, but they shall be priests of God and of Christ, and shall reign with Him a thousand years. (Revelation 20:6)

The reason for telling Marie's story in the previous section goes far beyond the benefit of witnessing the redemptive process through which God has taken one of His own. God loves us and wants our lives to be healed and to be fulfilling to us, which is compelling in its own right. But it is even more astonishing when we begin to see what God has in store for us from His perspective and for His purposes. Jesus intends to present you and me to His Father as glorious, holy beings, fully prepared for God's pleasure. God the Father, in return, intends to present you and me to His Son as His suitable partners, who will rule and reign with Him in a literal way, on the earth, for all eternity. We have a future that is nearly indescribable, a destiny beyond imagining, but yet more real than anything else we have experienced before.

Another very exciting dimension to this whole story is the fact that we can begin to exercise this power and authority now, in this present age, even as we wait for Jesus' return to the earth. However, a surprising revelation faces those who desire to have authority on earth as it is in heaven. True power comes only to those who embrace the process of becoming like the One who has all the authority, Jesus Christ. He is going to share His power, but only those who are conformed to His character and likeness will be able to stand under the weight of the glory He is beginning to release.

One of my favorite New Testament stories is from the tenth chapter of the Gospel of Mark. Two of Jesus' disciples, James and John, approach Him to inquire about their destiny in the kingdom of God. They want to sit in positions of glory and power when Jesus establishes His earthly reign, one at His right hand and one at His left. It is an audacious request, one that left the other disciples irritated at James and John. It is essential to notice, however, that Jesus does not rebuke them for their interest in having power. If positional authority was not part of their future, Jesus would surely have corrected them. Instead, He lays out before them the cost of inheriting that kind of power with a sober, even chilling, response:

> *"You do not know what you ask. Are you able to drink the cup that I drink, and be baptized with the baptism that I am baptized with?" (Mark 10:38)*

The two young and zealous disciples respond with predictable bravado, saying in effect, "Of course we're ready." But Jesus had to demonstrate that He was qualified to stand in the authority He has been given by a process of discipline and hardship. The book of Hebrews tells us that He was perfected by means of the things He suffered. His sufferings qualified Him to bring all who obey Him to the place of salvation.[1] In His question to His friends, Jesus was laying out the pathway to power, the cost of reaching one's power potential. There is a cup to drink and a baptism to embrace. And in somewhat startling fashion Jesus declares to James and John that they will indeed drink His cup and be baptized with His baptism. They will be qualified for authority *in the same way that Jesus was to be qualified for it!*

1   See Hebrews 5:8-9

Jesus was not speaking of some religious rituals of drinking and dunking (or sprinkling, as the case may be). The cup and the baptism that Jesus embraced was the process of laying down His life for the sake of the Father's will, becoming the redeemer of those He loves. The God-Man relinquished control over His human existence. He embraced what one writer profoundly calls "the utter freedom of absolute dependence." He resolutely trusted His Father to bring about the fullness of His plan; He never one time sought His own will but deferred to the Father in every instance. He was the perfectly obedient and responsive Son, living out the will of God as a man in a body. In response to that trusting obedience, the Father released to Him all power and all authority in heaven and on earth. The meekest and most submissive man becomes the one who inherits all the power. Unbelievable!

In the perfection of being God's son, Jesus stood in as our substitute. He allowed the rage of Satan against humans and the wrath of God against sin to be fully visited upon Him instead of on us. When Jesus went to His crucifixion He accepted the guilt of every human being who has ever lived. All our sins, all our sorrows, all our shame, all our sickness—it was all laid upon Him who was blameless.[2] The perfect man became the perfect sacrifice, and He died in our place—yours and mine. Though He deserved nothing but praise and worship, He took what we deserved instead and thereby was proven worthy to receive all the power, honor, glory, and dominion forever and ever.

Watching Mel Gibson's movie *The Passion of the Christ,* I was gripped by a scene that portrays the depth of Jesus' substitutionary death in a way I had never experienced until I saw it on screen. It occurs when Jesus is being scourged by the Roman soldiers. The beating goes on interminably, and then the exhausted Jesus falls to the ground. The soldiers stop the whipping, looking coldly satisfied that they have beaten Him into submission. Then, in a moment beyond imagination, the viewer sees the hand of Jesus—trembling with anguished pain—reach up to grasp the handle of the whipping post once again. He staggers to His feet, and once more assumes the necessary posture for the scourging to continue. The Roman commander and the soldiers look at one another in disbelief and then resume the beating with full demonic fury.

2   Consider the stunning reality of Isaiah 53:1-12

As I watched that scene unfold, I screamed out within myself *Why is He getting back up?! Isn't it enough already?* The thought that immediately came into my mind was, *He had not yet taken the stripes that were reserved for you.* Tears flooded down my cheeks as I saw the reality and horror of what Jesus did to win my heart. He embraced the cross, the most cruel and shameful vehicle of death, because He loves me and wants me to realize all that He created me for.

In His death, Jesus fully embraced the broken condition of the human race. He took on the death that was promised to those who disobey the commands of God.[3] When Jesus went to the cross in obedience to His Father, He became fully identified with sinful humanity. He became like us so that He could stand in our place, taking the punishment that was due to us. The crucifixion of Jesus is a nearly incomprehensible act of love on God's part, sacrificing His own Son so that He could have relationship with the very people whose sin caused the death of Jesus.

In 1996 director Ron Howard made a film entitled *Ransom*. It is the story of a well-to-do businessman whose life is interrupted by the kidnapping of his son. The story is built around the passion of the father to redeem his son, no matter what the cost to him and his estate. At the time the movie was produced, some people within the Christian world saw this story as a metaphor of what God had done for us—showing the willingness to do anything for our redemption. As true as that is, however, it does not go nearly deep enough into the heart of God's love. The truth of God's love is that He allowed His Son to be declared guilty of the crimes of all mankind and to be murdered by the ones who were in fact the guilty ones. Here's the stunning reality: *He did it so that He could have relationship with the murderers!* God didn't spend money to get His Son back; He let His Son die so that He could have a love relationship with you and me, though our sin caused Jesus' death! Unbelievable, isn't it?

Jesus' death was a dark and unthinkable fulfillment of the promise in the heart of God that this "man would leave His Father . . . and cling to His wife, and the two would become one flesh."[4] In coming to the earth Jesus left His Father. By embracing all of mankind in love, Jesus left the exclusive embrace of His mother nation, Israel. Through His

---

3   See Genesis 2:17
4   See Ephesians 5:31-32 in fulfillment of Genesis 2:24

death, Jesus became fully identified with sinful humanity and took the punishment for all our sin and brokenness.[5] He became one flesh with us, and will live as a man forever.

This act goes far beyond getting us out of hell. It elevates our relationship with Jesus to a level of intimate partnership that can only be spoken of in romantic terms, in terms of marriage, in fact. Jesus did not die that we might become mere servants, friends, or even family members. We *are* all those things, and they are wondrous in their own right, but Jesus' death was for more than that. He died so that, having become like us, we might become *like Him,* His Bride, His Beloved! He became fully like us, took our sin into Himself, and died in that sin. He was declared guilty in place of us, and He suffered the punishment of that guilt.

But because of the purity of His life, His full and glad obedience to the Father's will, He was qualified to be raised from the dead by the power of God. He was given a new title: "the Firstborn among many brethren"[6] and became the prototype of a whole new race of people. When Jesus was raised from death, He ensured the redemption of all who put their trust in Him. He redeemed from hell those who had been held in the captivity of humanity's brokenness.[7] He raised them (and us) up with Himself to an entirely new kind of existence, one like Paul speaks of in his letter to the Galatians:

> *I have been crucified with Christ; it is no longer I who live, but Christ lives in me; and **the life which I now live in the flesh** I live by faith in the Son of God, who loved me and gave Himself for me. (Galatians 2:20)*

Paul is speaking here of a whole new kind of existence—life in the flesh but lived in the power of faith in Christ. This is no mere doctrinal standing, no simple propositional truth that we blandly accept intellectually and then spend all our energy struggling with the same old sin issues. This new life in Christ is a life empowered by His love, energized by His Spirit, and focused on living by the will and the Word of the Father. It is for us today as much as it was for Paul in his day.

5   See Isaiah 53:6ff

6   See Romans 8:29

7   See Ephesians 4:8

Jesus is offering to you and me the full privilege of being sons and daughters of God, the inheritors of the kingdom of God in this life and in the age to come. He means for us to live as He lived and to walk in the same power that He had as a man on earth. But why is the matter so urgent? How do we access this power in the here and now? And how do we learn to live in the dynamic flow of authority on earth as it is in heaven? These questions give rise to the focus of the remainder of this book. Our prayer is that the Holy Spirit will grant us wisdom and understanding from the mind of God so that we might comprehend what He has in store for us who believe.

Why Is This Such An Urgent Thing?

The urgency of becoming like Jesus is clear for one main reason: the time of Jesus' physical return is near. There is no doubt in my mind that many who are alive right now will see Jesus' bodily return. He really is coming back to earth, and only those who have grown into His likeness by the power of the Holy Spirit will be qualified to stand with Him in His authority. This is a call to maturity in a day when many believe in a form of grace that places no demands for righteousness upon anyone. Grace is not permission to remain in weakness and immaturity. The grace that is poured out by the work of the Holy Spirit is the power to be made like Jesus!

Many passages in Scripture underscore the thesis of this book. Consider for example the beautiful but challenging text of Psalm 24:3-6:

> *Who may ascend into the hill of the LORD?*
> *Or who may stand in His holy place?*
> *He who has clean hands and a pure heart,*
> *Who has not lifted up his soul to an idol,*
> *Nor sworn deceitfully.*
> *He shall receive blessing from the LORD,*
> *And righteousness from the God of his salvation.*
> *This **is** Jacob, the generation of those who seek Him,*
> *Who seek Your face.*

The inarguable point is made in the question articulated in verse 3: who is the one who may stand in the presence of the Lord and presume

Wedding feast

to wield His power? The answers are focused on the person with purity of heart and deed. That person will receive blessing from God and be granted an eternal standing in righteousness.

Another passage speaks powerfully about the issue of righteousness and its relationship to the message of intimacy with Jesus, which we call the Bridal Paradigm. In Matthew 22:1-14 Jesus gives a potent picture in the parable of the king's wedding feast. The story is familiar: the king is giving a wedding celebration for His Son, and those who were invited found many reasons to be excused. In His anger at their refusals, the king commands that the masses in the streets be brought in so that the feast will be full.[8]

As the king comes to the feast, He notices that one man is not dressed in the appropriate garments of a wedding feast. When the king asks this man why he is not dressed, the man is speechless with fear. The king orders that he be bound hand and foot and thrown out into "outer darkness," a euphemism for being given over to judgment. This parable seems very difficult to comprehend if we approach it with a theology that makes no demands on those who accept the invitation to the wedding. We must realize, however, that righteousness and holiness are essential accompaniments of salvation and that we cannot be in the presence of God without them. Let's look at some other Scriptures that underscore the meaning of this parable.

The wedding garments speak of the character of Jesus that must inevitably emerge when we receive the grace of God. In Colossians 3, for example, we are exhorted to clothe ourselves in the character of Jesus:

> *Therefore, as **the** elect of God, holy and beloved, put on tender mercies, kindness, humility, meekness, longsuffering; bearing with one another, and forgiving one another, if anyone has a complaint against another; even as Christ forgave you, so you also **must do**. But above all these things put on love, which is the bond of perfection. (Colossians 3:12-14)*

In these verses the character of Jesus is to be put on by us precisely because we are chosen by God and dearly loved. When the grace of God

8   It is not my intention here to explain the full parable. I have done so in my book *Come To Papa: Encountering the Father that Jesus Knew,* (Oasis House, 2003), 131-146.

Clean
Clothes;
purity
cleanness
righteousness

Matt 22
Col 3
Zech 3

has its effect, we have the power to grow into His image, and it is our responsibility to respond to this grace with obedient faith.

Consider also this segment from Revelation 19:

> *And I heard, as it were, the voice of a great multitude, as the sound of many waters and as the sound of mighty thunderings, saying, "Alleluia! For the Lord God Omnipotent reigns! Let us be glad and rejoice and give Him glory, for the marriage of the Lamb has come, and His wife has made herself ready." And to her it was granted to be arrayed in fine linen, clean and bright, for the fine linen is the righteous acts of the saints. (Revelation 19:6-8)*

In his vision, the apostle John sees a Bride dressed to meet the Bridegroom whose coming is only moments away. He sees that she has been granted authority to clothe herself in righteousness, and she is filled with inexpressible joy, knowing that she has been made ready to meet her Beloved. The force of the original language is this: *"It was given to her to clothe herself in fine linens."* The grace was made available, and the Bride made use of the grace to obey and become conformed to the image of Jesus.

One final passage is taken from Zechariah 3, where the prophet is shown a dramatic encounter between God, the high priest Joshua, and Satan:

> *Then he showed me Joshua the high priest standing before the Angel of the Lord, and Satan standing at his right hand to oppose him. And the Lord said to Satan, "The Lord rebuke you, Satan! The Lord who has chosen Jerusalem rebuke you! Is this not a brand plucked from the fire?" Now Joshua was clothed with filthy garments, and was standing before the Angel. Then He answered and spoke to those who stood before Him, saying, "Take away the filthy garments from him." And to him He said, "See, I have removed your iniquity from you, and I will clothe you with rich robes." And I said, "Let them put a clean turban on his head." So they put a clean turban on his head, and they put the clothes on him. And the Angel of the Lord stood by.*

Then the Angel of the LORD admonished Joshua, saying, "Thus says the LORD of hosts:
'If you will walk in My ways,
And if you will keep My command,
Then you shall also judge My house,
And likewise have charge of My courts;
I will give you places to walk
Among these who stand here.'"
(Zechariah 3:1-7)

grace & obedience

The purification of the priest, symbolized by his change of clothing, is his qualification to stand in the place of authority God has appointed for him. But again, there is the perfect balance of grace and obedience. The angels clothe Joshua in clean garments of righteousness as an act of pure grace, but then the priest is given the condition—now he must walk in the ways of God and keep His commands. He has been granted the ability to do so—now he must follow through and obey.

So How Do We Get There from Here?

The first question to consider when we realize that we are intended to live like Jesus is, *How do I get there from here?* The life and power of Jesus seem so out of reach, so beyond our ability, that it seems foolish to even dream that we could be like Him. And yet our soulful longing is focused exactly on a life like His, a life lived to the fullest potential, with joy, authority, significance, and impact—in short, life on earth as it is in heaven.

The way into this life is the theme of the rest of this book. We are designed for fullness of life and will find no satisfaction until that is our experience. Finding the doorway into this fullness is, therefore, of paramount importance to us. We must know how to get there from where we are, how to discover the pathway that will lead us to the fulfillment we crave.

Through the teaching of Jesus in Matthew's Gospel, chapters 5-7, this life of power becomes accessible. Popularly called the Sermon on the Mount, this compilation of Jesus' teaching is so revolutionary, so disruptive to business-as-usual living, that most Christians of our time have disregarded it as unrealistic and impractical. Some have gone so far as to assign it to life in the millennial kingdom, supposing that by doing this they can avoid its demands and the implications of taking it seriously. But the simple fact is that in the Sermon on the Mount, particularly in the first section, called the Beatitudes, Jesus has given very practical principles by which we may enter into His life and by which we may continue to grow into His image throughout our days. The Beatitudes are the pathway to power, the roadmap to reaching our power potential. The Beatitudes direct us to our destiny for what God created us to be.

Through the rest of this chapter we will present an overview of the Beatitudes, leading us into a more in-depth study that will make up the remainder of the book.

Hitting the Wall: Recognizing Our Need for God

God's desire for human beings has always been that we would come to fully realize our potential, the thing for which He created us. His Spirit yearns jealously for us,[9] and He is passionate in His desire for us to be with Him, to live in the fullness of our destiny.[10] Therefore, God inserts Himself into our lives with focused passion. He leads us into situations designed to bring us face to face with His purposes in our lives. These situations have three common denominators that lead us to the place of encounter with God.

The first is the awareness of our potential and of how far we are from actualizing it. Our frustrations are often God's strategy to bring us to Him. We can ignore them or come to some measure of fulfillment apart from a relationship with God, but we will never find what we are looking for. Whether or not we know it, we need the God-life, and we will not be satisfied until we lay hold of it.

The dilemma presented by this issue is profound, and it is the basis for all human desire. We know we ought to be great, and the pursuit of greatness drives our choices, our passions, our longings. The fear that we might never reach our potential motivates us to all sorts of activity. Then add into the mix the strategies of Satan to sabotage the process by stealing our hearts and passions with far less satisfying counterfeit affections. His attempts to bring us to death are tireless, always focused

9   See James 4:5
10   See John 17:20-26

on the false promise that we can get what we want by our own measures, by taking control of our lives instead of trusting God. If we fall prey to Satan's lies, we may redouble our efforts and work harder, summoning all our human energies in the pursuit of our goals. We may manipulate people and justify the use of many tactics to achieve the things we long for. And when we fail to achieve our most important longings, we may medicate ourselves to the point of oblivion—anything to escape the pain and fear of falling short of the mark.

The second common denominator is that eventually we are faced with the reality of the person of Jesus. The effect of this encounter can range from producing mild interest to provoking stark terror. Like Saul on the road to Damascus, we may encounter the living Christ in a terrifying revelation that blinds us to everything else and absolutely alters our perceptions of reality.[11] Or, we may gently encounter Jesus as He woos us with kindness and patience. But, whatever way Jesus chooses, He will be relentless, for He means to have us completely or not at all. Sooner or later we will be forced to deal with the fact that this man is the Lord of all creation and that He alone has the legitimate claim on us as the one who created us and who bought us back after we sold ourselves to the Evil One.

As we consider Jesus' life as it is revealed in Scripture, we find ourselves alternatively drawn to this man, captivated by His beauty and grace, or wanting to run from His unrelenting demands of holiness and the single-minded pursuit of God's agenda. When we consider Him, we soon begin to realize that *He* is what we want to be—powerful, authoritative, yet kind and gracious, full of compassion and mercy. He is like no one we have encountered before, and He forces us to deal with Him one way or another. Either we find ourselves falling in love with Him, our hearts filled with worship and adoration, or we curse Him and avoid interaction with Him at all costs. Those who choose the latter option will have to deal with the person of Jesus later in life. He is unavoidable in His position as the center of all things, the unifying force that holds together all creation.[12] He is the one to whom has been given all authority in heaven and on earth,[13] and every knee will bow before Him

---

11 See Acts 9:3ff
12 See Colossians 1:17
13 See Matthew 28:18

in acknowledgment of His supremacy and Lordship.[14]

The key point of our encounter with Jesus occurs when we experience what happened to Simon Peter, one of Jesus' disciples who became a chief apostle in the early Church. Luke 5 records the event:

> *[Jesus] got into one of the boats, which was Simon's, and asked him to put out a little from the land. And He sat down and taught the multitudes from the boat. When He had stopped speaking, He said to Simon, "Launch out into the deep and let down your nets for a catch."*

> *But Simon answered and said to Him, "Master, we have toiled all night and caught nothing; nevertheless at Your word I will let down the net." And when they had done this, they caught a great number of fish, and their net was breaking. So they signaled to their partners in the other boat to come and help them. And they came and filled both the boats, so that they began to sink. When Simon Peter saw it, he fell down at Jesus' knees, saying, "Depart from me, for I am a sinful man, O Lord!" (Luke 5:3-8)*

In this encounter with Jesus, Peter came face to face with humanity as it was intended to be: fully in harmony with God and fully in harmony with creation. There was no distortion because of sin, only the prototype man, Jesus, doing what God intended man to do—have dominion over all of creation. Peter's encounter with this man in his little boat simply overwhelmed him, and he came to a very important awareness: "I am a sinful man." In other words, "I do not have what it takes to live like man was created to live."

This experience is in fact the third common denominator that prepares our hearts to be changed by the grace of God. We must come to see that apart from the grace of God we have no hope of becoming what we are supposed to be. Something in us is broken; some internal mechanism got so fouled up that despite our best efforts we simply fall short of what God had in mind when He created us. From the beginning of His creative process, God has desired to fully combine the divine and uncreated reality of His life with the created, material substance

---

14   See Philippians 2:10-11

of our earthly existence. His eternal purpose is to bring *all things in heaven and on earth together in the person of Jesus Christ.*[15] All things spiritual are destined to be fully united with all things material, and the focal point of His purpose is the perfection of humanity in the image of Jesus. We cannot come to fullness of destiny apart from God, because the life of God *is* our destiny!

The First Step Is Poverty of Spirit

To begin to realize this is to come to the first step in the process of reaching our power potential. Jesus calls it "poverty of spirit." It is the essential realization that we do not have within us the resource to become what we are created to be. Without the power of God living in us through a relationship with Jesus Christ, we cannot become what we long to be. Apart from the grace of God being poured out in our lives day by day, we will never know our own destinies, never realize the fullness of the desire that burns in our bones. We cannot get there from here. What can we do but call out to God for mercy and help?

The astonishing result of this realization is that those who embrace it are called "blessed," or happy and fortunate, and are promised that the kingdom of heaven will belong to them. The things we want—power, authority, significance, destiny—are all pledged to those who realize their poverty of spirit and approach God on that basis.

This is just a tidbit of the exciting journey you are about to begin. The first Beatitude will remove the barriers that have kept you from divine power. Be open and prepared to receive the revelation and Holy Spirit anointing that the Lord intends for you as you read the next parts of the roadmap.

The Second Step Is to Mourn over the Present Reality

When we hit the wall of our own poverty, our inability to produce what we long for, we find ourselves facing an even more difficult step of humility—that of mourning over the condition in which we find ourselves. We'll say this again in the chapter on the second Beatitude, but mourning over our brokenness is really a lost art in our culture. Because we want to have positive feelings about ourselves, we tend to avoid deep self-examination, thus hindering us from heading where God wants to

---

15   See Ephesians 1:9-10

take us. Instead, we continue on by making a career change or altering our marital status, or by reading a new self-help book (maybe someone has discovered the magic formula!) or trying a new church, or perhaps, by medicating ourselves in some deeper and more damaging way.

Jesus has shown us the way, but it requires a significant choice for humility on our part. We must allow ourselves to mourn and grieve. This mourning requires a time to reflect, to consider what we have missed out on, the relationships we have lost, the opportunities that have passed us by. We must face the reality of our choices that have damaged us and those around us. Most significantly, we must face the anguish we have brought to God, who created us for His own great pleasure, but to whom we have brought nothing but pain.

Though mourning is a difficult posture to take, the reward is proportional to the cost: those who mourn will be comforted. In other words, the pain that we feel when we consider the broken condition of our lives will be assuaged, and we will know the comfort of the One who has the authority to give it at the deepest possible levels.

As you journey into this chapter on the second Beatitude, you will be overjoyed at the freedom you will feel. Isn't it a hopeful feeling to know that the Lord has so much more for us! As you begin this chapter, it would be very helpful to have a friend praying with you as you mourn. What a beautiful bonding experience you are going to have with the Lord.

The Third Step Is to Stand in Meekness

Meekness is a fascinating term, perhaps one of the most misunderstood concepts in our vocabulary. It can be defined as "gentle," in the sense that describes a wild and powerful horse that has been trained to respond to its master. Meekness is strength under discipline.

To stand in meekness implies that we acknowledge that our lives do not belong to us. Each of us must acknowledge: There is One who created me for His own pleasure, and who redeemed me from the clutches of Satan. So by the dual right of creation and redemption, my life belongs to Him. Since God is the one who "thought me up" in the first place, it is only He who can define me. Only He can tell me who I truly am, and only He can impart the grace to me to become that which He sees.

Meekness is the quality of steadiness, peace, and patience that emerges out of accepting and standing in what God says about us, regardless of the situations and contrary opinions we encounter. The constant effort of Satan is to convince us that we cannot trust God to give us what He has promised and what we desire. The enemy does not care if we come to despair over this issue and simply give up in hopelessness and shame, or if we take the other extreme and attempt to achieve our destiny by the strength of our own resources. Either extreme keeps us from the grace of God that produces in us what He requires. Satan's greatest fear is that we will embrace what God has planned for us, that we will accept God's definition of our lives on a daily basis without question.

The promise of God to those who are meek is that they will inherit the earth. Once again, the things we crave at the deepest levels are promised to those who will acknowledge their need for God and live by His power according to His definitions and parameters. The inheritance that comes from God is not given to those who seize the day by dint of will and force of personality, who strategize the best or are the most creative in marketing.[16] Though they may seem to have the edge for a season, the fact is that the meek will inherit the earth, and the wisdom of their choices will be vindicated and demonstrated when the Kingdom of God is established here on this planet.

God's perfect order of the first two Beatitudes sets us in a place to make a decision and say "Yes!" to meekness. As you engage the chapter on meekness you, will begin to recognize a change taking place in you. Do not be discouraged if it is not immediate. The Holy Spirit sometimes does these transformations gradually as you say, "Yes, Lord, come and do this in me." Then as you begin to embrace meekness, you will also begin to realize that people will want what you have. They will see a change taking place and they will follow your example. God will give you the power to lead by example.

---

16 We make no objection to strength of personality, leadership, creativity, or wisdom in the context of the systems of life. All these things are gifts of God that, operating under His grace, can serve us in realizing His promises. What the Scriptures condemn is a misplaced confidence in these human resources that discounts or neglects our need for God.

The Fourth Step Is to Hunger and Thirst for Reality to be Established

Our hope is that you are beginning to grasp the natural and necessary flow of the Beatitudes. Awareness of our poverty leads us to mourn our condition. As we grieve over what has been lost and over the impact our brokenness has on God's heart and ours, He comes to comfort us. Part of that comfort is the further revelation of who we really are in His heart and of His commitment to bring us to that fullness if we will trust Him and embrace His ways.

The more we see of what God has for us, the more we begin to desire it. The more we are frustrated in our own attempts to produce by strength what He would give us by grace, the more we cast ourselves on Him in utter dependence. As He speaks to our hearts concerning His plans for our lives, our hunger grows deeper to have these things established in our lives. The more we consider the person of Jesus and open our hearts to fall in love with Him, the more He touches us with His own desires to make us complete. While He is comforting us, He is also stirring us to desire what *He* deeply desires. He answers our longings by giving us greater longings, taking us to the place where we are famished and parched for want of His nourishment.

That is what righteousness is: the fullness of God's design being realized in practical reality. It is a mistake to think of righteousness as merely the patterns of our external behavior, when in fact righteousness refers to conformity to God's nature and design. Righteousness is everything operating as it was designed to, in line at every level with God's pattern and purpose.

When Jesus declares, "Blessed are those who hunger and thirst for righteousness," He is saying that He desires people whose greatest longing is to think, feel, and act like He does. His promise to them is that they will be satisfied, satiated with righteousness to a degree greater than they can fathom.

This matter of hungering and thirsting for righteousness is central to God's purposes being realized here on earth. This fourth Beatitude is the pivot point in the list of character traits that Jesus outlines in Matthew 5. The first three Beatitudes lead up to it, and the final four proceed from it, moving into the positive expressions of Christ's character. As the satisfaction of this hunger and thirst begins to occur, other qualities emerge as a natural result.

The first three Beatitudes have cleared the way for you to receive astounding revelation from God. Because you have mourned and taken a posture of meekness, you are prepared to yearn for more of what Jesus has in store for you. The grieving and mourning has been supplanted by a sincere yearning. So let's move on to learn about God's power encounter!

The Fifth Step Is to Become Merciful

As we begin to be conformed to the character of Jesus in our search for power, we also begin to realize how Jesus exercised the authority that was given to Him. We begin to see things as He sees them and to respond to people and situations with the mercy and compassion that characterizes the heart of God in His dealings with us. In another section of the Sermon on the Mount, Jesus says that as we give mercy to those around us, particularly to those who are undeserving of it, we begin to demonstrate our intimate relationship with God as our Father, who is merciful and kind to those who are wicked and ungrateful.[17]

Being merciful to evil and unthankful people does not seem like the way to greatness, at least to those who are accustomed to living in the me-first, cutthroat world of contemporary culture. But we must be reminded that mercy is the way of God, and He is the one who defines all things. It is He who gives power to those who wait upon Him and are conformed to His ways. He promises those who are merciful that they will receive mercy, both for themselves and as a resource to give to those who need it.

Mercy is such an essential dynamic in God's kingdom because that it provides a context in which people can truly be transparent about the condition of their hearts and lives. In the New Testament letter to the Hebrews, the writer provides a profound understanding for the context of mercy established by God on our behalf.[18] Citing the temptations that Jesus faced as a man on the earth, the writer says that these pressures made Jesus compassionate and merciful toward the rest of us when we face such trials. Because Jesus is sympathetic due to His own

17   See Luke 6:32-36
18   See Hebrews 4:15-16

experience of testing, we can come into the presence of God in the confidence of full self-disclosure, knowing that mercy, not condemnation, awaits us. As we experience mercy as the first result of encountering God, we are enabled to give mercy to others, opening a way for them to be transparent about their concerns. The freedom to be real and transparent in a non-defensive way is integral to spiritual growth and lasting change, and the extending of mercy as the first response sets the context for that growth.

When God finds people who are becoming merciful, He extends even greater mercy to them. One of the great dynamics of the kingdom of God is that whatever one gives away is returned in greater measure. In Luke 6:38, just a few lines after Jesus teaches about mercy, He says that what we give will be returned to us, compressed and increased in proportion to how we gave it. Though many people have applied that principle mostly to the giving of finances, Jesus is talking primarily there about mercy and forgiveness. As we become conformed to the character of His kingdom, we become recipients of the graces of His kingdom. We give mercy to those who need it, setting in motion the release of additional mercies to us.

You can begin to take on the characteristics of Jesus. It will be a supernatural change in your life. As you continue to say yes to Jesus, He will begin to pour out on to you His mercy and you will begin to see life through His eyes, which are merciful and kind. The Holy Spirit will transform your old spiritual DNA into the Lord's DNA with an abundance of mercy for others. Watch the blessings that come into your life as a result.

Step Six Is Becoming Pure in Heart

Apart from Jesus Himself, King David was a man who understood authority perhaps better than anyone ever has. He ruled the nation of Israel during its ascent to the pinnacle of power among earthly kingdoms, and he gave much energy to contemplating authority and what is required of those who will exercise it. In Psalm 24 David gives us insight into the authority structure of heaven and the requisites for receiving that heavenly authority here on the earth. Consider these words:

The earth is the LORD'S, and all its fullness,
The world and those who dwell therein.
For He has founded it upon the seas,
And established it upon the waters.
Who may ascend into the hill of the LORD?
Or who may stand in His holy place?
He who has clean hands and a pure heart,
Who has not lifted up his soul to an idol,
Nor sworn deceitfully.
He shall receive blessing from the LORD,
And righteousness from the God of his salvation.
(Psalm 24:1-5)   ~everything operating as it was designed to pg 52~

David acknowledges that all the fullness of the earth belongs to the Lord God. He is the supreme authority by right of creation and redemption, and all who dwell on the earth belong to Him. Then he focuses on who will be qualified to share in the Lord's authority: "Who may ascend into the hill of the Lord, or who may stand in His holy place?" In other words, who is the one who can stand before the Lord in confidence to share in His authority?

The answer is concise and pointed: "He who has clean hands and a pure heart, who has not lifted up his soul to an idol, nor sworn deceitfully." David takes the issue of qualification right past the question of behavior to the deeper matter—the condition of the heart. The one who may confidently stand in God's presence is the one with a pure heart, who has no falseness or deceit in the foundations of his personality. Because the heart of God is absolutely pure, with no hint of improper motives or deceitful agendas, He is able to exercise His authority in such a way that brings maximum grace and fulfillment to all who come to Him. He doesn't use people for His own glory at their expense. Rather, He shares His identity and authority with them so that they may be exalted and glorified, thereby bringing even greater honor to Him.

Those who will share His authority must be conformed to His character. They will be the same on the inside as they are on the outside; God desires us to have *"truth in the inward parts."*[19] As we grow in conformity to God's character, a greater revelation comes to us: God allows us to see Himself. We can hardly imagine the depth of this reward.

19 See Psalm 51:6

King David, in the context of his own magnificent earthly kingdom, said that his greatest desire was to be in the house of the Lord, gazing upon the beauty of God, and inquiring in His temple.[20] David knew that God's self-revelation was the ultimate prize, worthy of the total focus of his own heart.

How many of us have cried out to the Lord: "If only I could see You!" As you pursue this chapter on purity of heart, you will be amazed at what God will reveal to you about His nature. You will realize more deeply that Jesus loves you and intends to give you everything He has. He does this so that you can live in that place of divine power that He has promised for so long.

The Seventh Step Is to Become a Peacemaker

The New Testament understanding of making peace goes far deeper than merely working for a compromise between two or more parties to diminish hostilities. Peacemaking is a costly, self-sacrificing reality that finds its fullest expression in the life, death, and resurrection of Jesus, who invites us into the same kind of sacrificial life. Consider this passage in Paul's letter to the Ephesians:

> *For He Himself is our peace, who has made both one, and has broken down the middle wall of separation, having abolished in His flesh the enmity, that is, the law of commandments contained in ordinances, so as to create in Himself one new man from the two, thus making peace, and that He might reconcile them both to God in one body through the cross, thereby putting to death the enmity. And He came and preached peace to you who were afar off and to those who were near. For through Him we both have access by one Spirit to the Father. (Ephesians 2:14-18)*

Jesus was the ultimate peacemaker; He sets the definition for what that term can mean. Jesus as a man was fully and completely obedient to God, perfectly living out the character of God in the flesh. He is the one man who did it right every time! Because He is the author of life, and all of life is contained in Him,[21] when He demonstrated His perfec-

---

20   See Psalm 27:4
21   See John 1:1-4

tion through His life on earth, He became the prototype of a whole new human race. It is as though He gathered up into Himself all who would believe in Him and brought them to peace, reconciling them to His Father through His life.

Because we have been reconciled to the Father, we no longer have to strive to find our identity and destiny. As we live in communion with God, we hear our Father's voice telling us over and over who we are, how much we are loved, what our task is, and the destiny to which He has invited us. His love and power assure us that these things will be fulfilled, and therefore we can be at peace. When we are at peace with God, striving ceases, and we can relax. We can trust the Holy Spirit to lead us into the Father's perfect plan for our identity and destiny. And as a result we can come to peace with one another.

Those who make peace stand in the direct flow of the ministry of Jesus. As we live in loving obedience to the Father, people are drawn to Him through us as they were through Jesus. The opportunity presents itself to establish peace between those individuals and God as their Father. As the reality of peace with God is absorbed into their lives, it becomes possible for them to make peace with others. Because this effect stands in such harmony with the ministry of Jesus, the reward that comes to peacemakers is at the level of fundamental identity: they are called "the sons of God."

Recently, Marie was at a party and overheard a conversation. Someone was talking about their mother, who always seems to be happy and at peace. She is enjoyable to be around because of her steadiness and even disposition. In other words, she is a peacemaker. What a legacy to leave behind, and what a trait to model to children and friends!

When you finally arrive at this step, the first six Beatitudes will have paved the way for the Lord to begin to supernaturally give you this gift of being a peacemaker. You will understand that this is the total opposite of holding in your feelings for the sake of peace. Instead of anger or passive aggressive behavior, you will begin to be a peacemaker because you *have* peace. What a negative reality that people in our culture are stressed, striving, and anxious most of the time! So hang on and get ready for the peace that goes beyond your understanding and passes smoothly onto others who are around you.

Step Eight Is the Blessing of Being Persecuted for the Sake of Righteousness

The final stage of being qualified to stand in the authority of heaven on earth is that of being persecuted for the sake of righteousness. We must see that persecution comes *for the sake of righteousness,* and not for any other reason. Persecution for the sake of anything else is not what Jesus is speaking about here. It is not about being political activists or doctrinal watchdogs, or adopting extreme positions on controversial issues. It is about being people who are consumed with God, passionate that all people and things become what they ought to be according to God's design, and who have given their lives to the pursuit of humility, meekness, and love.

People like this are received well by the general population. Although we have a longing and desire to be like God, we also have a deep ambivalence rooted in our determination to be the god of our own little world. It's a pathetic posture, really, a position polluted by megalomania. The assumption that we have what it takes to rule our world is unrealistic and patently untrue. No matter how much we can control, so many other factors are beyond our control that any human ability to exercise authority apart from God dangles by the most fragile of threads. History has proven this again and again, and we ignore the truth to our own detriment.

Yet it is an immensely unpopular stance to challenge the sovereignty of the individual and ask people to give up the right of self-direction for the sake of submitting to God. Though some people—prepared by the Holy Spirit and wooed by the heart of God—will hear that invitation and respond gladly, many will resist it to the point of persecuting those who stand with Jesus. Persecution has been the real experience of godly people through the ages, and Jesus promises that we will experience it as well. But He wants us to see the real blessing behind the experience and to rejoice that we are numbered with the faithful through the centuries. We will be faced with trouble as we preach, teach, and live these principles. This is the way of the Kingdom of God.

Onward to the Blessing!

So, let us venture onward into the place of the greatest promises in the Word of God. We can and will be like Jesus. We can and will become the most blessed, the happiest, and the most powerful people in the universe! We can and will reach our power potential, having authority on earth as it is in heaven. As we walk in the ways of Jesus, in the power of the Beatitudes, the inheritance will be ours.

POWER POINT OF THIS CHAPTER:

Jesus fully intends to share His power with His Bride, the people who have been conformed to His image as revealed in the Beatitudes.

FOR DISCUSSION AND REFLECTION:

1. Reflect on your own attempts to achieve your potential outside the context of intimate friendship with God. Make a list of the barriers you have hit as you tried this path.

2. How have you dealt with the person of Jesus Christ in your own journey? Is He simply a teacher or a good example? Have you come to see Him as the King and Lord of all, to whom you owe your life? How will the reality of His identity affect your daily lifestyle?

3. Are you beginning to recognize that you will never come into your destiny apart from an intimate friendship with Jesus? What would it look like in your day to day existence to have Him as a close friend and advisor?

4. You have made your way through this overview of the Beatitudes. Now list several things that impacted you. What do you feel the Holy Spirit is saying to you as you begin this journey into your power potential?

CHAPTER TWO:

POWERFUL PEOPLE HAVE
GREAT REWARDS

His lord said to him, "Well done, good and faithful servant; you were faithful over a few things, I will make you ruler over many things. Enter into the joy of your lord." (Matthew 25:21)

As we approach this study of the Beatitudes, it is necessary to give some focus to the payoff that comes to those who embrace this journey. We're working with the premise that greater power and authority are given to those who become conformed to the image of Jesus. And so, in this final introductory chapter, we want to examine the statements of Jesus and other Scriptures that give insight into the nature of the true power and authority that is given to the Bride of Christ.

It is important to consider the fact that Jesus is big on rewards for right choices and right behavior. Sometimes in our religiosity we think that we ought to be motivated purely from the desire to please God and to do the right thing, and that any thought of reward is somehow beneath the dignity of the true Christian. However, when we try to take that posture, we are attempting to be more holy than God, for He promises great rewards at every turn. Jesus Himself was fully obedient to the Father "for the joy set before Him,"[1] His own heart set ablaze because of what the Father had promised Him in return for His suffering. The prophet Isaiah was

---

1   See Hebrews 12:2

clear: "He shall see the labor of His soul and be satisfied" (Isaiah 53:11).

In addition, Jesus' parables are consistent in the promise of reward for those who do the right thing. The servants who were faithful stewards of their master's estate were rewarded upon his return from his journey, while the one who was not faithful was met with judgment and punishment.[2] Reward is a big deal in the economy of the kingdom of God.

We are promised great rewards for heeding the commands of Jesus given in the Beatitudes, and we are foolish to ignore them. It is never wrong to do something for the right reward, and the pursuit of the character of Jesus for the sake of inheriting the power of the kingdom of God is exactly the right thing to do.

The Continuity between This Present Age and the Age to Come

As we wait for the full release of power and authority in our lives, we must realize something very important in God's plan. This present age, polluted as it is by sin and its effects, is merely the staging ground for the imminent reality to be realized on the earth in the coming age. But this does not mean that the present is unimportant. Far from it! The time we spend here and now is a preparation, a training for our life in the age to come. The very limited authority that we have now is given to us for the purpose of training us for the real authority that will be released to us when Jesus returns. Remember, He really is a man in heaven who is coming back to the earth to set up a literal government. All the nations of the earth, every king and every authority figure, will bow before the Son of God and acknowledge His supreme rule and reign.

The startling reality is that Jesus will have a huge "management team" that will assist Him in governing the universe. His Bride is being made ready to fill those management positions, and the little piece of authority we are given now is for the purpose of our training. Jesus was clear about this in the parables of the faithful servants, cited above. Jesus is pictured as a wealthy man who goes on a journey to a far country. He leaves his estate in the hands of his servants, with the challenge to manage the estate in a profitable way until he returns. Upon his

---

2   See Matthew 25:14-28 and Luke 19:12-27

return, he summons all the servants to account for what they did with the resources entrusted to them. As the faithful servants give a report, the master informs them that their reward is to be rulers over many things.

This parable speaks directly of the return of Jesus at the end of the present age. He has given each of us assignments to carry out in this life—some in the business world, some in the work of ministry, some in education, or science, or entertainment. Wherever the Holy Spirit has positioned you, you have been given the resources to invest for the kingdom of God in the arena of your influence. The key here is not how large your sphere of influence is but how faithfully you manage what you have been given. The master's measuring stick was the faithfulness of his servants, not the scope of their influence. Those who were found faithful were rewarded in precisely the same way, whether the piece entrusted to them was large or small. The reward of faithfulness was rulership over many things, plus the experience of the joy of the master.

When Jesus returns He will demand an accounting just like the master in the parable. He will assess the faithfulness that we have shown with the resources we have been given. Those who are found faithful, who have cooperated with the journey into the likeness of Jesus, will have much authority in the age to come. This authority will be exercised here on the earth. Again, the kingdom of God will be established in fullness on earth! Our eternal destiny is not in heaven but in the kingdom of heaven established on the earth. There will be continuity between this age and the age to come, and we will be given the authority of Jesus to rule and reign with Him.[3]

This Is Not Just "Pie in the Sky"

Even though the fullness of these things will be established after Jesus' return, we can also anticipate a significant release of power and authority now, in this life. Again, the parable of the faithful servants is our reference point. Before the master leaves for the far country, he gives his servants real resources, real wealth to manage in his absence. In the same way, Jesus has given *us* resources so that we might occupy until He comes again. To some He gives financial resources. To others He gives abilities and skills in science or education. To still others He

3   Please consider Revelation 5:8-10; also Revelation 20:6, as well as 2 Timothy 2:12.

gives the responsibility of teaching and training His people according to the Scriptures. To all He gives the presence and power of the Holy Spirit so that we might begin to live in the same kind of intimate partnership with the Father that Jesus experienced in His time here. In the management of these resources, we will be trained for power and authority to be given to us in fullness.

What Are the Rewards That We're Promised?

In these times, Jesus is not primarily looking for bigness or success according to the world's system. He is looking to see who will exercise his or her authority in the same way He did—in the character and nature of the kingdom of God. Those who do that will be rewarded in ways that are beyond our imagination. Let's look at the things that are promised to those who embrace the Beatitudes and exhibit the character expressed in them.

The Poor in Spirit Will Receive the Kingdom of Heaven

The promise of the kingdom of Heaven (which is the same as the kingdom of God) is made to those who exhibit the first and the last Beatitudes. Those who are poor in spirit and those who are persecuted for the sake of righteousness are promised that the power and authority of God's reign will be at their disposal.

The kingdom of Heaven speaks of the rule and reign of God over all created things. This kingdom is to be expressed on the earth now, increasing in its influence as the Church grows in maturity, coming to literal fullness at the return of Jesus. When He came to earth the first time, Jesus declared that the kingdom of God had come to earth, invading the present evil age. The task that was before Jesus was to restore all things to their original intent and design, and He did this one encounter at a time. Every time He spoke the Father's Word, Jesus established the kingdom of Heaven. Every time He healed the sick or gave sight to the blind, He took ground for the kingdom of God. Every time Jesus revealed the nature of God in such a way that people were renewed in their faith, the kingdom was built a little more completely.

Jesus has given us the same authority and power to build the kingdom in the situations of our lives. We have been given His Spirit, and we've been given the privilege of prayer and intimate friendship with God, so that we can communicate with Him and hear back from Him what He wants to do through us in any given situation. We've also been given the written Word of God, the Bible, to direct us and to give us understanding for the circumstances of our daily existence.

This authority works itself out in many ways from day to day, and we can fully expect to do any of the things Jesus did in the course of His life here. As we go step by step through life, we are to announce that the kingdom of Heaven is here and do the things that kingdom people do. This includes preaching the gospel to the poor, healing the sick, raising the dead(!), and driving the demons out of the demonized.[4] The businesswoman who is growing in the character of Jesus can pray before the sales meeting and receive a sense from the Holy Spirit about the direction and focus of the meeting. The college student can ask God for clarity of mind to remember things studied in the late hours of the night before a big exam. The grade-school student can pray for their sick friend and fully expect the power of God to be released to heal them. The CEO of the big corporation can wait before the Lord and discern the timing for the important deal; he can get a clear sense from God about how to bless his employees, and can understand how to use the profits to benefit the poor of the earth. As people approach their arena of influence and responsibility in these ways, they will have the confidence that God is going before them, preparing the pathway so that their life and influence will reach its full power potential.

Consider these two passages that speak directly to this issue:

The steps of a good man are ordered by the Lord, and He delights in his way. (Psalm 37:23)

For we are His workmanship, created in Christ Jesus for good works, which God prepared beforehand that we should walk in them. (Ephesians 2:10)

God has prepared every situation of your life for the purpose of discovering your power potential. There is no situation that He does not fully understand. There is nothing about which He lacks wisdom, and

---

4   See Matthew 10:7-8

He gives it freely to those who ask for it.[5] Every encounter of your life is a stage on which the kingdom of Heaven is to be acted out. You are the representative of God in that encounter, fully empowered for every good work by the Holy Spirit.[6] As your character grows into the likeness of Jesus through the journey of the Beatitudes, God will make even your enemies to be at peace with you.[7] Nothing is withheld from those whose character has been formed into that of Jesus. He asserts this with powerful clarity in His conversation with the disciples in John 15:7: "If you abide in Me, and My words abide in you, you will ask what you desire and it shall be done for you."

This promise is strengthened for us later in that same chapter, where Jesus reminds His disciples that He chose them and appointed them precisely for this kind of authority and effectiveness in their lives. Verses 15 and 16 make a startling declaration of God's intention for His followers, and the statements are just as applicable to us now as they were to these men to whom Jesus was speaking face to face:

> *No longer do I call you servants, for a servant does not know what his master is doing; but I have called you friends, for all things that I heard from My Father I have made known to you. You did not choose Me, but I chose you and appointed you that you should go and bear fruit, and that your fruit should remain, that whatever you ask the Father in My name He may give you. (John 15:15-16)*

According to these words, the disciples were chosen and appointed for three things. First, they were to be fruitful in their lives and ministry. They themselves would grow fully into the character of Jesus, exhibiting His power and authority as the evidence of His presence with them by the Holy Spirit. In addition, their lives would effectively influence the lives of other people, directing them toward relationship with God as their Father and with Jesus as their Bridegroom. The people whose lives they touched would grow into the character of Jesus and would exhibit the same quality of life that the disciples had.

Second, their fruit would remain. The disciples would be

---

5   See James 1:5-8

6   See 2 Corinthians 9:8; also see 2 Timothy 2:21

7   See Proverbs 16:7

unshakable in their commitment to Christ, not deterred by the difficulties and discouragements of their own growth processes. Neither would they be halted by the resistance of the enemy. His tools are the persecutions that Jesus promised to those who love Him and are conformed to His image. On top of that, the people they affected would continue in their love relationship with Jesus through all the seasons of life, giving evidence of the ongoing work and presence of the Holy Spirit both in character and in power. Throughout their days the fragrance of Jesus would be upon them, both in the character of their relationships and in the power exhibited in dealing with life's situations.

Finally, they would have the confidence of answered prayer. It's a stunning promise: "Whatever you ask the Father in My name He may give you." That promise is a blank check signed by Jesus on His Father's bank account! It's *carte blanche*, a free pass into the supply house of heaven! To those who are poor in spirit, who recognize their total dependence upon the presence and the mercies of God, and who joyfully endure the persecution that is promised to those who live in the character of Jesus, He makes this pledge: the Father's kingdom will be at their disposal. It is a staggering reward and should serve to motivate us to respond however we must in order to realize this reward. You will want to go on into the meat of this book to discover the paradoxical power of poverty of spirit so that you can truly understand the inheritance you were created to have.

Those Who Mourn Will Receive God's Comfort

Those who are in touch with the beauty and desirability of the kingdom of God are filled with seemingly conflicting and contradictory emotions. To the degree that our hearts have been opened to the beauty of Jesus and the wonder of His coming rule on earth, we are filled with love for this One we have not seen yet, and we "rejoice with joy inexpressible and full of glory" (1 Peter 1:8). At the same time, we struggle with our immaturity as believers while grieving over the gap that separates us from where we want to be. The promise is that this grief over our own condition and that of the broken people and fallen creation will be comforted in the actual presence of God.

This consolation comes in two ways. First, we are given the presence of the Holy Spirit, who in John 15:26 is called "the Helper," or "the

Comforter." One of the main functions of the Holy Spirit in our lives is to teach us the truth about who Jesus is, and how things really are in His kingdom. As we gain God's perspective, our hearts are comforted through knowing that the present situations are merely temporary. In the perspective of eternity they will seem like a light mist on a windy day. One of the difficulties when we are suffering times of trouble is that they seem as though they will never end; in turn, this hopelessness can be an enemy of our souls.

As we are writing this in the spring of 2006, Marie and I are part of a group of people praying for the healing of four men who are quadriplegics. In addition, one is blind, one is deaf, and one is mute. These men are trapped in the very personal prison of having bodies that do not respond to their wishes, and the battle to remain hopeful can often be fierce. And it is no less difficult for those who are the primary caregivers to these men, for their lives are consumed as well with the ordeal of the mundane, day-to-day realities of managing life. In one recent time together, the wife of one of these men shared deeply and painfully out of her own battle with despair, a battle she is forced to wage every day as she waits for the coming deliverance.

Only the Holy Spirit can release hope into situations like that. Only by the revelation of the beauty of Jesus and the certainty of His intervention can we find the comfort necessary to face life every day and remain upright. The temptation is to reach for the false and slight comforts of compromise, making the pain a little more bearable while we wait. But God's promise is that if we will truly mourn over these situations and call out to God, He will release the true comfort of His presence now in the person of the Holy Spirit, and in the age to come with His own personal and powerful touch. A day is really coming when the Lord Himself will bring the fullness of comfort for which we all are longing. Consider this passage from the book of Revelation:

> And I heard a loud voice from heaven saying, "Behold, the tabernacle of God is with men, and He will dwell with them, and they shall be His people. God Himself will be with them and be their God. And God will wipe away every tear from their eyes; there shall be no more death, nor sorrow, nor crying. There shall be no more pain, for the former things have passed away." Then He who sat on the throne said, "Behold, I make all things new."

And He said to me, "Write, for these words are true and faithful."
(Revelation 21:3-5)

We are truly comforted by the present ministry of the Holy Spirit who reveals the beauty of Jesus and the truth of His promises. We will be ultimately and eternally comforted in the literal presence of God in His earthly kingdom in which there will be no pain at all, ever again. Oh, the comfort that is ours, now and in the age to come! If your desire is to know the comfort of God beyond your imagination, you will want to digest the contents of this book thoroughly, for the way to these rewards is the way through the Beatitudes. Let's go on to the next reward!

Those Who Are Meek Shall Inherit the Earth

There is something in every human heart that is God-breathed, and it is the yearning to have a little piece of real estate to call one's own. Marie and I currently live in Kansas City, Missouri, in a lovely home built on a half-acre lot less than a mile from the International House of Prayer, (IHOP). Though it's a very nice place, greatly convenient in terms of access to IHOP, it has a few shortcomings. It's too close to a very busy road, so often we keep our windows closed because of traffic noise. Also, the ground is typical Missouri clay, which is almost impossible to work with if you have any interest in gardening. So there's something of a longing in both our hearts to have a place that is a little more secluded, with a combination of some woods and some open meadow. It would be a place where our dog could roam freely and where we might even be able to board a horse for Marie's pleasure.

No doubt many people would be absolutely thrilled to have our current living situation, and so we are grateful for what the Lord has given us for this season of our lives. The point, however, is that we have a longing for more, a sense that there is a better place for us, a dream location that would fulfill all our yearnings and desires. The pursuit of the fulfillment of similar desires has shaped the course of history, for the chronicles of mankind are filled with accounts of engagement and conquest, often centered around the issue of possessing a certain portion of land. It is a desire for power, for ownership, for control over one's environment, and it is universal among human beings. It's like the old quote: "I just want what is mine, and that which is next to that which is mine."

In March of 2006 Marie and I had the privilege of being in Germany and Switzerland on a ministry trip. As we were being driven through the countryside near the border of Germany and France, our host pointed out a particular hill and told us how in 1939 Adolf Hitler stood on that hill, gazing covetously across the Rhine River into France. The beauty of that land gripped his heart, and in his demonic lust Hitler set in motion the war machine that he thought would give him the ownership of the earth. If only he could have understood that God has promised the earth to those who are meek!

Whether it comes in the form of a personal desire for a place to call my own or the megalomania of a military conqueror, this longing arises out of the fact that God planted the desire to own the earth in the hearts of His created sons and daughters. It has always been God's plan to give the creation to human beings, and now He has promised to give the earth to those whose character matches that of Jesus Christ. There will come a time—an actual time—in which the Lord of heaven and earth will allot our inheritance, a portion of the earth over which we will be given authority.

In addition, as God's community, followers of Jesus will be given the authority to govern the creation in the way it was intended from the beginning. We will come to understand what Paul means in Romans 8:19-21 when he says that the creation itself eagerly awaits the revelation of the people of God in the true expression of their glory as God's children. The earth itself will be restored and reclaimed under the rule of God's people who have been fully conformed into His character and power. As this happens, we will speak the blessing of God over the creation, which will be restored to the beauty that it had before the fall of man into sin. The curse will be removed, and the ground will yield its increase once again as it was designed to do. Consider the beauty of the promises of Psalm 85, to be fully realized when Jesus returns to the earth:

Surely His salvation is near to those who fear Him,
That glory may dwell in our land.
Mercy and truth have met together;
Righteousness and peace have kissed.
Truth shall spring out of the earth,
And righteousness shall look down from heaven.

Yes, the LORD will give what is good;
And our land will yield its increase.
Righteousness will go before Him,
And shall make His footsteps our pathway.
(Psalm 85:9-13)

Here King David was reminded of the promise that the Lord God had made to the nation of Israel from the very beginning—that they would inherit a Promised Land, a place set apart for them by God. In that place they would enjoy the full measure of His presence and blessing, His provision, His protection, and the incredible prosperity that would cause the nations of the earth to tremble with wonder and jealousy.[8] The Israelites attached so much emotion and such a sense of well-being to dwelling in this land that when God's judgment came upon the nation, the most profound punishment He could bring to them was to remove them from the land and leave it desolate behind them.

This is why there is such intensity in the battle over the land surrounding Jerusalem today. From a purely natural perspective, it makes no sense that a little piece of real estate the size of New Jersey would command the attention of the whole earth. But we must understand that when God promised that portion of the earth to the nation of Israel, He was giving us a prophetic picture of the age to come. One day the whole earth will be given as an inheritance to spiritual Israel, the Bride of Christ made up of Jews and Gentiles, people from every tongue, tribe, and nation brought together as one new man because of Jesus Christ.[9] In that day we will experience the absolute fullness of the presence of God. Every promise will be fulfilled, every dream will be realized, every longing for intimacy and authority will be met, and we will finally know what it is like to be at home where we belong.

While we wait for the day when the fullness of that promise will be released upon us, we can enjoy a growing measure of dominion as we grow into the likeness of Jesus. Marie and I have heard stories of people who have envisioned a particular place to live, only to have it become available at some point along the way. We have some dear friends in Kansas City who have followed the Lord intensely over the years of their marriage. They have given everything they own for the sake of obeying

---

8   See Jeremiah 33:6-11
9   See Ephesians 2:14-18; Revelation 5:8-10

the Lord and so have full confidence in asking Him to supply what they need. Recently they spotted a house on a hill that they thought would be a lovely home for them. They already occupied an adequate spot, but they simply began to ask the Lord for that house. They had no money to make any normal overtures; they merely prayed. Not long after this they heard that a Christian brother had bought the house. And not long after that, they received a phone call from this man, asking them if they would be interested in renting the home. They told him they were interested but did not have enough money to meet the rent requirements. Soon he called them again, offering to let them stay in the house for free, and eventually he has ended up paying them $250 a month to live in it for him!

This little story illustrates in a real way that God really does own all the real estate and likes to give what He owns to His children who will trust Him with their lives and futures. The principle that Jesus stated in Mark 10:29-30 is true: those who leave everything to follow Him will be rewarded *in this life* with a hundredfold blessing of houses and brothers and sisters and mothers and children and lands—and, oh yes, persecution! But the beginning of the promise is there. God will make abundant provision of earthly necessities and desires for those who give everything for the sake of being obedient to His voice.

The promise of inheriting the earth also has implications for governing things that have been given to us as a stewardship in this life. In the parable of the master and the servants,[10] the master prepared the servants for eternal rulership over cities by giving them a financial portfolio to manage with wisdom and discretion. We must see that the finances the Lord has already entrusted to us are not our reward. They are His vehicle for training us in faithfulness and righteousness, and we must understand that principle if we are to gain true riches in the age to come. If we learn to rule over our financial stewardship in a way that is consistent with the values of Jesus and His kingdom, we can be confident of the Lord's pleasure upon us and the certainty of increased authority over the earth in the coming age.

The Hungry and Thirsty Shall Be Satisfied

The yearning to be satisfied at every level is central to the human experience. We have this vague sense of how things ought to be, and

10   See Matthew 25:14-23 and Luke 19:12-27

we think that if only this thing or that thing were in place, all would be complete. The longing for satisfaction comes to us directly from God and cannot be realized in any other way except for God's kingdom and righteousness to be released in our experience. Pascal's statement about the human soul's inability to find rest except in God is born out in every human experience. The Rolling Stones were right—there is no satisfaction—except in the fullness of God's presence and likeness.

Our yearning to be satisfied is a reflection of the yearning in the heart of Jesus. His desire to have a people formed in His own image, with whom He can have full and uninhibited communion, and with whom He can fully share His power and authority, has driven His activity with mankind from the beginning. We tend to compare ourselves to one another, wishing that somehow we could attain to some measure of earthly satisfaction. God looks at us from the perspective of what He had in mind when He created us and will not be satisfied until we fulfill the longing in His heart. The only way God could make that happen was by the suffering, death, and resurrection of His Son, Jesus Christ, and His desire for intimate friendship with us was so great that He was willing to pay that price.

The prophet Isaiah knew this as well, and under the inspiration of the Holy Spirit, he wrote about the process of bringing satisfaction to the heart of God:

> *Yet it pleased the LORD to bruise Him;*
> *He has put Him to grief.*
> *When You make His soul an offering for sin,*
> *He shall see His seed, He shall prolong His days,*
> *And the pleasure of the LORD shall prosper in His hand.*
> *He shall see the labor of His soul, and be satisfied.*
> *By His knowledge My righteous Servant shall justify many,*
> *For He shall bear their iniquities.*
> *Therefore I will divide Him a portion with the great,*
> *And He shall divide the spoil with the strong,*
> *Because He poured out His soul unto death,*
> *And He was numbered with the transgressors,*
> *And He bore the sin of many,*
> *And made intercession for the transgressors.*
> *(Isaiah 53:10-12)*

A day is coming when Jesus will see the fruit His labor, and will be fully satisfied. In other words, our salvation, which God held in His heart from the beginning, will be realized, and we will be the people He had in mind at the start. Think of it! God will look upon you and me and be fully satisfied. We will stand before Him as He gazes upon us in the beauty of His holiness, and everything that He had in mind concerning you and me will be complete. I cannot imagine what it will feel like. The thought of standing in the presence of God in His wholeness and having Him completely satisfied with me is beyond comprehension. But, Scripture says it will indeed be so: "He shall see the labor of His soul and be satisfied." What a stunning thought!

God asks us to get excited about what excites Him. The desire to become everything He has in mind for us—a hunger and thirst for righteousness, conformity to His will—must motivate us. When it does, He will be satisfied, and then *we* will finally be satisfied. The main thing that satisfies the child is the delight and approval of the Father. The main thing that satisfies the Lover is the knowledge that the One beloved is delighted and fully satisfied in her. As the desire for righteousness takes the central place in our hearts, we are assured that He—and we—will be satisfied.

Remember the initial premise of this book: God created us to have power, to be in His likeness. The desire to be like Jesus was inserted into our souls at creation, and it has never left. The only way to find satisfaction is to become like Him. Consider what the writer says in Psalm 17:15:

As for me, I will see Your face in righteousness;
I shall be satisfied when I awake in Your likeness.

Then again in Psalm 65:4:

Blessed is the man You choose, and cause to approach You,
That he may dwell in Your courts.
We shall be satisfied with the goodness of Your house,
Of Your holy temple.

Until the yearning in our souls is realized and we come to rest, it burns in us and motivates us to attain something more than we have known to this point. We may attempt to medicate that longing by trying to find satisfaction in lesser things, but we will never be contented until we are with Him and fully like Him.

Praise God that one day we will be like Him! As we await the day of fulfillment, we are comforted by the knowledge that He is taking us there, one step at a time. Paul tells us that as we meditate on the beauty of the Lord, gazing upon Him with the eyes of the spirit, we are being transformed—literally metamorphosed—into His likeness from one level of glory to the next.[11]

The Merciful Shall Receive Mercy

One of the most profound promises in all of Scripture is found in Isaiah 55, where God is speaking through Isaiah to those who have come to Him in recognition of their need for His help:

> *Ho! Everyone who thirsts,*
> *Come to the waters;*
> *And you who have no money,*
> *Come, buy and eat.*
> *Yes, come, buy wine and milk*
> *Without money and without price.*
> *Why do you spend money for what is not bread,*
> *And your wages for what does not satisfy?*
> *Listen carefully to Me, and eat what is good,*
> *And let your soul delight itself in abundance.*
> *Incline your ear, and come to Me.*
> *Hear, and your soul shall live;*
> *And I will make an everlasting covenant with you—*
> *The sure mercies of David. (Isaiah 55:1-3)*

The bottom line promise from God to those in this circumstance is "sure mercy," not just any mercy. It is the mercy that is promised and given to David, who was called "the man after God's heart." Let's consider a passage that will help us understand the term "sure mercy."

There are many Psalms that speak of God's mercies to David, but one in particular has grabbed my attention over the years. It is Psalm

---

11 See 2 Corinthians 8:16-18

18, which was written during a time of deep compromise in David's life. The future king of Israel was running for his life from the demonized King Saul and was in a crisis of personal faith. Over about an eighteen-month period David made a number of poor choices—he lied and got a number of people killed, and had a temper tantrum that almost resulted in another massacre, among other things.[12] At the end of that season, when God delivered him in a most profound way, David wrote Psalm 18 as a hymn of thanks and praise to his Lord. Two verses in the Psalm grab my attention and encourage my heart. In verse 17 David speaks of how his enemy was too strong for him and had almost overpowered him. But then God delivered him in a mighty way, and David gives us a wonderful insight into the motivations of God's heart. Even in his time of weakness, David was precious to God, and his testimony about God is that "He delivered me because He delighted in me."

To know God's delight and deliverance during a time of weakness and compromise is a deep experience of mercy, and when we claim the promise that the sure mercies of David will be our reward, it is powerful.

The second promise in Psalm 18 that thrills me is found in verses 35 and 36, where David says this about his God:

Your right hand has held me up,
Your gentleness has made me great.
You enlarged my path under me,
So my feet did not slip.

My soul is so encouraged by these words, because *my* greatness is not dependent upon *my* efforts. Instead, greatness is bestowed upon me by God's grace and gentleness. God's mercies will sustain me in the day of trouble, and if I will simply cooperate in the power of His grace, greatness will be the result.

The second half of the verse is just as powerful. David insists that when he came to a place of trouble where he was in danger of slipping off the pathway of righteousness, *God made the path wider!* I love that so much, because we might think that God would say something like "Be careful now, young man. The path is narrow, and if you slip, you'll be in trouble." But no. God is gentle, and our greatness is His agenda.

---

12   See these stories in 1 Samuel 21-25.

When difficulty or danger comes, He makes the path wider so that we can find it more easily.

The sure mercies of David are a wonderful promise from God to those who demonstrate their willingness to be merciful as He is merciful. Living in the mercy of God is one of the most desirable positions a person can imagine. The term "sure mercies" has the meaning of determined kindness, that God has set the recipients in such a place that mercy is their inevitable experience. Many Scriptures have wonderful things to say about the mercies of God, awakening us to the anticipation of great joy. Consider these passages:

> *Through the LORD's mercies we are not consumed,*
> *Because His compassions fail not.*
> *They are new every morning;*
> *Great is Your faithfulness. (Lamentations 3:22-23)*

The compassion of God never fails! We get to begin fresh every morning with a new flow of mercy from the well of God's great faithfulness. It's a wonderful blessing! Here's another powerful passage:

> *Have mercy upon me, O God,*
> *According to Your lovingkindness;*
> *According to the multitude of Your tender mercies,*
> *Blot out my transgressions.*
> *Wash me thoroughly from my iniquity,*
> *And cleanse me from my sin. (Psalm 51:1-2)*

In these verses written by David in his season of repentance over his sin with Bathsheba, the king of Israel appeals to God's masculine, committed love as well as to the tender mercies of God's feminine side! The word that is translated "tender mercies" here literally means "the womb" and refers to the mothering instincts that are found in the nature of God. How good it is to know that when we are in trouble, even because of terrible sin, we can appeal to the mercies of God and be confident that we will find them at our disposal. The requisite for receiving this sort of mercy is to be merciful to those around us who are in places of need. If we respond to God's mercies by giving mercy to others, we will know what it is to receive it.

This principle is clearly shown in this final passage that is so tender in its approach. It is found in Luke's version of the Sermon on the Mount, where Jesus says these powerful words:

Love your enemies, do good, and lend, hoping for nothing in return; and your reward will be great, and you will be sons of the Most High. For He is kind to the unthankful and evil. Therefore be merciful, just as your Father also is merciful.

Judge not, and you shall not be judged. Condemn not, and you shall not be condemned. Forgive, and you will be forgiven. Give, and it will be given to you: good measure, pressed down, shaken together, and running over will be put into your bosom. For with the same measure that you use, it will be measured back to you. (Luke 6:35-38)

Here the motivation for giving mercy is that when we do, we are judged to be like our Father, who is merciful. When we give mercy to those who are undeserving, we are acting like our Father God and therefore can expect great reward. Jesus says that reward will be mercy given back to us "pressed down, shaken together, and running over," measured back to us in the same way we dealt it out.

The Pure in Heart Will See God

The idea of seeing God has captured the imaginations of history and has motivated countless individuals to give themselves to a lifetime of devotion, prayer, and self-denial. Seeing God in His glory, termed "the Beatific Vision" by those who have followed the contemplative calling, is the highest reward imaginable, for to see Him is to become like Him.[13]

The passion to see God is articulated powerfully in several places in Scripture. Moses found himself bearing the weight of incredible responsibility in leading the children of Israel—some three million people!—through the wilderness toward a promise that seemed far out of reach. As he persisted in his assignment, the thing that motivated and sustained him was his ongoing relationship of intimacy with God. Moses had regular encounters with the Presence of the Lord, and he witnessed the beauty that surrounds God. But the more he followed

---

13   See 1 John 3:2

and obeyed, the more deeply he felt the longing to *see* God. Finally, Moses came to God in the aftermath of the great sin Israel committed with the golden calf, and in effect said to God, "If I'm to lead this group of rebellious people into Your promises, I need to know for certain that You are personally with me. I need to see You, so please God, show me Your glory."

Here is God's response to Moses in Exodus 33:

So the Lord said to Moses, "I will also do this thing that you have spoken; for you have found grace in My sight, and I know you by name." And he said, "Please, show me Your glory."

Then He said, "I will make all My goodness pass before you, and I will proclaim the name of the Lord before you. I will be gracious to whom I will be gracious, and I will have compassion on whom I will have compassion." But He said, "You cannot see My face; for no man shall see Me, and live." And the Lord said, "Here is a place by Me, and you shall stand on the rock. So it shall be, while My glory passes by, that I will put you in the cleft of the rock, and will cover you with My hand while I pass by. Then I will take away My hand, and you shall see My back; but My face shall not be seen." (Exodus 33:17-23)

The key phrase in this passage is the Lord's statement concerning Moses: "You have found grace in my sight." In other words, God is saying that Moses has cooperated with God's power to transform his character and now he can survive the weight of the revelation of the beauty of God. If we will allow God's grace to have its effect in our lives, the power of God's self-revelation will be given to us.

Another compelling portion of Scripture is the testimony of Job in the midst of his troubles. In this story, which is foundational to understanding the ways of God, Job has been made the object of Satan's rage under God's sovereign permission in order to demonstrate Job's qualifications for authority. As this godly man endures his trouble, he wrestles with God and with his friends, trying to find some anchor point of hope in his life. The following statements, found in Job 19:25-27, show us the depth of longing and comfort that attend the thought of seeing God:

For I know that my Redeemer lives,
And He shall stand at last on the earth;
And after my skin is destroyed, this I know,
That in my flesh I shall see God,
Whom I shall see for myself,
And my eyes shall behold, and not another.
How my heart yearns within me!

As Job struggles to find meaning in his time of pain, a powerful revelation comes to him: the conviction, the deep knowledge in his heart, that God lives and that Job will see the living God standing upon the earth.[14] Job understands something deep in his soul, and the knowledge that his own eyes will behold the living God both sustains him in crisis and produces a deep yearning inside him. This longing to see God motivates him to complete his journey, painful though it may be. The promise of seeing God is a powerful thing.

A passage in the New Testament that touches this longing in our hearts is found in the fourteenth chapter of John's Gospel, where Jesus has a significant conversation with His disciples. He tells them that if they truly perceive who He is, they will both know and see the Father. It's an amazing statement, and one of Jesus' followers, a man named Philip, gives a poignant response: "Lord, show us the Father, and it is sufficient for us."

This is quite a statement. If we could just see God, then all our other issues would be settled. So the promise of seeing Him provides a strong motivation for us to purify our hearts. In fact, the apostle John writes in his first letter that to see God is to become like Him, and if we truly have that hope, we will do whatever is necessary to purify ourselves, even as He is pure.[15] The promise of seeing God is one of the strongest and best promises in all of God's Word. Open your heart to God in prayer so that the richest blessings in the heart of God may be fulfilled in your life.

The Peacemakers Shall Be Called Sons of God

It is so significant that the reward promised to those who conform to the image of Jesus is a reward of relationship and intimacy. The foundational cry of the human heart is to know one's Father, to be loved and

14 See Zechariah 14:4
15 See 1 John 3:2-3

recognized as significant in present relationship, as well as to have an inheritance in days to come.[16]

The primary blessing of sonship is to have the confidence that we are not an accident of nature, not a product of chance. The Holy Spirit makes it clear in John 1:13 that as God's sons and daughters we are here by His will and desire, not because of any other factor. It is precious and powerful to know that you are here as an individual because you were chosen and desired by God and that He has infused into you everything you need to become just like Him.

To stand in a family relationship with God is to be the inheritor of wonderful things. Such wonder is attached to being able to call God "our Father" that Jesus found Himself in significant difficulty with religious leaders simply by asserting that God was His Father. John 5:18 says that the Jewish leaders sought to kill Jesus precisely because He called God His Father, "thus making Himself equal with God." These religious leaders understood better than we do the power of calling God "Father." They perceived the truth that it implied an honor of equality and authority beyond our ability to comprehend.

Jesus responds to their indignant accusation by fueling their fire with more language of intimacy and authority:

> *Then Jesus answered and said to them, "Most assuredly, I say to you, the Son can do nothing of Himself, but what He sees the Father do; for whatever He does, the Son also does in like manner. For the Father loves the Son, and shows Him all things that He Himself does; and He will show Him greater works than these, that you may marvel. For as the Father raises the dead and gives life to them, even so the Son gives life to whom He will. For the Father judges no one, but has committed all judgment to the Son, that all should honor the Son just as they honor the Father. He who does not honor the Son does not honor the Father who sent Him. (John 5:19-23)*

The authority of sonship, promised to those who are peacemakers, is an incredible reward. A level of revelation is opened to them, rooted in intimate affection that includes everything the Father is doing. Jesus

16 For an in-depth treatment of the character of God as Father, see my book *Come To Papa: Encountering the Father that Jesus Knew,* (Oasis House, 2003).

asserted that even greater things than the healing of a life-long para-
lytic would come through the revelation of the Father to the Son and
that these wondrous things would cause the leaders of Israel to marvel.
The list included raising the dead and standing in the authority to judge
all things.

Someone might respond and argue that Jesus was speaking only of
Himself in these statements and that it has nothing to do with us ordinary believers. But in John 14:12 Jesus informs the disciples that these
greater works would not be done by Him personally *but by His Spirit
working through those who believe in Him.* In John 15:15-16 Jesus declares that He has told His friends everything the Father made known
to Him, He promises that whatever they ask of the Father, He will do for
them. In addition, the apostle Paul tells us in 1 Corinthians 6:3 that we,
the believers in Jesus, will judge angels and therefore are qualified to
judge all things that pertain to this life.

The authority and power of sonship is an incredible thing. But
there is one reality that Jesus holds in even higher esteem than raising
the dead or judging angels. In the tenth chapter of Luke, we are given
the record of Jesus sending His disciples out to preach the gospel of
the kingdom of God and to do the works that He had been doing. When
they returned, they were filled with excited amazement, because the
Spirit of God had honored their obedience by releasing works of power
through them. Jesus rejoiced with them over this good report, but then
in Luke 10:20 He gives His friends an essential insight, saying, "Do not
rejoice in this, that the spirits are subject to you, but rather rejoice
because your names are written in heaven."

Jesus understood the incredible value of relationship with God as
His Father, and He wanted His disciples to comprehend this as well.
The most important thing is not the authority to tell demons what to
do but the far greater blessing of being sons of God. When we stand in
the reality of sonship with God, we stand as co-heirs with Christ, sure
to receive everything the Father has to give. In order to receive these
promises, we must become peacemakers, even as Jesus is the ultimate
peacemaker. Your understanding of this essential character quality will
be deepened as you continue your journey through the Beatitudes.

Those Persecuted for Righteousness' Sake Will Receive the Kingdom of Heaven

Here we come full circle. The first promise to the poor in spirit is that the kingdom of heaven is theirs. Now we find that the same promise is made to those who are persecuted for the sake of the kingdom, for the sake of righteousness, and for the sake of the Name of Jesus. God has given great and mighty promises to those He loves precisely so that we will be motivated to grow into the character of Jesus. The prospect of having the fullness of God's kingdom, His authority, His power, and His resources available to you is worth any investment you will make, even to the degree of giving your life as a sacrifice.

The journey is intense at times, but you will always be accompanied by the Holy Spirit. You will be given the wonderful fellowship of a growing company of Christians who perceive the central importance of this journey of growth into the image of Jesus. You will be empowered by His grace as you make decisions to obey and to trust Him, and the rewards that come—both during the journey and on the other end of it—will be beyond your expectations.

May the Lord bless you as you begin this journey to reaching your power potential. May the authority of heaven be yours on the earth as you come into the character of Jesus by way of the beautiful Beatitudes.

POWER POINT OF THIS CHAPTER:

God motivates His people to become like Jesus with the promise of great rewards, both in this life and in the age to come.

FOR DISCUSSION AND REFLECTION:

1. Consider the fact that everything we do is motivated by the desire to have pleasure, even if in the short term it might cost us something.

2. Discuss with your group the fact that God loves to motivate His people with the promise of great rewards.

3. As you reflect on this chapter, list the rewards given in the order of their importance to you. Talk about your conclusions with your discussion group.

4. Set your heart in prayer to pursue the rewards that God promises in such a way that you will be certain to receive them.

CHAPTER THREE:

POWERFUL PEOPLE ARE
POOR IN SPIRIT

Blessed are the poor in spirit, for theirs is the
Kingdom of Heaven. (Matthew 5:3)

Marie:

Deep inside we hide our secret sins and our deep hurts. We think
that if we keep them to ourselves, they will eventually heal by themselves. We think that what happened to us years ago has no relevance
today because we cannot go back and change the events. Or perhaps
if we make enough money and have the right marriage partner, everything will be okay. If this were true, society would probably be far less
afflicted by alcoholism, drug addiction, sex offenses, and people who
are overweight, depressed, and anxious.

As a young businesswoman in the 1980s, I became very wealthy and
powerful. Yet I lost the will to live, because I felt disconnected from
other people and lonely and empty. Instinctively I knew there had to
be another way to achieve my need for significance and love. I reached
a point where I recognized and acknowledged my personal bankruptcy,
and I allowed God to reveal my brokenness. I found myself reacting to
difficult events in predictable and dysfunctional ways rather than growing in maturity and grace.

To illustrate this, let me tell the story of a wealthy friend of ours who was abused severely by his father and witnessed many times his mother's blood by the hand of his father. Today, this man believes the past has no effect on his present behavior. He says he cannot change the events that happened and that he has forgiven his father. But his wife tells a different story. She says that he has many outbursts of verbal anger directed at her, accusing her of never doing the right thing. He judges others harshly and is critical.

When we are doing well, the concept of acknowledging our need for God can be offensive to us, because we feel confident in our own strength and sufficiency. As a result, God is quite willing to allow circumstances to come that reveal to us our true condition of need before Him.

In the past few years I have been involved as a fundraiser for the University of the Nations, the training arm of Youth With A Mission. We organized many "Kona Encounters," bringing donors to the campus in Kona, Hawaii, to expose them to the work of YWAM. During these encounters my husband and I would teach on "The Father Heart of God." I continue to be surprised at the number of Christian leaders, teachers, and businesspeople who for years have hidden their hatred of an absent, abusive, or just plain neglectful father. One example in particular comes to mind.

A certain man became wealthy through building many businesses. His father abandoned him early in his childhood. In fact, the father denied his paternal relationship with his son to the point of writing him out of his will, thus inflicting a final hurtful blow after his death.

This tall, good-looking man stood in front of our class and read the letter of forgiveness he had composed to his deceased father, crying so hard that his voice was barely audible. He was so broken in his spirit. And the God who knows his pain continues to bless and love him. Psalm 51:17 says, "The sacrifices of God are a broken spirit; a broken and contrite heart...." In other words, apart from an intimate and transparent relationship with God, we will never be able to please Him by our works or our outward actions. It is the attitude of our hearts that concerns Him. He wants us to be so broken and humble that every time we commit a sin, no matter how small it may seem to us, we realize that it hurts our relationship with our children, spouses, friends, and especially Jesus. Ezekiel 6:9 (New Living Translation) says, "They will recognize how hurt *(other translations say crushed or grieved)* I am by their unfaithful hearts and lustful eyes that long for their idols."

Pain from our past and shame or low self-esteem because of a broken spirit can keep us from experiencing the presence of God. As long as we hide our secrets of shame, anger, bitterness, and low self-esteem, we continue to harbor the old life. If we turn to Him in our brokenness, however, He has promised us the kingdom of heaven. Recently a prophet friend fasted and prayed for many weeks asking the Lord what troubles Him about our sins. God spoke to her about His coming judgment regarding the exaggerations and outright lies we tell. A couple of weeks later Gary was reading Fox News on the internet and a headline read, "Americans Are Liars." It went on to say that, based on a national survey, most Americans lie because of a lack of self-esteem, or because of fear or a desire for power.

It has taken me over nine years to write my portions of this book. At times I would set it down for a year or more, because I knew that the Lord was not yet finished with me or the book. I was right, because in the fall of 2004, after leading my mother to the Lord, I was in Kona again, overseeing a group of people for a teaching on "The Father Heart of God" at YWAM's University of the Nations. Everything was the same as before except for one major change: we had a new speaker/teacher named Gary Wiens.

As you read my story of amazing healing, you will see that the Lord purposely put Gary in that classroom in order for me to heal from a major stumbling block in my life—the shame of my previous marriages and the conviction that no God-seeking man would want me. I could still not comprehend that God had erased all of my old record because of His love for me. I did not trust that God would put it in someone's heart to bless and love me unconditionally. This short story demonstrates how God orchestrates healing.

Before meeting Gary personally, I had come to know that he had recently lost his wife to cancer. A couple of months later, when I walked into the first day of teaching that Sunday morning, I was taken by Gary's love for the Lord and his demonstrative way of describing Jesus' love for us. He also talked about his children with deep love and devotion. Listening to him, it occurred to me that this was exactly the kind of man I had been praying for. But the old secret messages began to resound in my head: *Just wait until he finds out about your life. Who are you to think that he or anyone would want you once he finds out about your marriages?*

Yet, the Lord had a strategy that week for my deliverance and healing. Through the course of that Kona Encounter, I began to pray with some friends who were in attendance that God would start something between Gary and me. Nothing seemed to be happening in his heart, and I was confused about that as the week went on.

During the Thursday morning session, Gary was speaking about shame issues that keep us from God's purposes in our lives. He told the story of a man at the International House of Prayer in Kansas City, who had a long-standing addiction to pornography that his wife had discovered. He confessed and repented, but after some time she caught him again. In his shamed state, the man tried to commit suicide by shooting himself through the heart, only to fail in the attempt when the recoil of the pistol caused the bullet to miss his heart by a fraction of an inch. The worst possible scenario was now reality, because now everyone would know, and he would have to face all the issues instead of escaping them.

The wonder of the story to me was how Mike Bickle, as the director of the House of Prayer, along with his leadership team, embraced this man in his shame and restored him to a place of leadership and honor. I began to have reactions of physical anguish and emotional distress as I listened to Gary tell this story in class. Eventually I had to leave the session with excruciating stomach pains, because I realized that I had hidden my shame and it was eating me up inside. I managed to recover in time for dinner, but the agony recurred during the evening session to such a degree that I had to leave again.

My difficulty continued through the night to the extent that on Friday morning I called my supervisor at the Kona Foundation. I poured out my heart, confessing the situation to him, along with my belief that no godly man would ever want me. As I wept over the phone, he assured me that this was a lie and that if I could see myself as the Lord and others at the university see me, I would come to peace in the situation. He prayed with me, and through the Lord's tenderness I was able to come to a measure of peace, at least for a day. The Kona Encounter ended that day. Gary left for a teaching assignment in Denmark, and

I remained in Kona, rather discouraged that nothing had come of our meeting because I had an attraction to him and several people there had thought he would be perfect for me.

The next afternoon, I was sitting around a table at the hotel I was staying at with about seven or eight friends who had attended the teaching. One of the men asked me what the week had meant to me, and immediately the Lord spoke to my heart saying, "It is time." Tears came to my eyes as I revealed my secret shame. Several in the group began weeping with me and praying over me. Suddenly, my dear friend Julie Livens looked deep into my eyes and asked me if I was ready to be delivered of this shame and the pain it caused me. I said yes, and we headed off to my hotel room to pray through the issues of deliverance and healing. The Lord met me in a powerful way in my poverty of spirit and set me free from the things that had held me captive for so many years. Within just a few days, my correspondence with Gary began. God was now free to bring to me what He had desired to give me, and now after nearly two years together our romance feels as though it is just beginning.

A wonderful promise comes to us in the Bible that, if we will bring our secret shame issues out into the open, we can deal with them and be forgiven. A man named James, who was Jesus' brother, wrote this passage in his letter to the believers of that day:

> *Confess your trespasses to one another, and pray for one another, that you may be healed. The effective, fervent prayer of a righteous man avails much. (James 5:16)*

Most of us keep our shame issues secret, fearing that they will cause us to be rejected and condemned. We may confess them to God, probably many times, but we wonder why they continue to have power over us. James' statement gives us the answer: confess those things to another person who will pray for you that you might be forgiven and healed. It's as simple as that.

Only the poor in spirit confess their sins to one another. Those who are proud, who have a reputation to maintain, don't do that. It's too costly—at least it seems that way. The fact is, however, that it is less costly over the long-term, because through poverty of spirit, healing actually comes, along with great personal freedom and the promise of great blessing.

My secret shame no longer has a hold on me, and had God chosen not to bring someone into my life, I would have continued to have peace. I have been blessed through my work with YWAM with the privilege of helping others heal. I know now that God purposely brought this godly teacher with his wonderful stories just when He did, because He knew it was time for me to receive this healing. Isn't the Lord precious in His timing? The wonder of this story is that, just a few weeks after the Kona Encounter, Gary and I began to develop a relationship that led to romance, and then to marriage, and even to writing this book!

God wants us to recognize our own inability to please Him with our own striving and effort. We must give our will to Him in complete brokenness, humility, and confession, acknowledging that apart from Him we are nothing. We do not earn or deserve our salvation—it is a gift of God's grace to us through faith, a gift that God wants to give us because He loves us so much.

C. S. Lewis once wrote of this experience:

Whenever we find that our religious life is making us feel that we are good—above all, that we are better than someone else—I think we may be sure that we are being acted on, not by God, but by the devil. The real test of being in the presence of God, is that you either forget about yourself altogether or see yourself as a small, dirty object. It is better to forget about yourself altogether.[1]

In the Amplified Bible, Matthew 5:3 reads "Blessed…are the poor in spirit—the humble, who rate themselves insignificant—for theirs is the kingdom of heaven!" The New International Version Study Bible explains the "poor in spirit" as being those who are not spiritually proud or self-sufficient. We are poor in spirit when we realize our own utter helplessness, ignorance, and inability to live in the power that God intended for us. We must realize that we are completely dependant on God, needing to put our whole trust in Him.

In the beginning of our journey, Gary and I realized our own pov-

---

1   C.S. Lewis, *Mere Christianity* (New York; Macmillan Company, 1960), 111

erty of spirit because we did not see much power for signs and wonders related to our prayers, and we have seen for the most part a power-less Church in our nation. Yes, there are pockets here and there where healing power is being released, but in our poverty of spirit we are cry-ing out, "Why not more?" We are mourning for those who are going to church crippled and leaving crippled, for those who are blind when they come and blind when they leave. We cry out for those who come and say, "I am no longer satisfied; isn't there more?"

In your personal journal, write down times when you have felt com-pletely isolated and alone. Now think about the emotions, fears, and stress that accompanied these times. Ask God to heal those thoughts of condemnation, shame, and self-hatred. Just as the Lord intervened in my life through the revelation of His character, He will also bring about circumstances in your life that will help you heal.

We must realize that sin cannot be taken away by our own efforts or by the words or efforts of anyone else. Only God, through the death of Jesus on the Cross, can free us from sin and the hurts of the past. We must realize that apart from God we can do nothing. Only God is abundant in spirit; we are poor in spirit. We must be conscious of our complete dependence on God, and that we come to Him spiritually bankrupt.

A wonderful passage in Isaiah 57 gives us understanding about this:

And one shall say, ". . . Prepare the way,
Take the stumbling block out of the way of My people."
For thus says the High and Lofty One
Who inhabits eternity, whose name is Holy:
"I dwell in the high and holy place,
With him who has a contrite and humble spirit,
To revive the spirit of the humble,
And to revive the heart of the contrite ones."
(Isaiah 57:14-15)

When we face our sins and repent of them, we remove the barriers, the stumbling blocks, that keep us from being poor in spirit. When we cling to sinful thoughts and behaviors, we hold on to things that sepa-rate us from God. It is only when we confess these things and turn away from them that we can come to the Lord in true poverty of spirit and receive His power and authority for our lives. The good news is that God loves to be around people like this, people that know how much they need Him. He loves to fill them with power and authority, or in other words, to give the kingdom of heaven to them! It is His pleasure to give us authority on earth as it is in heaven.

Poverty of spirit can be compared to a company that is not able to pay its bills because of loss of customers, competition, the poor economy, or theft. Eventually the company will reach a point where it has no further recourse for financial help and no other source of revenue. It will then file bankruptcy. In the same way, we, too, need to acknowledge our spiritual bankruptcy before God. This bankruptcy is not only our condition when we *feel* helpless. Remember, God always intended His divine life to be joined to our earthly, human life. When we recognize that apart from Him we can do nothing, and then cry out to Him, God will deposit in our spiritual account all that we need as we depend on Him for our spiritual and emotional wholeness.

A widow friend of mine had just returned from a mission outreach in Fiji. People who loved her financed her trip. Even though she had previously participated in a Discipleship Training School through YWAM, she still emerged with a low self-esteem, which was then reinforced by an incident on the outreach in Fiji. Her low self-esteem was hindering her from fulfilling her dreams and from attaining the fullness of God's plan for her life. During a time of prayer for her, God gave me a delightful picture which I shared with her.

The image the Lord showed me was of a donut company, which I will call Crème Puff Donuts. He also showed me a computer company, which I will call Nikkensoft. The Crème Puff Donuts stock was very volatile, whereas Nikkensoft stock was rock solid. The business friends who had donated money for her Discipleship Training School and outreach to Fiji had invested in the solid stock—which was her. I told her that they had not invested in the fad-driven Crème Puff Donuts stock, which would get stale in two days and be smashed flat. I pointed out to her that these friends did not make poor investment choices and that this is why they had invested in her.

I told her to always visualize herself as the rock-solid stock that God and others invested in as a worthwhile investment. She went from being poor in spirit to being whole, knowing who she is in God's sight. Ephesians 1:3 says, "Blessed be the God and Father of our Lord Jesus Christ, who has blessed us with every spiritual blessing in the heavenly places in Christ." And 2 Peter 1:3 says, "His divine power has given to us all things that pertain to life and godliness through our knowledge of Him." During a teaching time in Seattle a few years later, I ran into this friend and I was thrilled to see her growth in the Lord. She was with a wonderful man who cared for her greatly. It will be interesting to see the future that God has in store for them.

If therapists and doctors were really so successful at healing people of their emotional wounds, their offices would not be so busy with repeat customers. The truth is, no one but Jesus can reveal our brokenness and the work that must be done in us so that we can heal. We are poor in spirit, and when we cry out to Him, He brings all the riches of the kingdom of heaven to bear in restoring our poverty-stricken spirits. Jesus' instruction to us to deny ourselves and take up our cross and follow Him means that we surrender our will to the will of God. In doing so, we learn to desire what He desires.

Charles Stanley once told a story on his radio broadcast about a man who came to him and said that he was interested in being involved in a missionary trip sometime in the future. The man said, however, that he would probably never *really* be able to go on such a trip because he had so many responsibilities. He had house payments, car payments, and other debts to meet. Charles Stanley warned this man that God could take all his possessions away from him, and then he would have no excuses.

This is what happened to me. I lost everything. Then, when I could not find a job in my field and was broken, God sent a man to me from a nonprofit Christian crisis relief organization. Later I realized that he could only have been sent by God. Determined to meet me, he had crashed a female-only luncheon! Because of his boldness, I became associated with Northwest Medical Teams, and I entered into a series of encounters that transformed my life.

Out of one of the most broken times of my life came one of my greatest, life-changing stories. I traveled to orphanages in Romania, a children's hospital in Moldova, and remote areas of Mexico to serve God's children. Because I was so broken in my spirit from my personal losses, when I saw these children without proper clothing or food, absolutely devoid of books or toys, God began working in my heart. I was able to see God's priorities for His kingdom.

In my brokenness and poverty of spirit, God began to birth in me a vision and the purpose He had for me. He could not have reached me without this brokenness because I would have continued in the for-profit world, making more money and seeking worldly power. God promises that if we are poor in spirit and acknowledge our bankruptcy through confession and depend on Him, we will have peace and the assurance of His open door to heaven and authority. Complete dependence on God and trust in Him is the foundation of obedience to Him. Our obedience to Him releases power and authority to us as citizens of God's kingdom.

Jesus puts this Beatitude first, because being poor in spirit is the foundation for all the other character traits that follow. His promise is, "yours is the kingdom of heaven." This Beatitude could be restated like this: "Oh, what joy and gladness you will have when you realize that your ability is limited and you can be so helpless and broken at times but still put your trust in God. In your awareness of your inadequacy and your obedience to God, He will show you the kingdom of heaven which will be your inheritance and authority on earth as it is in heaven."

Gary:

As we begin the process of reflecting on the Beatitudes as the measuring stick for those who are being qualified to have authority on earth as it is in heaven, the first thing to notice is the order in which they are given. There is a purpose to their order, a progressive encounter with God's character requirements which must be formed in our lives that we might fulfill His desires for us.

Therefore, it is significant that the first requirement for heaven's authority to be released is poverty of spirit. There is no great mystery as to what the words mean. Poverty is a condition of having no resources, of being totally dependent upon the resources of another. One who is poverty stricken is one who is at the end of his means, who has no hope of changing his circumstance by his own strength. For most of us, living as we do in our affluent culture, we see poverty only at a distance; it rarely touches us except in a secondhand way.

Once in awhile, however, some circumstance emerges that allows us to touch poverty more personally. In the late summer of 2005, a massive hurricane named Katrina pounded the Gulf Coast of the United States, bringing great destruction to a huge region of the nation. We sympathized with those who were forced to leave everything and escape the storm's fury. We watched with horror as people who had made the decision to stay in their homes rather than evacuate experienced the terrifying reality of nature's strength. It was a gripping scenario, and for days the nation's news agencies were riveted on this story.

In the midst of that event, one vignette that captured my attention involved a group of people who had been vacationing in New Orleans. They were people of means, but suddenly their wealth meant nothing, as they were completely unable to make arrangements to get out of town. They had paid $25,000 to charter a bus to come into the city to take them away, only to find that the armed forces in the city commandeered the bus before it could get to them. In that circumstance, these people had no recourse, and though they eventually found a way out, the anger and frustration rooted in fear was obvious in their faces as they told their story.

Poverty of spirit is like that. It is the sometimes shocking awareness that when it comes to living up to the values and expectations of God's heavenly kingdom, all of us are weighed in the scales and found to be too light. The statement of Paul the apostle in Romans 3:23 is pointed and powerful: "For all have sinned and fall short of the glory of God." Poverty of spirit is the realization that nothing we do will set us straight with God or produce the kind of powerful life we were created to live in and enjoy.

A story in the New Testament gives us a wonderful example of Jesus' attraction to people who are poor in spirit.[2] He told the story as a parable—a real-life situation used to illustrate a spiritual principle. The story involved a man who was a tax collector and was therefore despised among the Jewish people because of his involvement with the Roman government and because of the greed that was so common among those of that profession. This tax collector, however, went to the temple to pray, and he called out to God for mercy on his sinful existence. Je-

2   See Luke 18:9-14

sus pointed out the contrast between this prayer and the prayer of a self-righteous Pharisee, who gave thanks for his own spirituality that made him "so much better" than the tax collector.

Jesus' praise was reserved for the sinner. This man came to God in recognition of his need for mercy, instead of justifying himself and pretending to have no need. This awareness and acknowledgement of the need for God's help and mercy is poverty of spirit, and it is no accident that it is first on the list of the Beatitudes. We have no way forward out of the stuck places of our lives without first standing before the Lord in humility and brokenness of spirit, acknowledging how much we need His intervention. And make no mistake—all of us are in stuck places in comparison to what God desires and has in store for us! The tragic figures of life are not mainly those who have trouble. The tragic figures of life are those who think they are all right, who do not see their need for God and therefore do not call out to Him for help.

Jesus and Poverty of Spirit

It is necessary for us to see that Jesus Himself lived in the constant awareness of how much He needed the help and strength of God, His Father. This is shown clearly in His encounter with the Jewish religious leaders, recorded in chapter five of the Gospel of John. Here's the scenario: Jesus has just healed a crippled man in a wonderful way, and the Jews are upset because He healed on the Sabbath day. Jewish tradition and religious legalism had turned the day of rest into a spiritual and social prison by restricting activity instead of calling the people to a day of intimate communion with God designed to bring rest to their bodies, souls, and spirits. So, when Jesus revealed the tender mercy of God by healing this man on the Sabbath, the Jewish leaders missed the whole point and were furious.

When they questioned Him about the event, Jesus gave this surprising reason for healing the man:

Most assuredly, I say to you, the Son can do nothing of Himself, but what He sees the Father do; for whatever He does, the Son also does in like manner. (John 5:19)

Here's the startling truth of this confession: Jesus, the Son of God, is declaring that He can do nothing on His own initiative! The most powerful man in the universe is admitting that He has no strength unless the Father gives it to Him! Jesus goes on in the next verse to reveal the delightful dimension of intimacy with His Father that releases this strength and authority in His life:

> *For the Father loves the Son, and shows Him all things that He Himself does; and He will show Him greater works than these, that you may marvel. (John 5:20)*

It is so important that we grasp what is being shown us here! Jesus, the ultimate man, is declaring that He has no ability to do anything on His own.[3] Jesus can't do anything for God; He can only do what God gives Him the strength to do in the context of their intimate friendship. He is completely dependent upon His love relationship with His Father to know what to do and to have the ability to do it. Jesus realized that He had come to fulfill God's mysterious plan of bringing all heavenly things and all earthly things together in Himself. He was a man, but one who was full of the Spirit of God. In His merely fleshly existence, He could do nothing of power on His own initiative.

This is poverty of spirit at its best, and the example is given to us that we might embrace the same reality in our lives. The realization that in our mere flesh we can do nothing is the essence of poverty of spirit. If Jesus could do nothing on His own initiative, how much can we do on our own?

But God designed us to participate in *His* life. Jesus models true humanity by cultivating His relationship with the Father, listening to Him, watching Him with the eyes of the Spirit, and doing whatever the Father is doing. The wonderful news is that the Father loves the Son and shows Him everything He Himself does. Because the Father shows the Son what He is doing, Jesus is empowered to do those same things, and therefore *we* have the reward that comes to those with poverty of spirit—the kingdom of heaven!

Every time Jesus did what the Father was doing, the earthly and the heavenly came together. The man operated in poverty of spirit, and the Father released signs and wonders. The one who was poor in spirit received

---

3   The Greek word used here is *dunamis,* referring to the ability or power to do something.

the kingdom, and modeled the life of true humanity for the rest of us.

We must not confuse God's motives here. He is not a controller, limiting our activity so that He can pull the strings of our lives like some sort of cosmic puppeteer. That image of God is a horrible caricature and is true of Satan, not God. The God that Jesus knows as Father desires His children to live in the full reality of His power and liberty. Jesus walked in the freedom of that power on earth because every moment He recognized His need for God's life to be lived through Him.

We are created to live every day in the power of God. Yet we don't often see that reality lived out in our day. I believe this is because the vast majority of God's children don't even know that He desires for us to live like Jesus did, much less that He has made the power available for that kind of living. For this reason the Holy Spirit is raising up the message of intimacy, righteousness, and power flowing from God to His people at this time in history so that we might be transformed into Jesus' DNA and experience authority on earth as it is in heaven.

The Father spoke to Jesus of the greater works that would be shown to Him. In John 14:12 Jesus promises that those greater works would be done by believers after He departed to be with the Father in heaven. Do you see? This inheritance that Jesus touched in His daily experience is given to us, and we will receive it in exactly the same way as He received it. We come in poverty of spirit, acknowledging that we can do nothing on our own initiative. And we are also aware that the Father loves us and is willing to show us everything He is doing! When we learn to see with spiritual eyes and listen with ears of the heart, we will find ourselves doing the things that Jesus did, with the anticipation of even greater works being released as our faith increases.

The Reward: The Kingdom of Heaven

Jesus makes an astonishing promise to those who will come before the Father in poverty of spirit. He says "the kingdom of heaven will be yours." In other words, those who embrace the character qualities of the Beatitudes will become participants in the life God intended for them here on earth now and in the fullness of the kingdom of God in the age to come. This is the life Jesus lived, a life fully established in a relationship of intimate friendship with God. It's a life filled with His attitudes and expressed in His character. It's a life characterized by the power and authority that Jesus had.

There is a story in the Old Testament about a king that illustrates in some key ways what we are speaking about in this chapter. Manasseh was a king in Jerusalem, reigning over the southern kingdom of Judah, and he was wicked in his ways. He did not seek the Lord, and he in fact promoted idolatry in the land. God brought him into a season of severe corrective discipline by the king of Assyria, who bound Manasseh with chains and deported him to Babylon, located in present-day Iraq.

Manasseh's response to this trouble was to humble himself and cry out to the Lord for mercy. His plea before God was effective:

Now when he was in affliction, he implored the LORD his God, and humbled himself greatly before the God of his fathers, and prayed to Him; and He received his entreaty, heard his supplication, and brought him back to Jerusalem into his kingdom. Then Manasseh knew that the LORD was God. (2 Chronicles 33:12-13)

God's purpose is always for His people to live in the fullness of His provision, blessing, and authority. However, when we become arrogant, as Manasseh did, and try to manage our lives apart from the presence and the will of God, things will eventually go very sour. The only effective thing we can do at that point is to humble ourselves, call upon the Name of the Lord, and turn back to making intimacy with Him the priority of our time and energy.

As we do this, God responds to us like He did to Manasseh. He receives our prayers, hears our cries, and restores to us the things that He allowed to be taken away. His promises of blessing, protection, provision, power, and authority begin to be released in our lives again as we continue to recognize how much we need God for every situation of our lives.

Marie and I had an experience of this sort of restoration during the first year of our marriage. Having been married only seven months at the time, we were still very much in the process of discovering who we are together and what we each bring to this relationship. The Holy Spirit had been probing us both because of His determination for us to walk in a manner consistent with His calling on our lives.

This particular situation revolved around the fact that in past years I had used my position as a teacher and writer to draw attention and affirmation from people in ways that were inappropriate and damaging. Because many personal disappointments had accumulated over years of ministry and family life, I justified my behavior and created scenarios in which my ego could be massaged to the degree I thought I deserved.

Through some prophetic insight given to Marie personally as well as through an intercessor friend, the Holy Spirit began to probe my heart, revealing my dark motives and damaging decisions. These things had a powerful and negative effect on Marie, and she began to feel mistrust and a deep fear that I would again lapse into those old patterns.

Over about a three-day period, we began to hammer out the very difficult and exhausting process of confrontation and acknowledgement, repentance and forgiveness. A wall had emerged in our relationship that terrified both of us. We both had sensed that God has something profound for us in days to come, and suddenly those promises seemed threatened at a basic level. We were both frightened and uncertain how to proceed.

So we began to call out to God in our broken condition. The amazing reality of the gospel is that God loves and even enjoys us while we are in weakness. He is delighted when we trust Him with our deepest pains and issues. All either of us could do was to weakly say, "Jesus, help me." In our poverty of spirit, there was no other prayer we could pray.

Over the space of a couple of days, God heard our cries and gave us courage and strength to persist in the process. In the past both of us would have turned away in fear or discouragement, but the Lord Jesus infused into us a determination to not move away from each other. As we moved toward each other in forgiveness and mercy, the Holy Spirit kept His part of the bargain and began to release a deeper quality of love and affection than we had known before. What could have been a disastrous and undermining event has instead become one of the anchor points of our marriage, a stone of remembrance that has deepened our commitment to holiness before the Lord and faithfulness to one another at every level.

We want you to understand what was so helpful to us in this situation: the Holy Spirit helped us weeks ahead of time by helping us cultivate a listening ear so that we could respond to His prompting at the right time. The Lord had spoken to Marie earlier in that year about time with Him in "the courtyard," where she would be given understanding. We interpreted this to be the place of worship and intimate prayer, and in that environment of communion He focused the issues that eventually would be addressed. These hints from the Holy Spirit are not given for the purpose of punishment or humiliation, but for the purpose of restoration and healing. However, God is purposeful about His desire for His beloved. He means for us to be holy even as He is holy, and He means to have a Bride who is a helper comparable to His pure Son.

The Value of Trying Circumstances

In his first letter to the Corinthian believers, Paul writes these words:

No temptation has overtaken you except such as is common to man; but God is faithful, who will not allow you to be tempted beyond what you are able, but with the temptation will also make the way of escape, that you may be able to bear it. (1 Corinthians 10:13)

Temptations come as probing points in our lives. The original word for "temptation" simply means a trial, or a probing test. The issue is not whether we will be probed; we most certainly will be. The issue is this: in the time of testing, will we run to the place of personal gratification and short-term pleasure, or will we run in poverty of spirit to the Throne of Grace "to receive mercy and find grace to help in our time of need."[4]

Psalm 34:11-20 shows how the Lord describes His attitude toward the ones who run to Him in this way:

Come, you children, listen to me;
I will teach you the fear of the LORD.
Who is the man who desires life,
And loves many days, that he may see good?
Keep your tongue from evil,
And your lips from speaking deceit.
Depart from evil and do good;
Seek peace and pursue it.

---

4   See Hebrews 4:16

The eyes of the LORD are on the righteous,
And His ears are open to their cry.
The face of the LORD is against those who do evil,
To cut off the remembrance of them from the earth.
The righteous cry out, and the LORD hears,
And delivers them out of all their troubles.
The LORD is near to those who have a broken heart,
And saves such as have a contrite spirit.
Many are the afflictions of the righteous,
But the LORD delivers him out of them all.
He guards all his bones;
Not one of them is broken.

There is a way of escape from the temptations that the Lord allows for the purpose of revealing our hearts. It is the way of poverty of spirit, and He is jealous over us to find that way.

This testing makes itself known in many ways. Let me share another story that illustrates the point. I have a dear friend who is a businessman in Madison, Wisconsin. Dave owns and operates two fitness centers in that city and has been enormously successful over the past couple of decades. Over 25,000 people in Madison have memberships at the Princeton Clubs, and the favor and blessing of the Lord rests upon Dave and his family in a profound way. This, I believe, is mainly because Dave has learned how to live as a businessman, a marketplace guy, in the ongoing dynamic of intimacy with the Lord. His days are filled with constant and ongoing conversation with Jesus, even as he runs his business, leads his family, and meets many people on a daily basis.

The key is that he began to cultivate with God a relationship of intimate submission, and therefore intimate authority, years before the business became what it is now. Dave was a fledgling businessman in his mid-twenties when the opportunity came to purchase the fitness center that became the Princeton Club. He put together an investment group, raised the necessary capital (somewhere in the neighborhood of two million dollars), and felt as though the Lord was going to bless this venture. On the morning that the deal was set to close escrow, the Holy Spirit spoke to Dave in the quietness of his heart and asked him to lay the deal down, to not do it. He knew it was the voice of the Lord.

Dave was devastated. He had business partners to think of, and his own reputation as a credible businessman was on the line. He could have pressed past these very subjective feelings in his heart and rationalized the purchase of the club. He had the backing of reputable partners and the confidence of the men from whom he was buying the business. Deep in his heart, however, Dave realized that to move forward with the purchase would be to trust his own judgment and value his own reputation more than the voice of God. He would move out of the place of intimacy and confidence in the Lord's leading. He would save face in the short-term but lose that wonderful sense of partnership with God in his business ventures.

Dave went to the closing that day and shut the deal down. It was painful and humiliating, and he bore the price of that decision over the next couple of years. No one really understood why he had done what he did, and he himself was bombarded with thoughts of being ridiculous and hyper-spiritual.

A couple of years later, however, the Lord vindicated Dave's willingness to live as one who is poor in spirit, who knows how much he needs God. The men from whom Dave was going to buy the center called and asked to see him. When he walked into their office, they declared their inability to find a suitable buyer and their unwillingness to have anyone but him own the club. They then proceeded to *give* the fitness center to Dave—property, membership, machinery—everything! In one moment God vindicated the trust of His friend Dave and since that time has given favor to Dave in the marketplace of Madison. In 2004 Dave opened the second center, a $15 million structure that is a wonder to behold. Within a year of opening, the membership at the clubs doubled and a strong profit margin was realized.

As Dave has continued in that style of living and leading for nearly twenty years since that occurrence, God has shown Himself faithful to Dave and his family. The blessing of the kingdom of God is upon him, and his positive influence is profoundly felt by many people. In the summer of 2005, Dave and his family opened a House of Prayer for the city in conjunction with one of the clubs, and the blessing increases.

The promise of the kingdom of God being given to the poor in spirit is not only for this present age. The ultimate purpose of God is to bring all things in heaven and earth together under one head, namely, Jesus Christ.[5] His kingdom is going to increase eternally, and it will be governed by those who live in the same spiritual reality in which Jesus lived during His first venture to the earth. Tangible, physical, earthly reward is coming to all who embrace this reality. The wise will take heed, will seek the Lord with all their heart, and will love Him with everything within them.

Poor in Spirit - theirs is the K of Heaven

POWER POINT OF THIS CHAPTER:

Those who are aware of how much they need God to reach their potential will be given the full power of His Kingdom.

FOR DISCUSSION AND REFLECTION:

1. In your personal journal, write about a time when you felt completely alone, broken and helpless.

2. Ask the Holy Spirit to reveal to you the hurts, the sins, and the feelings of inadequacy that you face in your own heart. Ask God to bring His healing and forgiveness to you, and to reveal to you His plan and purpose for your destiny.

3. Share these things with a small circle of friends and ask them to pray for you, that the power of God would heal you and release you into His truth for your life.

---

5   See Ephesians 1:10

CHAPTER FOUR

POWERFUL PEOPLE ARE THOSE WHO MOURN

*Blessed are those who mourn, for they
shall be comforted. (Matthew 5:4)*

Marie:

The Navy was transferring my son, along with his wife and their children, across the United States. Saying goodbye to them was especially difficult. By this point in my life I had lost my business and was in the process of selling my home and turning the equity over to my business partner. I had also lost my car and my savings, and the man I was to marry had left me. Any comfort that I could claim in my church and Bible study group evaporated because of a horrible scandal that involved our senior pastor. My entire support system was gone. I used to joke that at least I had my dog, but then he was taken away also. I felt like a female Job.

One day I got down on my knees and cried so hard that I thought my insides would be drained of every ounce of fluid. I cried out to the Lord for every injustice, and every sin for which I was sorry. Pain over the mistakes I had made came pouring out in cleansing tears. This is what is called "holy mourning" or "godly sorrow." Holy mourning is when we are deeply sorry for our own sins and also for the pain we have suffered through no fault of our own. It is when we cry out to God to change us, because nothing else seems to be working. It is when we reach the end of our own means and realize that only God can help us.

All of us have hurts for one reason or another. We would not be human if we did not. Because we interact with people, we are bound to get hurt and have memories of things that have wounded us. The Beatitudes are designed by God to heal hurts that are chronic and those that are acute.

When I was in the treatment center in Ohio, I believed that I was in the wrong place because the abuse I had suffered as a child was not of an acute nature, at least not as I compared myself with the other patients. I soon learned that the Lord wants to heal all our wounds, and forgive all our sins. It is important to know that God is concerned about us and loves us so much that He wants to heal everything in us, no matter the origin of the problem.

Below are examples of hurts of a chronic and of an acute nature. It may be helpful for you to identify the source and nature of your pain. The Lord cares so much that, whether your pain is acute or chronic, He wants you to be set free so you can return to what He originally planned for you. Joy, peace, and love will shine through you and lead others to want to know your secret for living joyfully.

Example of Chronic Emotional Hurt

You came home after school every day as a young child, and no one was home. You had the responsibilities of an adult and none of the privileges of a child. Negative messages were conveyed to you about yourself on a daily basis. You might never have received hugs or tender, encouraging words. Maybe you were made fun of at school week after week, and no one stopped the insults.

Over time you began to believe the messages that you had no value, no worth to anyone, and so you developed defense mechanisms to protect yourself. Perhaps you vowed, like I did, to become strong so that no one could hurt you again. Or perhaps you gave in to depression and self-hatred and became lost in the pit of despair.

This Beatitude offers the only pathway to receive true comfort for the pain of those situations. Only the grace of mourning will bring you to the point where the Spirit of God can comfort you at the deepest levels of your need.

Examples of Acute Emotional Hurt

I read about a child who, every time he made his parents angry, was put in a cold shower without his clothes on. Time after time he cried for them to stop because he was so cold, but they ignored his cries. As an adult, this young man did not know that this was an inappropriate way to discipline a child, until someone told him. Can you imagine how he grieved and mourned when he discovered the truth? Can you imagine the anger he experienced?

Another example is of a woman I counseled for many years who has acute symptoms of abuse and will always deal with some sort of mental handicap until God heals her completely. He has already done miraculous work within her, and she is a beautiful witness to His great power. Her bad memories still remain, but the Lord has given her a toolbox full of His love and grace to get her through the tough times.

As a child, she was left alone in a car night after night while her mother got drunk in a bar. One night, at three in the morning, someone saw her sitting in the car crying and finally reported it to the police. She was sent to one foster care home after another. Eventually she was adopted but then was sexually abused by her stepbrother. Through her life she has suffered many physical and emotional problems. The reason she has come to some measure of healing today is because she recognized her brokenness and mourned her sins and the sins of those who harmed her.

Mourning the Pain of Others

This Beatitude shows us that we must be sensitive to the hurts of others, experiencing the brokenness they feel. We must mourn for the hurts they have suffered. God promises that if we mourn, we will be comforted. Yet mourning also refers to being desperately sorry for our own sin and unworthiness. The sensitive soul will grieve for its own sins and see them as a great offense against God.

God has never promised us immunity from sorrow, suffering, and pain. I recently heard a guest speaker on Dr. James Dobson's radio show tell about the deaths of her two Christian sons only months apart from each other, followed by the revelation of her only surviving son's homosexuality. One can only imagine the depth of grief and mourning that she has experienced in her journey.

Mourning can also be a comfort when we realize that we are going through God's "university" of learning who He is, what His character is, and how He teaches us through our suffering and trials. If we do not mourn and grieve, the results can be emotional depression, internalized guilt, repressed feelings, lack of trust, social isolation, short attention span, and inability to concentrate. Some of the losses you might have experienced include loss of childhood, loss of love, loss of choice, loss of joy and happiness, loss of belief system, and the loss of dreams and promises.

Hindrances to Mourning

James 4:7-10 gives us important insight into the necessity of mourning and lamenting over our brokenness and sin:

> *Therefore submit to God. Resist the devil and he will flee from you. Draw near to God and He will draw near to you. Cleanse your hands, you sinners; and purify your hearts, you double-minded. Lament and mourn and weep! Let your laughter be turned to mourning and your joy to gloom. Humble yourselves in the sight of the Lord, and He will lift you up.*

Since mourning over our situation is central to experiencing the blessing of God, you must be aware of those things that can hinder you from taking this step of mourning. If these hindrances are not removed, you will never experience the true healing of the Lord. The Beatitudes are in perfect order, and it would therefore not make sense to move on to the next Beatitude. If you cannot complete the mourning process, you will never know the blessing of being comforted by people who God places in your life or the peace that God imparts through His comfort. Some hindrances to mourning include the following:

- A loss of hope due to the circumstances of life. The resultant despair may become so overwhelming that true mourning is blocked.

- The love of sin. True mourning requires a desire to be done with sin, whereas a love for sin keeps us from the power of God to set us free.

- A lack of the sense of urgency. We think we have lots of time and do not consider that our lives are fragile and little more than a breath of wind.

- An attitude of self-righteousness. Self-righteous people have a façade of "holy" behavior, with little or no internal character behind it. Such people often are judgmental toward everyone but themselves.

- The lack of a prayer life. God responds to the prayers of His people; but when we do not pray, we eliminate the main avenue of connection with Him.

- A selfish, self-centered approach to life. People who seek their own way without regard for God's desires or the needs of others will not likely give themselves to mourning.

- And finally, the desire to maintain control. True mourning involves a willingness to let go of deep pain and to express anguish over things we have done, and things others have done to us. The need to maintain control blocks the expression of mourning.

The Blessing of Comfort

The best part of the mourning process is the blessing. Jesus promises a blessing for those who go through this mourning process. He says, "Blessed are those that mourn for they shall be comforted." The reality of this promise has been my experience. Here is what happened after I mourned my sins and confessed my pain to Jesus:

After I lost my house, I lived in a bedroom in the home of some friends for a year. I was very unhappy there. I was reminded in a number of ways that I was not welcome. As I cried out my pain, the Lord provided a guest home above a garage on a lake in the country. He also sent friends who helped me get back on my feet emotionally. He led me to a new church that was very loving and kind. He also provided a wonderful job for me. This gave me a real perspective of the Lord's kindness during a time of sufferings. He blessed me with vision and with success in the organization for which I worked.

I knew that God was showing me a pathway to my destiny, because had all these things not happened in my life, I would never have moved into a life of ministry. He used the abuse I experienced as a child and my dysfunction as an adult to help others. But first He wanted me to grieve over my life and to heal so that I could show others the beautiful map to righteousness and power He has laid out in the Beatitudes.

As we continue in this journey through the Beatitudes and ask the Lord to transform us, we will begin to experience a subtle change in our spirit, heart, and soul. We will begin to touch that divine power that God has been telling us about in His word.

As Gary and I were preparing to teach one morning in Dallas, Texas, in my spirit I heard the word *priest*. I recognized the voice of the Lord. I asked the Lord to reveal to me the meaning, and I heard, "Search out how they prepared to go before God in holiness." I went to the book of Exodus and was reminded that God was very specific about the garments that the priests were to wear such as the ephod, breastpiece, and robe. These garments symbolized how the high priest presented the people to God, and also represented God to the people. Today the Lord is taking us to a greater level of maturity and authority as priests so that we may see the miracles that He has promised. He is emphasizing this revelation in this day so that we will be a Church filled with His power. We are to clothe ourselves in righteousness via the pathway of the Beatitudes so that we may have power on earth as it is in heaven, power to do the greater works that He promised.

Gary:

I heard the grandfather clock in the living room chiming the hour at 4:00 AM. I was lying on the floor of our bedroom, calling out to the Lord in a place of deep anguish and desperation. Marie and I had been experiencing one of the divine ambushes that the Holy Spirit is so adept at arranging, and I had come face to face with several issues in my life that had profoundly negative implications for our relationship and the well-being of our family. As we had wrestled through the issues the previous evening, it was painfully apparent that I needed an encounter with the Lord at a foundational level.

As I pressed my face into the carpet in prayer, the specter of sinful choices made long before loomed over me like a street fighter over a defeated foe. I needed a breakthrough of a certain kind—the grace to deeply mourn over my sin and see the effects of that sin broken in my life. Minutes turned to hours as I struggled with God, finally coming to a place of peace that would allow me to sleep.

As Marie and I prayed together the next morning, the dam burst, and all the pent-up grief and accompanying fear came to the surface. We held each other and called out to God as we wept, and the breakthrough came—much later than I would have preferred.

The words of Jesus from Matthew 5:4 offer a strange but real assurance in times like that:

Blessed are those who mourn, for they shall be comforted.

Real mourning is a lost art in our medicated Western culture. Our extreme distaste for any experience of painful emotion drives us to all sorts of attempts to bring comfort to the situation in which real comfort stubbornly eludes us. We would rather do almost anything rather than endure a place of darkness. We drink alcohol, swallow pills, inject drugs, consume food, have affairs, spend money, leave town—anything to avoid an experience of real mourning. We desire comfort but seem unwilling to do the very thing that Jesus says is the root system of true comfort.

What is in view in this second Beatitude? The entry for *mourning* in Vincent's Word Studies speaks of grieving that is too deep for concealment. To underscore this interpretation, the word *mourning* in the New Testament is often used with the idea of weeping audibly. It implies that something comes into focus, some issue or pain, that is so dominating, so overwhelming, that we can't hide it any longer. All we can do in those times is mourn, crying out in agony over the situation in which we find ourselves.

Mourning Our Own Brokenness

Mourning is especially necessary when our own broken condition is the focus. When the reality of the effect of sin hits us in the face, the only right response is to face it bravely and allow its weight to have its maximum impact. The sinful condition of our lives involves the destructive things that have been done to us as well as our destructive responses to those situations. Our sinfulness also directly involves owning our own damaging choices rooted in selfishness and rebellion against God and His ways. Real healing and restoration can only begin in our lives when we are willing to squarely face the responsibility that we have for our situations—sinful responses to the acts of others and the sinfulness that arises out of our own dark hearts. We must allow the Holy Spirit to convict our hearts of our own sin, to feel the weight of it, and to begin to mourn over the whole thing.

A powerful example of this mourning occurs in the New Testament example of Peter in the aftermath of his denial of Jesus during His trial and crucifixion. Luke's gospel tells us that when Peter claimed for the third time that he did not know Jesus, a rooster crowed (just as Jesus had predicted) and Jesus' eyes locked with Peter's. Peter was immediately filled with agonizing conviction of his failure, and his response was to mourn over his sin. He went out and wept bitterly.

At some point in our lives we must come face to face with the fact that we have chosen again and again to follow our own agenda rather than the will of God. Peter denied knowing Jesus because he was operating in fear and self-protection at the expense of his commitments to his Lord. When he realized what he had done, it grieved his spirit beyond measure, beyond his capacity to contain it. Each of us must come to that place. There must come a time when the reality of our failure and the gaze of Jesus are focused on us, and when we feel the depth of our sin and can no longer excuse it or explain it away. At that point our only alternative is to mourn.

More Barriers To Mourning

One of the great problems with our fallen human nature is that we will do almost anything to avoid facing the reality of our situation. But we must face reality in order to mourn over it and move forward. In our contemporary culture we have grown to hate the thought of taking any kind of responsibility for the circumstances of our lives. We have cultivated a culture of blame shifting; we would rather find fault with something outside ourselves than to reckon ourselves responsible. We would rather blame the food industry for filling their products with fat and chemicals than face the fact that we are gluttons, unwilling to discipline our appetites. In the fall of 2005, the courts of the United States issued an amazing ruling that people who are obese can no longer bring lawsuits against fast-food restaurants! We would rather blame the government for taking prayer out of schools than acknowledge the fact that we are prayerless people. We want to put an interpretive spin on our situations so that we appear in the best possible light. So, we construct elaborate and devious schemes so that someone else—anyone else—will be forced to take the blame for our condition.

Another way that we avoid true mourning is by keeping our grief at a superficial level. We feel sorry for ourselves in the face of troublesome circumstances rather than allow the situation to expose our deeper issues. An example of this is seen in a biblical story found in Genesis 19, which speaks to this avoidance tendency in a powerful way. A man named Lot, the nephew of Abraham, had taken up residence in the wicked city of Sodom. Over time, God became fed up with the evil practices of the citizens there, and He determined to bring judgment to the city by raining down fire from heaven to destroy it. Three angels came to Lot to warn him of the impending disaster, and they urged him to take his family and leave town immediately. The angels specifically warned Lot and his family not to look back at the destruction of the city. I believe they received this warning to avoid being caught themselves in that judgment. Lot's wife ignored the advice, looked back as they were leaving, and was turned into a pillar of salt!

Some might think that the reason she looked back was that she was mourning the loss of her home and friends, but the mourning called for in the Beatitudes requires a deeper process. Lot's wife had a more basic issue. Deep in her heart this woman had a love for the ethos of the city, an attraction to the lusty lifestyle that surrounded her.[1] She had allowed her heart to become attached to a compromising situation. Instead of truly mourning the duplicity in her own heart and rejoicing in the true comfort of God's deliverance, she felt sorry for herself and gave herself to yearning after the lost pleasures of Sodom. She thus received judgment instead of real comfort and freedom.

1   See Luke 17:28-33

Shame as the Greatest Barrier

Another issue that causes us to avoid true mourning is the matter of shame. The Encarta World English Dictionary defines shame as "a negative emotion that combines feelings of unworthiness, dishonor, and embarrassment." My own personal definition of shame is the presence of an issue or condition that we fear will condemn us and cause us to be separated from everyone and everything that we care about.

Some years ago I was talking with a friend who was a pastoral counselor. I had been giving some thought to the problem of shame, so I asked him "Where does the issue of shame stand in the top ten list that people deal with from day to day?" His immediate answer was profound and disturbing. He said, "Shame is number one, and there is no number two."

Here's the problem with shame. When we are filled with shame, our universal response is to try to hide the issue or condition. We cover it up, keep it secret, and pretend it's not there. We avoid talking about it because we're convinced that if the truth comes out, we will be rejected. We can scarcely stand to admit the issue to ourselves, let alone to anyone else. When we do allow it to come to the surface, we often combine it with self-condemnation and regret. We take the role of judge upon ourselves and declare ourselves unworthy of love, dignity, and destiny—all those things that are essential components of people who are becoming truly free and powerful.

I am convinced that the only way to truly deal with the shame issues of our lives is to begin with deep mourning over those issues. More than feeling sorry for ourselves, more than despair over a past that cannot be reclaimed, mourning means to come before God in the depths of our anguish and throw ourselves upon Him to receive His mercy and grace. Again, a Biblical story helps us understand how this can work.

The Old Testament book of Second Samuel gives the record of an individual with a most unusual name—Mephibosheth. This strange name is the combination of two Hebrew words that mean "dispeller of shame." It literally means "to cut shame to pieces," which sounds like a powerful and good thing! What sort of situation did Mephibosheth live in that resulted in his having a name like that? My understanding of this began to emerge during a time of deep crisis in my own life.

Some years ago I was pastoring a Vineyard church in Aurora, Colorado. For a number of years the church had a positive presence of the Lord, an anointing for teaching and healing, and a wonderful spirit of worship that permeated everything we did. Over the years, however, the Lord allowed my bad leadership qualities and the reality of secret compromise in my heart to have its effect. In the early 1990s the church began to disintegrate, and we closed the doors in September of 1992. During this season I began to face some shame issues in my life, starting a long process of dealing with them.

As I was studying the Scriptures one day, I came across the New International Version's rendition of Psalm 34:5: "Those who look to [the Lord] are radiant, and their faces are never covered with shame." I was drawn to study that word, only to discover that the Hebrew word for "shame" is *bosheth*. Immediately I recalled two names from the Old Testament that incorporate this word. The first is the name Ishbosheth, which means "man of shame." Ishbosheth was the son of King Saul; he was installed by Saul's military commander Abner as a puppet king after Saul's death in an attempt to block David's ascension to the throne.[2] Rather than trusting that God would exalt him to a position of honor under David's leadership, Ishbosheth assumed responsibility for his own destiny by cooperating with the resistance. Motivated by fear of Abner and by the desire to find significance apart from God's purposes, he sided with the wrong group. He tried to bolster his ego by clinging to the outward trappings of royalty and honor. Ishbosheth, the man of shame, ended up being murdered in his own bed by men that he thought were loyal. Truly his life ended in shame and reproach.

The other individual with *boshet*" in his name was the man named Mephibosheth. I did the word studies and found that his name had the meaning of dispelling shame. I quickly turned to Second Samuel to research the story.

Mephibosheth was the son of King David's friend Jonathan. As a little child, Mephibosheth was dropped by a nurse and he became a paraplegic, crippled in his feet and unable to walk. He was also the descendant of Israel's first king, King Saul, who had a shameful career as the leader of God's people. Saul was beset by the fear of people's opinions, did not seek after God, and had the kingdom wrested away

---

2   See 2 Samuel 2-17 for the entire context of this story

from him and given to David. Mephibosheth was the last survivor of the house of Saul, and David determined to show him mercy for the sake of his friend Jonathan.

The reality of the story is that David had every right to eliminate all of Saul's descendants. It was the way of kings in those days to remove any possibility of rivals emerging from the previous regime, and this was usually done by execution. However, David had made a promise to Jonathan, and so when he came into power, he sought out Mephibosheth in order to keep his promise. This Scripture text recounts the first meeting between David and Mephibosheth:

> *And Mephibosheth, the son of Jonathan the son of Saul, came to David and fell on his face and prostrated himself. And David said, "Mephibosheth." And he said, "Here is your servant!" And David said to him, "Do not fear, for I will surely show kindness to you for the sake of your father Jonathan, and will restore to you all the land of your grandfather Saul; and you shall eat at my table regularly." Again he prostrated himself and said, "What is your servant, that you should regard a dead dog like me?" (2 Samuel 9:6-8)*

Mephibosheth was in a condition that should have meant death for him. He was a son of the former royal house, and he was crippled, thus making him useless as a worker or a warrior. His response to being summoned by David is significant. He threw himself on the floor, acknowledging the utter poverty of his own condition. David's response was to raise him up, receive him as a son, and to set him at the king's table for all his days. What a gracious and unexpected initiative on the part of King David! What a surprising turn of fortune for this young man! But the depth of what was happening in Mephibosheth's heart is not fully revealed in this portion of the story.

Sometime later, David's own son Absalom initiated a coup attempt, trying to steal the kingdom from his father. David, who was old and nearing the end of his years, considered that God may be finished with him as king. So he relinquished the throne for a time, waiting for God to make His will known more clearly. Mephibosheth had a caregiver named Ziba, who had been part of Saul's kingdom and who was still covetous of the material goods that could come to Mephibosheth through David's kindness. So Ziba, pretending to be loyal to David, told a lie, convincing David that Mephibosheth had become a traitor and joined ranks with Absalom. David believed him and transferred the inheritance to Ziba.

It was only after Absalom was killed that Ziba was exposed in his lie. David returned to the city of Jerusalem to take up his throne again and was met on the way by Mephibosheth. David discovered that the young man had been in a state of mourning during the king's absence. Mephibosheth had not cared for his feet, trimmed his beard, or washed his clothes during the entire time David was gone. When David inquired about the situation, Mephibosheth explained the deception and revealed his loyalty and love for David. When David vowed to give Mephibosheth his portion of Saul's estate, this "dispeller of shame" asked David to give the entire portion to Ziba, with this phrase added on: "inasmuch as my lord the king has come back in peace to his own house." (2 Samuel 19:30).

Here is what is significant to me about this story. Ishbosheth, the man of shame, tried to cling to the external trappings of a kingdom that had fallen. He refused to believe that God would have mercy on him through David, and he died in his shame. Mephibosheth, on the other hand, laid everything down in gratitude for the mercy of David and gave himself to loving the new king. When he had a chance to get his inheritance back, he refused it, saying in effect "All I care about is that the king is here! If the king is here, all else is good!"

We can apply this story in our life situations. There is a kind of mourning that is merely superficial, a feeling of sorrow and regret that things have gone badly for us. It is a narcissistic thing, self-focused and self-absorbed, and it only takes us deeper into the mire of depression and shame. The sorrow we feel comes because at the deepest levels we are consumed with shame and self-hatred. So we either totally disappear in the mire of our despair, or we focus all our energy on maintaining external appearances, conditions that we hope will give us significance. Ishbosheth, the man of shame, tried to preserve external things that would make him feel valuable instead of mourning his condition and making way for David to come to power. Had he done this, I believe that David would have had mercy upon him even as he did upon Mephibosheth.

True mourning happens when we set our eyes on the worth and beauty of the Lord Jesus and begin to understand how our self-centeredness has kept us from experiencing His love and freedom. Rather than trying to maintain any external appearance of dignity, Mephibosheth knew that his only hope was in the presence of King David. His identity would be established by the King. His destiny was wrapped up in the blessing of the king. Only in the king's presence would Mephibosheth come into the fullness of his inheritance. "It is enough for me that the king has returned!"

God's desire is that we would mourn over whatever prevents us from fully trusting in His love and grace.

Mourning That Reflects God's Heart

A second kind of mourning comes into view as we meditate on this Beatitude. It is the sense of grief and agony in the heart of God Himself as He considers the condition of the people He loves.

The Old Testament prophet Jeremiah has often been called the weeping prophet, because throughout much of his life he reflected the broken heart of God for the people of Israel. In one of the most poignant passages in all of Scripture, we see the mourning of God's heart poured out through this tortured prophet:

Listen! The voice,
The cry of the daughter of my people
*   From a far country:*
*   "Is not the LORD in Zion?*
*   Is not her King in her?"*
*   "Why have they provoked Me to anger*
*   With their carved images—*
*   With foreign idols?"*
"The harvest is past,
*   The summer is ended,*
*   And we are not saved!"*
For the hurt of the daughter of my people I am hurt.
*   I am mourning;*
*   Astonishment has taken hold of me.*
Is there no balm in Gilead,
*   Is there no physician there?*
*   Why then is there no recovery*

For the health of the daughter of my people?
Oh, that my head were waters,
And my eyes a fountain of tears,
That I might weep day and night
For the slain of the daughter of my people!
(Jeremiah 8:19-9:1)

A powerful dynamic is at work here in this passage. Jeremiah's ministry occurred during the forty years prior to and during the Babylonian invasion and subsequent deportation of the Jews in 586 BC. In this passage Jeremiah's anguished cry is the human expression of God's broken heart over the spiritual condition of the nation of Israel. Through their continuous and persistent idolatry, God's people have provoked Him to anger, and though His judgments are necessary and just, the impact of His judgments brings Him grief, not joy. In order to communicate the depth of His own grief, God draws a human partner close to Himself and pours out the emotion of His heart through the heart and words of the prophet.

Profound things are at work in this passage. The prophet is feeling the pain of God's people in their abandonment and desolation. Even though the circumstance is upon them precisely because they have rejected God and have been unfaithful to Him, their pain is still real, and it touches the heart of God. He is filled with anguish over the condition of His people, and He communicates that reality to His servant Jeremiah. Speaking by the anointing of the Holy Spirit, Jeremiah feels the despair of the people because God is feeling that pain and sharing it with him. The agony is so deep and powerful within him that all he can do is call out for a greater ability to weep—"Oh that my head were waters, and my eyes a fountain of tears…." Jeremiah sees that he does not have an emotional resource deep enough to express the pain of God's heart, but the misery does not dissipate. All he can do is to stay in the place of astonished mourning, stunned in his encounter with God's broken heart.

Mourning in the Experience of Jesus

The fullness of this prophetic picture of God's mourning comes into focus in the person of Jesus. Several times in the Old Testament God speaks of His desire to have a man who would join with His heart, feeling God's pain, and standing with Him in the ministry of intercessory prayer.[3] If He could find such a man to share in His agony, He would relent from His judgments and release mercy instead. Therefore, when the man Jesus—perfect in obedience, intimate in relationship with God—presented Himself to the Father as the ultimate intercessor, God poured out the fullness of wrath upon His own Son and the fullness of mercy upon all who would respond to His love.

It is a profound thing to consider that God desires to have human partners who will join Him in the expression of His emotions, whether positive or negative. We can scarcely imagine a God with such emotion, let alone one who desires to share that emotion with human beings. But if we can begin to see that this is where Jesus stood, and that God wants to have the same kind of relationship with us, we can begin to be open to the touch of the Holy Spirit that communicates His emotions to us.

This is precisely what Jesus had in mind when He asked His three best friends—Peter, James, and John—to accompany Him to Gethsemane on the night of His trial and crucifixion. Jesus was headed to the dark night of desolation and sacrifice. The experience, borne entirely in His body as a human being, was going to be utterly difficult and painful. The sufferings of Jesus would involve mourning at the deepest level as He bore the sin of humanity. And amazingly, Jesus was looking for friends with whom He could share this mournful experience, whose partnership with Him in this dark night would strengthen Him and enable them to have courage as well.

Jesus calls this dimension of mourning "blessed." Those who will come into identification with His sorrows will receive the most profound recompense—being comforted and rewarded by God Himself. The promise of comfort to Jesus is articulated in Isaiah 53, where the prophet declares the blessing that will come to God's suffering servant:

Yet it pleased the Lord to bruise Him;
He has put Him to grief.
 When You make His soul an offering for sin,
 He shall see His seed, He shall prolong His days,

3   See Ezekiel 22:30; Isaiah 59:16; Isaiah 63:5

*And the pleasure of the L*ORD *shall prosper in His hand.*
He shall see the labor of His soul, and be satisfied.
   By His knowledge My righteous Servant shall justify many,
      For He shall bear their iniquities.
Therefore I will divide Him a portion with the great,
   And He shall divide the spoil with the strong,
   Because He poured out His soul unto death,
   And He was numbered with the transgressors,
   And He bore the sin of many,
   And made intercession for the transgressors.
   (Isaiah 53:10-12)

[handwritten margin note: Blessed are they that mourn — they shall be comforted]

The mourning of Jesus was a precise fulfillment of this passage. In His humanity, Jesus presented Himself to the Father as one who would willingly share the agony of God's heart as well as bear the punishment due to the human race for their sin. Jesus said in effect "Father, You sought for a man to stand in the gap with You. Here I am! I will join with You, I will obey You in this, that Your heart might be comforted and satisfied."

Isaiah's prophetic promise over the life of Jesus is that when His soul is made an offering for sin, the pleasure of the Lord will prosper in His hand, and He shall be satisfied with the labor of His soul. In other words, He will be comforted by receiving the full reward of His suffering. That reward is nothing less than human beings fully redeemed from sin, and who are enabled to live in a relationship of intimacy and shared authority with Jesus forever.

What Does This Mean for Us?

When you and I begin to understand this, we will see that God invites us into an experience of mourning with Him. This will have two dimensions: the awareness of our own brokenness and need for healing, and the awareness of God's heart, which is in anguish for the broken people of the earth. As we draw closer to Him in prayer, desiring deeper intimacy with Him as our Father and with His Son as our Bridegroom, God will touch us with these essential dimensions of His will for us. We will be invited to mourn over our own condition and to experience

His emotions over the condition of His people. As we give ourselves to mourning, we can be sure that the reward of real comfort will be ours.

The comfort that comes to those who mourn is profound. The word *comfort* means "to be drawn near for the purpose of consolation," and it is ultimately expressed in our face-to-face encounter with God foreseen in Revelation 7:17 and 21:4. In both verses we are told that God will wipe away every tear from the eyes of those He has redeemed. We will be led to fountains of living waters, and there will be no more death or sorrow or crying.

But the promise of comfort is not reserved only for the ultimate future that we face. The Psalmist informs us that all our tears are placed in God's bottle, all our sorrows are written in His book (Psalm 56:8). Even as we await the full and complete comfort of the literal presence of God, we can experience the wonderful consolation of the love of God that is released to the hearts of those who mourn, sharing in the sorrows of Jesus. In addition, we are prepared for the revelation of our true identity in Christ, which is the basis for meekness, as we will discover in chapter five.

Finally, as those who mourn, we become comforters of others. For once we have received comfort from the God of all comfort, we can bring true comfort to those around us who are in seasons of difficulty (2 Corinthians 1:3).

The only pathway to the ultimate consolation of God's embrace is to lament and mourn with Jesus over the things that break His heart. As we do so, the comfort He finds in the Father's embrace will be our inheritance.

POWER POINT FOR THIS CHAPTER:

Those who allow the Holy Spirit to bring them to deep and thorough mourning over sin will experience the deep and thorough comfort of God's embrace.

FOR DISCUSSION AND REFLECTION:

1. Take the list of hurts and disappointments that you wrote in the last chapter and add to it anything that came out of reading this chapter on mourning.

2. Bring this list to the Lord in prayer and ask Him to help you mourn deeply over the situations you have faced—both for your sins, and for the damage done to you.

3. Once again, share these things with your small group of friends and allow them to be a vehicle of God's comfort to you.

4. Please do not be in a hurry to get out of the discomfort of mourning over these things. Let the Lord Jesus take you to a deep place of healing and true comfort as you wait for Him to set you free.

Jes us

CHAPTER FIVE:
POWERFUL PEOPLE ARE MEEK

*Blessed are the meek, for they shall
inherit the earth. (Matthew 5:5)*

Marie:

Because the Beatitudes are character traits that emerge by the power of the Holy Spirit's revelation and work in our lives, meekness is not a characteristic that comes naturally to us. Meekness does not mean being easygoing or nice. Rather, it is an attribute that is compatible with strength and character, with being a defender of truth while simultaneously having humility and self-control. It means speaking the truth with love, not saying things for the purpose of hurting someone or provoking them to anger. A study of the character of Jesus quickly reveals that He demonstrated the character quality of meekness through His words and actions.

The manifestation of true spiritual meekness as intended by God will be evident in our submission to God's will as we demonstrate an absolute belief in His promises concerning us. The Lord has identified the greatest fruit of the Spirit as love. If we are truly spiritually meek, with our hearts in tune with the heart of God, we will want to give to others and love them. We will be patient and kind to our spouses, our children, our friends, our families, and strangers. And we will then receive the promise contained in this blessing.

The experience of losing my home and business precipitated my own journey into meekness. In the depths of the losses, I constantly blamed myself for not being smart enough to save my money instead of investing in the restaurants. I blamed myself for not standing up to my partner when he told me I had to sell my home. I blamed myself for not hiring a consultant in the beginning to help me with my food and labor costs. I blamed myself for not being a good enough person to save the business. The reason I blamed myself so profoundly was that I was not yet aware of God's strategy to form meekness in my spirit.

A couple of months after the losses, I began to suffer disturbing physical symptoms, such as sleeplessness, despair, loss of hope, crying episodes, and lack of interest in people and activities. After reading an article about depression, I realized that I was physically exhausted and depressed because of the stress of working long hours for years while trying to hold the business together. I had worried constantly about what I was going to do and had tried so hard to get help that I had depleted my body of the natural chemicals it needed for normal functioning. I went to my doctor, and he immediately recognized the symptoms of clinical depression. A very reputable and responsible doctor, he put me on an anti-depressant.[1]

In about thirty days I began feeling better and was able to understand what had happened to me. I started remembering a prayer I had prayed in the early days of the business. I had asked the Lord to make me a gentle and kind woman. The storm had begun shortly after that. I take total responsibility for the mistakes I made, and there were plenty of them. But the Lord took my devastating circumstances and turned them for my good. He could use my life to teach others how to reach the blessings of living in God's power by supernaturally taking on the character of Jesus through the teachings of the Beatitudes. When we say yes to the Beatitudes, the Lord says yes to us. If we can grasp the fact that God either allows or causes events to happen in our lives in order to mold us into meek sons and daughters for His purposes and our

---

1   I want to make it clear that not everybody needs to go to a doctor for medication, but in my case I had gone through so much trauma for such a long time, that it made sense for me to seek a medical opinion. I was able to come off the medication within twenty-four months.

destiny, I think it makes the difficult times in our life seem a bit more tolerable. Isaiah 30:20 says:

And though the LORD gives you
The bread of adversity and the water of affliction,
Yet your teachers will not be moved into a corner anymore,
But your eyes shall see your teachers.

The best part of this chapter comes in verse 26, where the Lord says He heals up the wounds He inflicted upon us. Difficult times are easier to deal with when you know that the Lord inflicted them or allowed them in order to change us. Consider these words:

Moreover the light of the moon will be as the light of the sun,
And the light of the sun will be sevenfold,
As the light of seven days,
In the day that the LORD binds up the bruise of His people
And heals the stroke of their wound.

Being broken and poor in spirit and then mourning those things that separate us from God are critical stages in becoming meek. It is important to understand that it is not our human nature to be meek. Only the Holy Spirit can produce meekness in us. Meekness is the opposite of being willful and domineering. A person who is meek is not on the defensive or oversensitive about himself or always watching out for his own interests. He does not pity himself, does not seek revenge or retaliation, and does not express anger out of self-interest, but only out of godly righteousness in the interest of others.

A national best seller entitled *Good to Great* is about five Fortune 500 companies that have succeeded in going from "good to great" and have sustained their greatness even though their CEOs or Presidents have retired. I wondered what these men had in common that sustained this greatness, because most companies will begin to slide once their leader has left. What caught my attention was that these men never sought media attention. In fact, I had never heard of them before, even though I read business magazines and watched the news frequently. These men appeared to be very humble and meek. They didn't seem to seek the praises of men but instead grew the companies for the sake of sustaining them. We all know that what is exemplified at the top will be played out at the bottom. I am willing to bet that their employees felt the meek servanthood of these men and that it caused them to want to follow this behavior. "Blessed are the meek for they shall inherit the earth." In other words, people will follow the leadership of those who are meek.

In his book *Dealing with the Rejection and Praise of Man*, Bob Sorge says,

> *As long as you're seeking the acceptance of man, you are making yourself vulnerable to the rejection of man. If man's acceptance will build you up, man's rejection will devastate you. However, when you close yourself to needing the acceptance of man, you close the door to man's rejection. ...Man's rejections never penetrated Jesus' soul because He didn't allow man's praises to feed His soul.[2]*

It finally occurred to me one day that the reason I was not meek and mild-mannered was that I was stressing and straining to make myself known to others in order to feel validated. In my old state of brokenness, it seemed to me that if I became a mild and meek person I would not receive the attention and praises of man and would therefore be powerless. But it was the exact opposite! This opinion that I had formed and lived out for a good portion of my life demonstrated my lack of faith in God's promise that those who are meek and humble are blessed. I am now on a journey to meekness and have more influence with people because my heart and soul are more concerned about others than with my striving to be accepted through the praises of men.

Meekness cannot be equated with weakness. An example of a powerful man in the Bible who was meek and had great humility and love for God is Moses. Early in his life journey, before meekness had been developed in his character, he killed in anger an Egyptian who was attacking a Jew. That action led to forty years of wilderness training before he would be qualified for the authority required to lead God's people. But even after he was a proven leader with great meekness, he became angry when the people of Israel turned away from God and worshiped

---

2   Bob Sorge, *Dealing with the Rejection and Praise of Man*, (Oasis House, 1998), 30.

idols. This time, however, his anger was rooted in a righteous desire to see God's purposes fulfilled, not in self-interest, and it was an example of true meekness. Meekness is a gift from God. We must have the life of Jesus formed in us by the Holy Spirit in order to become meek.

Our Lord Himself said, "Come unto me, ...and I will give you rest. For I am meek and lowly in heart."[3] It can therefore be said that a meek person is a person whose character is one of submission and power under control, and who has a dependency on God. Jesus could have come to earth as a king or as someone with a notable position. But instead He came as a child with questionable parentage, as the son of a carpenter from a rundown place called Nazareth.[4] He slept in the homes of others or on the ground. He had no luxuries that we know of, spoke to those who were hurting and were the most needy, and healed those who were sick.

The definition of submission is to give over, to yield oneself to the power or authority of another, to defer to another's judgment, opinion, and decision. Submission does not mean giving up boundaries, being mistreated, being a doormat, being less intelligent or less worthy, being unequal, oppressed, bullied, or threatened. Jesus lived meekly every day, submitting His own strength to the will and purposes of His Father, and so was qualified to have all authority and power given to Him.

Meekness is best defined as power under control. Power under control is the ability to exert power over another person but to choose to use that power to serve, not to control. It is knowing who you are in God's design so that you do not have to assert control over others to prove who you are. It is setting boundaries, but not running over the boundaries of others. It is God's kind of love, which is demonstrated by love, joy, peace, patience, kindness, faithfulness, gentleness, self-control.

A wonderful example of meekness is my brother-in-law, Mike Erickson. Mike is a big man physically—six feet four inches tall and well over 225 pounds. Mike was a tough guy in earlier years, making his way in the streets of Minneapolis as a drug dealer. He learned at an early age to exert his power with his mouth and his fists. During one particularly critical moment of his life, Mike met Jesus in a personal way while in

---

3   See Matthew 11:28-29 (KJV)
4   Note Nathanael's scathing comment recorded in John 1:46: "Can any good come out of Nazareth?"

prison for his drug activity. A powerful encounter delivered Mike from his addictions and set him on a course of ministering to others who live in ways like he did. Today Mike and my sister Denise minister to broken people who desperately need the gentleness of Jesus yet the strength of those who can help them set boundaries and come to real healing. It's a ministry that requires meekness, and people are healed when they see this in action.

I will never forget how Mike sat with my dying father during the days before he passed away, reading the Bible aloud and praying in his spirit for my father's salvation. Mike's faithful, meek service was a significant factor in my father's reconciliation with Jesus just before he died.

The promise is that the meek will inherit the earth. When you have the character quality of meekness, there comes with it a sense of contentment, self-assurance, and high self-esteem. People will follow those who have those qualities, and a person with such qualities can be trusted with leadership.

In Matthew 11:28-29, Jesus says, "Come unto me, all you who are weary and burdened, and I will give you rest. Take my yoke upon you and learn from me, for I am gentle (meek) and humble in heart, and you will find rest for your souls" (NIV). Jesus is saying that He can teach us meekness, but only if we desire it enough to come to Him with all our burdens and humble ourselves to learn from Him.

The original Greek word for *meek* translates as "gentle, humble, considerate, and courteous." If this were used to describe a wild animal, it would mean a wild animal that has been tamed and trained. Similarly, when this word is used to describe a human, it means a person who has been gentled and molded by God to be quieted, especially during situations that normally produce anger and frustration. In other words, the meek person is a strong-spirited person who has been gentled and tamed through the surrender of his will to God.

When I left home years ago as a teenager, I was determined that no one would hurt me again. My behavior was exactly what is described in psychology textbooks. I gravitated towards men who abused me, and I became rougher and tougher in order to function in this world. Crying was so foreign to me that I was thirty years old before I was able to shed tears. I was in counseling one day when it was brought to my attention that I had so many walls that no one could reach me, not even friends. I told the counselor that I did not think people liked me, but she said that was not true. I learned that my rough edges and walls kept people at a distance, because I reasoned that if I didn't let people come close I couldn't be hurt or abandoned.

The process of shedding my layers of calloused skin began when I realized how broken and unhappy I was. I noticed that the people who were sweet and meek seemed to have less struggles and pain, and they seemed to have friends who wanted to be with them because they were easy to be around. The incredible blessing that God showed me is that people will follow you if you demonstrate meekness. They will want to be around you.

In my work as a consultant, I had a client who oversaw a nonprofit foundation. I reported to him, and on occasion we could both get uptight over a deadline or a decision. He was always kind and always meek in working out a resolution. I noticed that people wanted him to consult to their companies, and they confided in him their frustrations and business problems because he was comforting to be around.

It is pretty difficult to be meek (the opposite of passive-aggressive) if you do not have a healthy self-esteem and a confidence about your own identity in Christ. It is impossible to be meek if you are aggressively climbing the ladder for fear someone else will get to the top first. It is impossible to be meek if you need to be in control most of the time for fear you won't get your way. When you are truly meek, you bear the fruit of the Holy Spirit and shine with the gentleness of Jesus. The blessing comes because people want to know what makes you this way. They want to be around you because it is pleasant and relaxing to be in your presence.

One of the greatest examples in my own life of God's demonstrating His power over me in my journey towards becoming a meek woman was when the Lord spoke to me and said, "Ask for forgiveness [from a certain family member] regardless of who you think is right or wrong. Love this person unconditionally because I first loved you unconditionally." In meekness and submission to the Father, I picked up the phone, not knowing whether the person on the other end would even speak to me because there had been months of estrangement between us. She accepted my apology when I asked for forgiveness. I told her that I loved her and was going to accept her for where she was in her life—and I meant it! Two days later she became very ill, and she called to ask if I would come and stay with her and her baby in the hospital overnight.

If I had not done what the Lord had told me to do, in meekness, I would have missed that blessing. Can you now see the perfect order in which the Beatitudes are written? If you are not broken in spirit saying, "There must be more!" and yearning to see your life make a difference, you will not want or seek the growth of meekness in your life. The Lord will make this change in your spirit as you cry out, "Lord, change me into a meek and mild person, but with the gentle power of Jesus."

Gary:

How does the idea of meekness fit in your mind with reaching your power potential? For most of us, the word *meekness* conjures up an image that would seem on the other end of the spectrum of power. So what do we do with the fact that Jesus puts the term *meekness* in the same breath with "inheriting the earth"? Surely there are interesting and exciting things for us to discover as we look into this Beatitude.

The twelve men who were the closest followers of Jesus were in for a real shock as they came into the room that had been prepared for them to eat the Passover meal. They had become convinced (with the probable exception of Judas) that Jesus was indeed who He claimed to be—the Son of God in the flesh, the Messiah who would one day receive the authority written about through all the Hebrew Scriptures and promised to Him by His Father.

As Jesus had done consistently through His life, He was once again about to demonstrate His authority in a most unusual way. When the disciples entered what is called the Upper Room, they were met at the door by one dressed in the garments of a servant, who began to wash their feet. It was a common courtesy in that day to have one of the servants wash the feet of guests. Though it was a gracious gesture on the host's part that brought refreshment to the weary and communicated value to those on the receiving end, it was nevertheless a most menial task for the servant to whom it was assigned.

The startling thing about this encounter was that it was Jesus who had clothed Himself in the servant's garb and who proceeded to minister to His disciples in that most basic way. The first teaching He gave them that evening wasn't with eloquent words or profound thought; rather, it was a demonstration of tender love that showed them the power and authority of true leadership. Their comfort zones were shaken and the hidden motives of their hearts exposed as Jesus began His task. A long-standing dispute had existed among the disciples about which of them was the greatest[5] and which of them would get the privilege of being close to Jesus in the fullness of His coming kingdom. None of them would have given the least thought to taking the role of foot washer, and the idea of Jesus doing that task was simply incomprehensible. But there He was, and the shallow pettiness of their argument was being laid bare before them without a word being spoken.

The thing that captures me about this story, recorded in chapter 13 of John's Gospel, is the utterly unexpected foundation of Jesus' act of servanthood described in verses 2-5:

> *And supper being ended, the devil having already put it into the heart of Judas Iscariot, Simon's son, to betray Him, Jesus, knowing that the Father had given all things into His hands, and that He had come from God and was going to God, rose from supper and laid aside His garments, took a towel and girded Himself. After that, He poured water into a basin and began to wash the disciples' feet, and to wipe them with the towel with which He was girded.*

Try to get your mind around what we are being told in these few words. Jesus is already aware that one of His closest friends is going to sell Him out to the Jewish officials for the sake of personal gain. He is aware that every one of these men is going to abandon Him within just a few hours, when He is taken to His trial and crucifixion. Each of them, in his own way, is going to deny his love for Jesus and leave Him to die alone and abandoned.

But Jesus, the greatest and most powerful human being who ever lived, had a resource that enabled Him to take the low place of serving those who wanted to be great because He had created them to be great. Jesus could serve because He knew that "the Father had given all things into His hands." Because of His intimacy with His Father, Je-

5   See Luke 22:24

sus understood that by God's own promise He had authority over everything, both in that moment and in the coming age when God's kingdom will be established on the earth. Further, Jesus knew "that He had come from God, and that He was going to God." In other words, His sense of identity and His sense of destiny were fully established in His heart and mind. He knew who He was, He knew where He was going, and He knew His place of power. Therefore, He chose to exercise that power in the loving activity of serving His friends, even to the ultimate service of giving His life for their redemption. He would pour His own life out for them in anticipation of the day to come when His power and authority would be established in reality before all people.

It is this posture of serving others from a place of strength that the Bible calls *meekness*. The term literally means "gentleness," but not in the way most of us think about being gentle. We may at times think of meekness or gentleness as a quality of temperament that has more to do with one's natural personality than something that has been developed in one's character over time. But usually we perceive meekness and gentleness to be associated more with weakness than with strength. We envision meekness in a person who is trying to make the best out of a hopeless situation, exercised by one who has no power options and is trying to get along by being nice.

The meekness that Jesus speaks of in Matthew 5:5 and models in John 13:1-5 is not primarily about being nice. It is a character quality that chooses humility because humility is God's way. Meekness causes someone to do the right thing because it is right, but with a gentle style rooted in true strength. It is strength under discipline, a gentleness built upon the solid foundation of understanding one's revealed identity and destiny rooted in the sovereign love of God. Meekness is not a trait that many are born with, but rather one that is developed through years of forming and shaping by the Spirit of God. Meekness is not an optional character trait, but one that is essential in coming to possess true power, for Jesus promised that the earth itself will be given as an inheritance to the those who are meek.

In our journey to reach our power potential we must come to understand that at the end of the day Jesus' value system will truly be established. All other strategies for power will fail, and only His methods will be found to be true. To pursue power with wisdom and the certainty of attaining it is thus to pursue it in the way Jesus promises to give it. Power will be given as an inheritance to those who embrace His character and His methods, and that includes the character trait of meekness.

How Meekness Is Formed in Us

The process of forming meekness in any of us usually involves a series of stages, some of which are almost inevitably traumatic. I have long been convinced that only God knows the true identity and destiny of any given individual. Only God (or those who speak with an understanding of His opinion) can communicate to a person with the necessary authority to establish them in settled truth concerning who they are. If it were our natural inclination to listen to Him and receive His opinions as real and true, the journey to meekness and power would be less troublesome.

However, for most of us the process of discovering our true identity is saturated with difficulty. We have this inclination to try to make something of ourselves, to prove something to God and everyone else. We want to be great apart from relationship with Him, but this simply does not work. The only way to lasting greatness is the way of Jesus, and sooner or later we must either choose that way or face terrible and eternal consequences.

Someone might consider the options and decide that ruling their own life apart from God is still preferable to submitting to Him. A famous man once stated, "I would rather rule in hell than serve in heaven." That is a stunning example of the self-centered rebellion that characterizes the fallen human soul, but frankly that sentiment is not uncommon. The tragic deception here is that no one will be ruling in hell, not even Satan. The Bible presents hell as a lake of fire where there is nothing but eternal and excruciating torment for those who choose to go there.[6] Satan and all those who choose his way will be in a literal place of eternal torment *by their own choice.* No life and no authority exists apart from God, only agony.

So, sooner or later we must choose God's way. Most of us choose it later rather than sooner. And because God is the patient Father that He is, He allows us the choices that invariably leave Him out, at least at the beginning. So we try to become somebody and often find ourselves

6   See Revelation 20:10-14

hating who we've become. Or we succeed for a time and then cannot figure out why everything crashes down around us. Or perhaps we reach the pinnacle of the mountain we were trying to climb, only to find that satisfaction has eluded us, and we are no more fulfilled than we were at the beginning of the journey.

In my life, the journey toward meekness has unfolded like a series of trips around the same mountain, running into the same issues again and again at deeper levels in my soul. Though I had a clear sense from the Lord early in my life that I had a calling and a destiny placed before me, I spent over thirty years trying to produce that destiny by my own energies. For a variety of reasons, I could never get comfortable with the idea that God would give me this inheritance purely by His grace, without my striving for it. I would experience periods of seeming success followed by disillusionment and disaster. At one level I knew that only God's grace could produce His plan, and so I would call upon Him to do His work. But at another level I acted as though things depended on me, so I used people and resources for my purposes, lording it over them instead of serving them in meekness. As the inevitable crises happened, I continued to call out to the Lord in the seasons of difficulty. He graciously took me to deeper and deeper levels of confronting my issues of unbelief and self-determination.

We can never genuinely serve people until we accept God's way of doing things. We must become convinced that God will honor and reward those who are meek, who use their strength to serve and bless rather than to control. Until we believe that the meek will inherit the earth, we will either strive to gain control of our world by the exertion of our own strength or give up and decide that power and authority are beyond our reach.

A decisive point of confrontation happened between the Holy Spirit and me in the spring of 2004. My family was in a crisis time because Mary, my wife of thirty-two years, was in the last stages of breast cancer. She died in June of that year. In the weeks before Mary's death, I had entered an extended season of fasting and prayer, seeking the Lord for what He had in store for us. One day He spoke to me in clear and disturbing tones. His voice rang inside my head in that mysterious "internal, audible" communication that those who know Him experience from time to time. He said "Gary, you think you are contending with Me, but I am contending with you." Suddenly, I realized that I had settled for far less in my life than God intended to give me and that this season of tragedy for my family was in fact God's way of shaking me out of my complacency.[7]

A touch of anointing on my life and ministry, mingled with a measure of secret compromise, had been good enough for me, but it was not good enough for God. I began to realize that He is determined that we have the full inheritance that He planned for us from the beginning, and He will do whatever it takes to bring us to the reality of it. God demonstrated to me that He is quite willing to frustrate me in the short term in order to produce the life of Jesus in me over the long term.

As I cried out to the Lord during that season, I came face to face with points of failure in my life, primarily my failure to be the kind of husband God had intended for me to be. With a sense of desperation that increased over the weeks leading to Mary's death, I called out to the Lord to give me another chance to be a godly husband. I didn't know at that point whether He would heal Mary or how the answer would come. All I know is that I was at a point of desperation and grief over the situation.

In the aftermath of Mary's death came a period of confusion and depression. I continued to travel and teach, but something had gone out of my heart. Though I still loved God and worshiped Him, I no longer felt confident that He would bring about His promises in my life. I remember one day as I was complaining to the Lord, I began to focus on one dimension of destiny that had been promised but had since faded into hopelessness. Over the years, I had received many prophetic words from people who had the impression that one day my wife and I would stand together and teach God's Word to His people. That dream had once been precious to me, but it had faded over the years, and died with Mary.

As I talked to God that day, I began to pour out my frustration by asking Him what happened to that promise. Almost immediately that quiet voice of His came into my thoughts: "Gary, that promise is still good." With that little statement a flicker of hope got rekindled in my

---

7   God does not send sickness to teach or discipline us. Sickness is a work of Satan that Jesus came to destroy. But in His mercy, God speaks to us in these times of heightened awareness to bring us to deeper fulfillment of His purpose in our lives.

heart, and I began to think that perhaps God was not finished with me, that maybe He had something in mind that was beyond what I could produce on my own. It was only a few short months later that I met Marie, and the next season of destiny began to unfold.

As we fell in love, Marie began to speak to me of what God had showed her concerning my life and concerning our life and ministry together. Through her love God began to heal my heart, and her confidence in God began to restore mine. The Holy Spirit began to speak to us more and more clearly about what He has for us in the coming years, and together we are coming to believe Him. We are beginning to see that only by embracing His ways and His character can we receive from Him the things He has to give us, those things that deep down in our hearts we know should be our inheritance. We are beginning to stand in meekness, knowing who we are in His plan and trusting Him to fulfill all things in His way and His time.

God uses the frustration of our attempts to fulfill our life goals to bring us to the place of calling out to Him for help. He knows that we can never reach our power potential without His input, because having designed us and made us, He holds the secrets of our identity and destiny. But He will never impose that knowledge on us. His desire is that we choose Him and seek for Him as a child would seek after his father or as a lover would seek after her beloved.

Some people, in the foolishness and stupidity of their own pride, keep banging their heads against the wall of self-discovery, thinking that if they keep doing the same old routine, maybe this time the result will be different. It's really insanity in action! Those folks will never know who they are, where they came from, where they're going, and the authority that is theirs for the asking. They are stuck in their foolishness, and as long as they persist, nothing will change. Others give up in hopelessness, tired of striving but too disappointed to trust God anymore. They roll over and die inside, convinced that God is powerless, or worse—cruel and uncaring. They say "God will use me, but He won't answer my prayers."

Still others, however, whom the Scriptures call wise, learn to call upon the Lord in their times of distress. Consider this representative list of steps that characterize those who are coming to the place of meekness:

- Having seen that apart from God they do not have what it takes to attain the greatness for which they were made, they begin to acknowledge their poverty.

- Having faced the rebellion in their hearts toward God and His Son Jesus, they begin to grieve and mourn over their own sin and the pain it has caused Him.

- They begin to pray, to ask God's forgiveness for their self-centered rebellion.

- They begin to search the Bible for clues about their existence.

- They begin to socialize with people who are discovering that identity and destiny are rooted in what God says about them, and that apart from that reality there can be no fulfillment in life.

- They begin to spend large amounts of time just thinking about the person of Jesus, reading about His life in the Bible, and asking the Holy Spirit to help them become like Him.

- They learn to worship God and thank Him for the way He has led them to Himself and for the blessings that He has in store for them as they follow His ways.

- They begin to serve one another as Jesus served the people around Him.

The wondrous thing is that as we give ourselves to activities like these, God begins to reveal the truth concerning who we are and what we are about. Our sense of destiny begins to emerge, along with the authority we need to come into our full inheritance of power, both here and in the coming age. This change happens supernaturally from God. Little by little, from one level of glory to the next, we begin to look and sound and act like Jesus. The more we become like Him—treating people like He did, serving instead of demanding to be served—the more we step into our own place of authority. The more we taste of this life, the more we hunger and thirst after it. Having become meek, we begin to inherit the earth.

POWER POINT OF THIS CHAPTER:

Meek people know that they have come from God, that they are going to God, and that God has given them everything they need for doing what they have been created to do.

FOR DISCUSSION AND REFLECTION:

1. In your personal journal, write down some of the things you have looked to for your sense of identity and destiny. This may include things like the opinions of others, job success, income level, and educational background.

2. Consider the rough edges in your life that are contrary to meekness. Write down a list of things you would like for God to change in you.

3. Begin to ask the Lord to break these bondages and deliver you from these chains. He did not intend for us to be critical, edgy, sarcastic, short in our answers, and abrupt in our conversations.

4. Write down the characteristics of meekness that are the opposite of the harsh behaviors and that you would like to develop in your life.

5. Talk these things over with your small group, and pray together that the Holy Spirit will establish you in meekness.

CHAPTER SIX:

POWERFUL PEOPLE HUNGER AND THIRST FOR RIGHTEOUSNESS

Blessed are those who hunger and thirst for
righteousness, for they shall be filled. (Matthew 5:6)

Marie:

Did you know that there are amazing promises for those who seek and hunger after righteousness? The day I discovered them in Psalm 112, I remember thinking that this is like a parent telling his or her child, "If you believe in Jesus, and if you hunger and thirst after righteousness, I will give to you these gifts, because of my love for you:

- you will be confident
- you will be fearless
- you will have influence and honor
- you will be long remembered
- you will be compassionate
- you will be generous
- your children will be successful
- an entire generation of godly people will be blessed
- you will be blessed

- you will be wealthy
- you will not be overcome by evil."

I remember thinking, *Lord, I want all of these. Would you please show me more of your revelations?* When I was a single woman, on many evenings I would make a date with Jesus to be alone with Him and the Bible. My craving to know Him more increased as I discovered more ways to connect with the Lord. Through this process He spoke to my spirit about certain events, and I gained new understanding. I began to see what it meant when people said that the Lord tells His friends His secrets. I believe if you comprehend this chapter, you will understand the power that the Lord wants to pour out onto His people. I believe this is the most important part of the Beatitudes. The Lord showed me this very clearly one day. As I was praying, I had an impression of a house that was bursting with power and flames. The Lord showed me that the address of this house is RIGHTEOUSNESS, and the road map to the house is the Beatitudes. I finally realized that the Lord was saying, "if you want those things in Psalm 112 and if you desire to experience my power to heal up the wounds of my people, both physical and spiritual, you must recognize that the way to this power is the Beatitudes." How exciting to discover that the Lord is revealing His pathway to power in this day.

Gary:

Marie and I enjoy looking at cars and dreaming about what it would be like to tool down the motorway in a variety of luxury SUVs or sports models. Marie is captivated by the Nissan 350Z, and she fantasizes about the thrill of driving one. I particularly like BMWs, and am intrigued by their motto: "The relentless pursuit of perfection." The motto points to the elusive but conceivable goal of the company—to produce cars that touch perfection. What a wonder it would be to drive the ideal road machine, the perfect car! Now, if there is a reality in the realm of automobiles that can be termed "perfection," that means there is a standard that draws our thoughts and serves as a reference point for our dreams. That standard would be the objective reality against which every car would be measured.

We tend to look at life this way. We long for perfection and are exhilarated when our experience touches something that approaches it.

When we or our situations fall short of perfection, we are disappointed, although we eventually resign ourselves to accepting less than the ideal. The fascinating thing is that the teachings of Jesus in the Bible encourage this pursuit of perfection. As a matter of fact, Jesus indicates very clearly that perfection exists for us who will seek after it. He calls it "righteousness."

The difficulty that we encounter when we think of perfection is that it makes us feel like we have to live up to something foreign to us. We think of ourselves as fundamentally flawed, and we have no hope that we could ever live up to a standard called righteousness. But God created us for glory, not for frustration. The human race was broken by sin, but Jesus made the way clear for everything that was in God's heart to be restored to us. We long for perfection because it is our birthright, to be fully realized when we see Him face to face. But this perfection is not something merely to be attempted in an external, behavioral way. Our hearts were made to be captured by the perfection of Jesus, to fall in love with Him, and to be transformed in such a way that the actions of our lives would become like Him as well.

Essentially the term righteousness means to live in a way that is consistent with God's perfect pattern for our lives. This perfect pattern is the man Jesus. You and I were created to be like Him. To be righteous is to have our inner persons—our hearts, our thoughts, our attitudes—aligned with the pattern of Jesus, with His thoughts and attitudes. From that internal alignment we can begin to live externally, by the power of the Holy Spirit, in line with the behavior of Jesus. Righteousness means to be in perfect alignment with how God sees all things. God's point of view is the final reality that will be established on the earth, and He promises that those who seek after it with intensity will be fully satisfied. This line of thought may cause one to ask, "How do I discover what God thinks and how He sees all things?" The answer to that question is that in a spirit of worship and prayer we begin to search the Scriptures and study the person of Jesus, who perfectly reveals God's character.

The Bible is full of thoughts and actions that are attributed to righteousness and to the lifestyle of righteous people. Consider for example this list of character traits in the book of Proverbs that are attributed to righteousness:

- The Outlook on Life
  o They are hopeful (Proverbs 10:24)
  o |They are concerned about the welfare of God's creation (Proverbs 12:10)
  o They understand justice (Proverbs 28:5)
- The Response to Life
  o They are covered with blessings (Proverbs 10:6)
  o They give thought to their ways (Proverbs 21:29)
  o They persevere against evil (Proverbs 24:15-16)
- How the Righteous are seen by Others
  o They are appreciated (Proverbs 13:15)
  o Their conduct is upright (Proverbs 21:8)
  o They do not desire the company of godless people (Proverbs 24:1-2)
  o Others are glad when they triumph (Proverbs 28:12)
  o They care for the poor (Proverbs 29:7)
  o They detest the dishonest (Proverbs 29:27)
- The Quality of Life
  o They stand firm (Proverbs 10:25)
  o They are delivered by righteousness (Proverbs 11:6)
  o No real harm befalls them (Proverbs 12:21)
  o Their income results in treasure (Proverbs 15:6)
  o They avoid evil (Proverbs 16:17)
  o They are bold as lions (Proverbs 28:1)
  o They will be safe (Proverbs 28:18)
- Short-term Results of Righteousness
  o They walk securely (Proverbs 10:9)
  o They are rewarded with prosperity (Proverbs 13:21)
- Long-term Results of Righteousness
  o God protects them (Proverbs 10:29)
  o They are never uprooted (Proverbs 10:30)
- Eternal Expectations

- o   They will earn a sure reward (Proverbs 11:18)
- o   They will attain life (Proverbs 11:19)
- o   Their life will end only in good (Proverbs 11:23)
- o   They will stand firm (Proverbs 12:7)
- o   They will have a refuge when they die (Proverbs 14:32)
- • God's Opinion of the Righteous
- o   He delights in their good (Proverbs 11:20)
- o   He will cause evil people to bow to them (Proverbs 14:19)[1]

This is an amazing list of character traits and promises, isn't it? Those who pursue righteousness with all their hearts will indeed be a powerful group of people! We would encourage you to meditate on these things, asking the Holy Spirit to help you understand what it means to live in righteousness in such a way that these statements become true of your life.

The Gift of Righteousness

The biggest mistake we make is when we attempt to be righteous by our own energy and strength. Instead of focusing on falling in love with Jesus and allowing His Spirit to transform us, we try to "behave ourselves." We try to act like Jesus without first being transformed by His power. We want to be good enough to gain God's approval. This will lead us to frustration with absolute certainty. The Scripture is clear that, with the single exception of Jesus, no one is righteous, not even one person![2] If that is true, we have a huge dilemma! How can we live up to the demands of righteousness if no one can do it?

The answer the Bible gives us is that because Jesus lived as a righteous man, we, too, can anticipate living in His perfection by having a relationship with Him. We are told in Philippians 3:9 that righteousness does not come by our own strength but by faith in Christ as a gift from God. When we acknowledge our failure to live as humans were intended to live, and ask for His forgiveness, God's power changes us inside. He makes righteousness available to us as a gift. We are granted a new nature, a new kind of life in which righteousness is possible. Because

---

1   Adapted from *The Life Application Bible* (Wheaton, Ill.: Tyndale House, [1996]), 1,112-1,113
2   See Romans 3:10

of His sacrifice on the cross, He can impart righteousness to us as a gift and then give us the strength to grow up into that reality.

The Bible speaks of righteousness as a reality; it is the truth of how things really are, rooted in the character of God who created all things. There actually is a standard, a perfect reference point from which every particular thing takes its meaning. That standard is God, whose character is made visible and accessible to us in the person of Jesus Christ. Consider this passage from the writings of Paul:

> He [Jesus] is the image of the invisible God, the firstborn over all creation. **For by Him all things were created that are in heaven and that are on earth, visible and invisible, whether thrones or dominions or principalities or powers. All things were created through Him and for Him.** And He is before all things, and in Him all things consist. And He is the head of the body, the Church, who is the beginning, the firstborn from the dead, that in all things He may have the preeminence. (Colossians 1:15-18, emphasis mine)

Your life is part of the "all things" that Jesus created out of His own desire for relationship with human beings. God chose you before He created the universe,[3] and He designed you from the very beginning to be like His Son Jesus, in whose image you were made. You were His idea! Therefore, since God thought you up, only one definition of your life can possibly be right, and that is God's definition. He has a complete understanding of who you are, and Jesus is in full agreement with the Father about you. God means for you to look just like Jesus, and to the degree that you begin to look like Him in your attitudes and actions, you will begin to touch righteousness. God knows who you really are, and He is determined that you will receive everything you need to be just like He designed you.[4]

Jesus said in Matthew 6:33 that the most important thing is to seek the kingdom of God and His righteousness. If we will do that, everything else that can possibly seem important will be added to us as well. Nothing is more important than coming into alignment with how God designed us to be.

3   See Ephesians 1:3-4
4   See 2 Peter 1:3-4

The Importance of Agreeing with God's Opinion

Since these truths are most important, the only thing that really ought to matter to us is the discovery of what God thinks about us. Once we begin to understand His definition of reality in general, and our life in particular, then we begin to have the hope of coming to some sense of fulfillment and power. Martyn Lloyd-Jones writes of the ultimate importance of God's priorities being established in our hearts:

> We are not meant to control our Christianity; our Christianity is meant to control us. I am to be dominated by the truth because I have been made a Christian by the operation of the Holy Spirit within. I quote that striking statement of the apostle Paul which surely puts it so perfectly—"I live; yet not I, but Christ lives in me." He is in control, not I; so that I must not think of myself as a natural man who is controlling his attitude and trying to be Christian in various ways. No; His Spirit controls me at the very center of my life, controls the very spring of my being, the source of my every activity.

> You cannot read these Beatitudes without coming to that conclusion. The Christian faith is not something on the surface of a man's life, it is not merely a kind of coating or veneer. No, it is something that has been happening in the very center of his personality. That is why the New Testament talks about rebirth and being born again, about a new creation and about receiving a new nature. It is something that happens to a man in the very center of his being; it controls all his thoughts, all his outlook, all his imagination, and, as a result, all his actions as well. All our activities, therefore, are the result of this new nature, this new disposition which we have received from God through the Holy Spirit.[5]

Again, Jesus' point in Matthew 6:33 is that the pursuit of God's rule and of the conformity of all things to His character is the most important quest of the human heart. When righteousness is the goal of our seeking, God becomes involved in a profound way to add "all these

---

5   Martyn Lloyd-Jones, The Sermon on the Mount (Grand Rapids: Eerdmans, 1959), 97.

things" to our experience. The things spoken of here are the physical needs of life—food, clothing, provision—which fill our hearts with worry when righteousness is not the goal. But when righteousness is the goal of our seeking, and when in the power of the Holy Spirit we conform our expressions of life to that righteousness, then everything else that concerns us comes into place according to the purposes of God our Father.

Marie

Recently I was meditating on the story in John 21 and the events surrounding the restoration of Peter. Jesus, standing on the shore, encountered Peter and the other disciples in their fishing boats. Although the disciples had caught nothing through a long night of fishing, Jesus commanded them to cast their nets on the right side of the boat. After doing this, they caught 153 large fish. In fact, the fish were so big they could barely pull them in and there was danger of their nets breaking. In the passage it says that all the disciples, minus Peter, could not pull the fish into the boat because of the weight of the fish. However, when they were all standing on land with Jesus and He wanted more fish to cook, Jesus spoke to Peter, who single-handedly pulled the net ashore. We believe that this infusion of strength was a preview of the spiritual power that would come to Peter on the day of Pentecost. I think that because of Peter's restoration and his thirst and hunger for righteousness the Lord released great power and authority into him.

The Holy Spirit led me to understand that Jesus had a specific reason for commanding them to cast the nets on the right side. He impressed upon me that the casting of the nets on the right side is symbolic of casting our lives on the side of righteousness. The large catch of fish represented the power of God to give complete blessing in every area of life to those who would throw themselves into righteousness and depend upon Him.

What God desires in this season is for us to throw our whole selves into the pursuit of righteousness, which is simple if we just follow the roadmap through Matthew 5:3-12, the Beatitudes, and to eliminate everything that is contradictory to God's character and nature. As we do this, He will cause all good things to come to us—provision, blessing, effectiveness in work and relationships.

After the story of casting the nets comes the following story in John 21:15-19. The Lord asks Peter three times if he loves Him. And when Peter says yes, Jesus says to him, "Then feed my lambs." In other words, "take care of my people, then feed my people." Then the Lord said to Peter, "I tell you the truth, when you were young you were able to do as you liked; you dressed yourself and went wherever you wanted to go. But when you are old, you will stretch out your hands, and others will dress you and take you where you don't want to go." (my paraphrase)

Jesus had prepared Peter for his destiny and now Peter would follow the Lord, even to the point of death. We are called to follow Jesus as well, and it may not always be where we want to go. But the eternal rewards will be great!

Gary:

When righteousness is centrally established and becomes the goal and expression of our lives, there emerges a marvelous confidence that God Himself is our champion. We begin to realize that nothing can shake us from our place in His heart, and that He is the one watching over our every circumstance. King David was one who understood this principle to a wonderful degree. His writings reflect a deep confidence in the Lord his God, who would protect him in the situations of life and cause all things to be established in his favor. Meditate on this section of Psalm 7 that reveals the confidence of David's heart before the Lord:

The Lord shall judge the peoples;
Judge me, O Lord, according to my righteousness,
And according to my integrity within me.
Oh, let the wickedness of the wicked come to an end,
But establish the just;
For the righteous God tests the hearts and minds.
My defense is of God,
Who saves the upright in heart.
(Psalm 7:8-10)

The confidence of David's life was that he had made the righteousness of God the goal of his seeking. Therefore, because his life was in line with God's righteousness, he could pray in an amazingly bold way—"Judge me, O LORD, according to *my* righteousness, and according to *my* integrity within me!" David comes to the solid place of trust where he can depend fully upon the judgments of God, because he knows that his own heart is upright—he is as fully aligned as possible with the righteousness of God.

By contrast, there came a time in David's life when he acted in profound contradiction to righteousness. The story, recorded in 2 Samuel 11, concerns the situation in which David, as the king of the nation, should have been leading his troops in the war that they were fighting. However, he remained in his palace, where one evening he went for a walk on the roof of his house. From there he observed Bathsheba, the beautiful wife of Uriah, bathing in the open air of her balcony. David lusted after this woman, sent for her, and impregnated her. In order to cover up the situation, King David sent for Uriah, who was one of his military commanders. David tried to get Uriah to sleep with his wife, but the man was too honorable to enjoy the pleasures of home while his soldiers were fighting. So, in a fit of horribly wicked behavior, David arranged to have Uriah placed in the hottest battle zone, where he was killed. David then took Bathsheba to his palace and claimed her for his wife.

This situation was deeply displeasing to God, and it brought great displeasure upon the life of David and his descendants. God sent His prophet Nathan to confront David, who responded with deep repentance and wrote Psalm 51 as his song of confession. That Psalm contains a profound phrase that grips me each time I read it. Verse 6 declares that God "desires truth in the inward parts." This is the formation of righteousness in the interior of our souls—to have our inward parts—our thoughts, attitudes, and secret longings—conformed to the desires and ways of God. It is this alignment that God is after so that He might pour out His blessing on His people.

In that dark season of his life, David knew what it meant to have his clean heart polluted by his own sin. The presence of the Holy Spirit was taken away from him, and the joy of intimate friendship with God was removed from his experience. The dread of losing this joyful sense of God's pleasure and delight motivated David to repent from his sin and turn back to the Lord with all his heart.

The Intensity of Pursuing Righteousness

Marie:

Early in the spring of 2005 the Holy Spirit began to speak to me about getting in alignment with God. I began to realize that God wants us to be the same on the inside as we appear on the outside. He desires that our lifestyle at home and in private reflects accurately the things that we speak and teach about as followers of Jesus.

Years ago, when I was a new Christian, I began to read the Bible for the first time in my life, and the truth of God's ways began to have an impact on me. For instance, I remember coming to the realization and conviction that it is not okay to sleep or live with a man until you are married. It was as if the Lord had turned a light switch on in my head. I was hungry to find the truth about purity and righteousness. I wanted to know why this was such a big deal to the Lord and what the consequences were for this sin. Fortunately, a friend sent me a teaching tape on the subject, and my questions were answered. The Lord took me through the process of which He speaks in Isaiah 43:26: "Put Me in remembrance; let us contend together; state your case that you may be acquitted."

Hunger is a sign of life. *Thirst* is the signal our body gives us in order to sustain life. God used these two words to alert us to the fact that knowing Him and His righteousness is critical to our lives and to eternity. Since righteousness is being conformed to how things really are, it is essential that we come to agree with God's viewpoint.

My granddaughter and I went out for lunch one day. She was five years old at the time. In the car, she pulled the vanity mirror down, looked into it, and said, "Grandma, I love myself so much." Can you imagine having that much self-esteem? Her head was not filled with the struggles of a low self-worth. As adults we can receive the same assurance from God. This assurance comes when we make the pursuit of righteousness the focus of our lives.

When we begin to hunger and thirst for righteousness, the Lord will answer our prayer. A profound truth is revealed in Isaiah 48:18 that shows the powerful influence righteousness has on God's heart:

Oh, that you had heeded My commandments!
Then your peace would have been like a river,
And your righteousness like the waves of the sea.

God promises that as we obey Him, He will give us a peace that flows like a river and righteousness that is as powerful as the ocean waves. In his book *Unrelenting Prayer,* Bob Sorge talks about three characteristics of ocean waves.[6] In the first place, they are *incessant.* When we live in righteousness, doing kind and godly things regardless of our circumstance or the mood we're in, our righteousness pounds God's heart in an incessant way. It causes Him to desire to answer our prayers. Secondly, ocean waves are *thunderous.* One little act of kindness creates a thunderous sound in heaven, getting God's attention and creating a yearning in His heart to answer us. Thirdly, ocean waves are *impacting.* They keep coming and coming and coming, and every time they pound the shore, something shifts and changes. When we live in righteousness, the choices of obedience we make from moment to moment impact God. His heart is moved by our acts of righteousness, and He looks for ways to answer our prayers.

If we resist this urging to seek righteousness, we set ourselves up for great trouble. The Bible teaches that one of the dangers of sin is that it leads to a hardening of the heart.[7] But when we do seek righteousness, and when we pray continually for ourselves and for other people, God is faithful in answering. Those individuals who have no desire to be in fellowship with God, who have no craving to be in His presence and can never find the time to pray, will not be sensitive to the voice of God.

I remember when God started stirring my heart towards the beautiful Beatitudes. I had a great longing to go away alone to pray and write. I had a sense of urgency and a knowledge that God wanted to tell me something. So I did go away, and that's when this teaching on the Beatitudes started to emerge.

I believe that God is pointing out how to achieve a true happiness and authority through the Beatitudes. Remember, *blessed* means "blissful" or "joyful." It means being hopeful with joy in spite of our circumstances. If we desire purity and righteousness, and hunger for His

6 Bob Sorge, *Unrelenting Prayer* (Kansas City, Oasis House: 2005), 106-108.
7 See for example the story of how Pharaoh's heart was made hard through his resistance of God's purposes. This story is found in Exodus 5-15.

fellowship, we will find that happiness is given to us as a reward.

We must not deny the Scripture that says we were created in the image and likeness of God. We were made for intimate friendship with God, and our souls will never be satisfied unless we search for God and His ways. Sin blocks our desire by creating turmoil and pain.

Remember, the promise is that if we hunger and thirst after righteousness, we will be filled. When we truly love someone, we want to be in their presence. If they love you and want to be with you, they will also desire to share themselves with you. God wants to fill you with His knowledge of the truth and what your destiny is in His heart and mind.

God's Word is truth; man's word is distorted by his experiences and perception. To get at the truth, you must seek, and be open to see and hear, the truth. Look at Joshua, who was called to lead the Israelites into the Promised Land. The waters of the swollen Jordan River didn't part until the priests obediently took the first step into the water.[8] We can't find the truth and true happiness until we take that first step of being hungry and thirsty in our desire to know God.

From experience, I know that the Lord does not usually speak to me when I am in large crowds, involved in some program, or going to another Bible study. He loves it when we have our quiet time with Him, because then we get to know Him through His Word. This is one of the main ways that we grow in intimacy with God. We can only know righteousness by meditating on the character of God clearly revealed in the Beatitudes. In reading His Word, we need to ask ourselves these questions:

- What does this say to me?
- What does this mean to me?
- Is there a truth I need to see?
- Is there a sin I need to correct?
- Is there a promise I need to keep?

My relationship with my dad is a good example of how God brings righteousness into a situation. My sisters never gave up hoping that Dad would give his life to Jesus; they were hungry to see righteousness birthed in our father. The Lord answered their prayers, and in the process He taught me a lesson I will never forget. He showed me that He

8   See Joshua 3:1-17

can do anything at any time and that nothing is impossible with Him. My father and I had not had any relationship to speak of for twenty-five years. There had been a great deal of abuse in my family when I was a child. My parents divorced many years ago, and my father lived in denial regarding the damage he and Mom did to their children. Even though my sisters and I confronted him repeatedly, he chose to deny any wrongdoing. I, in turn, chose not to have a relationship with him.

Many years later, as I was contemplating the Ten Commandments, I asked God to show me how to honor my mother and father given the past circumstances and even their unacceptable behavior up to that very day. The Lord began to show me that my attitude and response to them was blocking my growing in righteousness before God. The Holy Spirit was definitely convicting me. God reminded me that He knows all things and is in control of all situations. When my parents sinned against me, God sovereignly used the circumstances to fulfill His purpose for me. While His original intent was not to have my parents sin and hurt their children, He had given them a free will to choose between evil and good.

As an adult, after many years of separation from my parents, I asked God what He would have me do. God said, "Go and see your father, and ask for forgiveness for your behavior and response to him." I'd had so much pent up anger from years earlier that my actions and thoughts toward him were not those of a godly woman. Many times I would say to people who asked about my father that he was an evil man who would end up in hell. Today I know that this was a judgment, and it was wrong. I found out that the Lord can do anything He pleases.

Admittedly, I did not pray much for my father, but my sister Denise never gave up on him. Three of my sisters would on occasion report to me regarding his same old behavior, and then I would feel justified in feeling about him the way I did.

Then, a few months before Christmas of 2003, Denise called to tell me that Dad had put away all his pornography. She was very happy, exclaiming that it was a miracle. My father had looked at porn all his adult life, and it became worse as he got older. With a very cynical attitude, I responded, "The day he picks up the phone and asks for my forgiveness is the day there will be a miracle."

On Christmas Day that year I was sitting visiting with my sister and her husband when the phone rang. It was my father. He said, "Please don't hang up on me, Marie. I just want to tell you I love you and I am sorry for everything." I immediately said, "You are forgiven, and I love you too." I was amazed at my own accepting behavior. But the Lord had taken me through the Beatitudes, and now I was seeking *His* righteousness.

My father had gradually gone blind because of diabetes, glaucoma, and cataracts. The Lord asked me to pick up the phone and pray with him because he was going in for eye surgery. The doctors were going to attempt to restore his eyesight at least so he could see shadows. Me, of all people, to pray with my dad! I was the one who had exposed my family's past abuse on national television and in newspapers and magazines, and who had humiliated him. But I knew that if the Lord was at work here, and if I had heard His voice, my dad would welcome my prayers.

I picked up the phone and told my dad how sorry I was to hear about his blindness. I asked him if I could pray with him, and he eagerly answered, "Yes." He then told me that he was very frightened about the coming eye surgery. My father had never been in the hospital before this, but he was desperate to have even a little of his eyesight restored.

A couple of weeks before this the Lord had said to me, "Bring him to Me—he is ready." I knew that familiar voice, for I had heard it many times before, when God had prepared someone to say yes to wanting Jesus in their life. However, I stubbornly ignored this command of the Lord. Of all people, why did the Lord have to choose me? Two days later I heard the voice of the Lord, again saying, "Bring him to me—he is ready." Again I ignored the Lord—until that day before my father's surgery. I had gone to my car after finishing a business meeting, when the Lord said, "Now is the time! And if he accepts Me into his life as Lord and Savior, then pray for a 20/20 vision healing of his eyes."

I got into my car and immediately called my dad. I asked him if he knew where he was going if he should die, and he said, "Well, I think to heaven, because I have been a good person." The grace of God came upon me, and I was able to gently correct that comment. I told Dad that we do not get to Heaven by our works, but by faith in Jesus Christ. I told my dad that he would need to pray and ask Jesus into his life. Dad said that he did not know how to do that. I asked him if he would repeat the words after me. He eagerly said yes. He didn't miss a word of the prayer, not even the part when I said, "Forgive me of my wretched sins."

After this I said, "Dad, I am going to pray for a 20/20 healing of your eyes, but you must pray that you never set your eyes on pornography again, because the Lord could take your eyesight again."

The next day was the day of my dad's surgery, and he came through it perfectly. The Lord Jesus was faithful and answered my prayers. My dad had 20/25 vision for the rest of his life; for the first time since he was thirty years old, he did not have to wear glasses. He could read the fine print in the telephone book. What a miracle! That is the kind of thing the Lord does in our lives when we hunger and thirst after righteousness. Surrender to God, and He will give you a hunger and thirst for Him. He wants your free will. Turn it over to Him, and He will fill you with happiness and contentment. I received a wonderful gift of knowing my father as a loving and kind man for a couple of years, and this brought great joy to my heart. Unfortunately he could not resist the devil and went back to pornography. Things went very badly from then on, and his health began to deteriorate. He passed away last year, and during his illness he recommitted his life to the Lord. I was happy but sad at the same time for all the wasted years.

A Picture of Righteousness

One morning, during the season in which God was speaking to Gary and me about righteousness, I awoke from a dream, having seen something that was amazing to me. The Lord showed me a round object in my dream, and He spoke to me and said, "This is righteousness." The object consisted of three thick strands of some kind of material that were intricately woven together. It had the appearance of a Celtic knot, only the strands were three colors—gold, silver, and white—that were intertwined. When I awoke from the dream, I asked Gary what the colors meant. As we talked together, we began to see that the silver color spoke to us of the cost of redemption—what Jesus did to win our hearts, and what we are called to do in response to His voice. The gold was the color of refining, like gold made pure in the fires of testing. The white color represented purity, the life of Jesus lived out in the "righteous acts of the saints" spoken of in Revelation 19:8.

The message of the dream has continued to become clearer as we have meditated and prayed over it. When we present ourselves before God and begin to agree with Him concerning our lives, we enter the journey toward righteousness. There is a cost to this journey—the cost of leaving the old life behind and embracing the new one that God offers. This costly decision was also made by Jesus, who chose to leave the joys of His heavenly existence for the greater joy—amazing!—of relationship with broken people. That decision cost Him His life, and the decision to follow after Him costs us our old existence as well. That is the silver strand, and we must be willing to pay that price to begin the journey into righteousness.

Following that decision, there comes the journey of purification. Psalm 12 says that the Word of the Lord is purified seven times in the fire so that it is proven to be trustworthy. Even as Jesus was proven in the fires of His earthly life, death, and resurrection, so we are made pure by the situations of life that we encounter. As we follow Him and trust Him through the times of life, allowing His Spirit to form us into His image, we become like gold, purified in the fiery furnace of life's experiences. This is the golden strand, and there is no way to come to righteousness without sufferings.

Finally, there is the white strand, which speaks of the purity of life, the righteousness that is established in reality as we continue in the journey. Even as Jesus was exhibited as pure and holy through the circumstances of His life, so we will be held forth as lights in a dark world, shining in bright righteousness, fully formed in the likeness of our beloved Jesus.

What was so interesting to me was the emotional impact of the dream. I felt such relief knowing that attaining to righteousness would not be that difficult. It was something I could do because Jesus had already done it, and now He was inviting me to participate in what He had already accomplished. The price I have paid to follow Him—though small in comparison to what He did—was seen as valuable to Him. The suffering I've experienced as He has refined me now makes sense because He too suffered for the sake of loving me. Whatever level of purity has emerged in my life is real and precious to Him because it is a reflection of His purity. It was as though Jesus were giving righteousness to me as a gift, and then inviting me to grow into it myself.

Gary:

There is an intensity about this pursuit of righteousness to which Jesus calls His followers. He challenges us to let this desire for alignment with God's character strike us at the level of the most powerful urges of our lives:

> *Blessed are those who hunger and thirst for righteousness, for they shall be filled. (Matthew 5:6)*

Hunger and thirst are two of the most basic and powerful drives known to human beings. Having created us with these drives, Jesus purposefully takes His listeners to this foundational level of need. When Abraham Maslow established his famous hierarchy of needs, the physiological requirements of human beings found their place at the foundational level of the hierarchy. He writes:

> *The first need for the body is to achieve homeostasis. This is obtained through the consumption of food, drink, and air, achieving adequate sleep, a comfortable temperature, and so on. When some needs are unmet, a human's physiological needs take the highest priority. For instance, if one simultaneously experiences the desire for love and the hunger for food, a human is more likely to seek to satisfy the latter need first. As a result of the prepotency of physiological needs, an individual will deprioritize all other desires and capacities. Physiological needs can control thoughts and behaviors, and can cause people to feel sickness, pain, and discomfort.[9]*

When Jesus calls us to hunger and thirst after righteousness, He is declaring that the most important need of the human soul is to be aligned with the way things are in the kingdom of God. Martyn Lloyd-Jones, the brilliant English pastor and writer, has this to say in his commentary on this Beatitude:

> *Well, what does it mean [to hunger and thirst after righteousness]? It obviously means some simple things like these. It means a consciousness of our need, of our deep need. I go*

9 *Maslow's Hierarchy of Needs,* Wikipedia, The Free Encyclopedia, http://www. en.wikipedia.org

*further: it means a consciousness of our desperate need . . .
even to the point of pain. It means something that keeps on
until it is satisfied. It does not mean just a passing feeling, a
passing desire. . . . "Hunger and thirst"—these are not passing feelings. Hunger is something deep and profound that
goes on until it is satisfied. It hurts, it is painful; it is like
actual, physical hunger and thirst. It is something that goes
on increasing and makes one feel desperate. It is something
that causes suffering and agony.*[10]

The central issue of life is to seek to be in alignment with the character of God. Nothing matters more than this, and the pursuit of this
condition is to be done with the intensity of the most basic requirements of human existence. The release of all other blessings depends
upon the pursuit and actualization of righteousness in our lives. This
is because God desires to pour out the full measure of His power and
blessing on us as those who are the focus of His affections. But in His
understanding that is rooted in His deep love, He knows that power
given to unrighteous people will lead to disaster, not blessing.

For many years, people like those who populate the International
House of Prayer in Kansas City have been crying out for the release of
God's power and blessing upon His people in that city, in the United
States, and in the nations of the earth. The truth is that God longs to
answer these cries for His presence to come and for His power to be
loosed. But because He is a merciful Father, He will not release the
fullness of His promise until we come into alignment with His character; without congruity between His character and ours, the power He
would release would kill us! In the same way that a flawed foundation
cannot bear the weight of a large building but would collapse under
the pressure of the structure, so we, the dwelling place of God, without righteousness in the foundations of our character, cannot bear the
weight of glory that will come when His full power is released. Without
righteousness the power of God's kingdom would corrupt us just like it
has corrupted leaders in business, in the public sector, and in the body
of Christ for generations. God desires righteousness, conformity to His
character, before He will release the fullness of His promises.

10 D. Martyn Lloyd-Jones, *Studies in the Sermon on the Mount* (Grand Rapids:
Eerdmans, 1959), 80.

Righteousness Is More Than External Behavior

It is essential to understand that the pursuit of righteousness is more than merely attempting to bring external practice into conformity with some code of ethics or behavior. The decisions we make concerning our lives have their roots in internal character, and it is this internal reality that is called into alignment with the character of God. This is why Jesus says in Matthew 5:20 that the righteousness we seek must exceed the merely external righteousness of people steeped in religiosity. There must emerge an internal quality of character that is fully aligned with God's character. From that internal reality, right behavior will be expressed as naturally as apples grow from healthy apple trees.

Through the course of writing this book, Marie and I have been experiencing the intense probing of the Holy Spirit as He works to bring us into this alignment with God. Recently we began to sense the Holy Spirit calling us to internal integrity, to become "the same on the inside as we are on the outside." Through the vehicles of Scripture, the prophetic ministry of friends who pray for us, and the internal work of the Spirit, we have been faced again and again with issues of the heart that would prevent us from living in the fullness of God's blessing and provision. The Lord has brought every motivation for ministry under scrutiny. He has put His finger on every misplaced affection, every compromise, and every dysfunctional communication pattern. We have found ourselves crying out to God in the night again and again, wrestling with Him to bring the broken places of our hearts before Him to be healed and set free. Repentance is our daily bread in this season. We are motivated by a sense of what the Lord desires to do with us and for us, but will not do until there is righteousness at the core of our being.

Hunger and Thirst in the Life of Jesus

If we are to come into our full inheritance of authority on earth as it is in heaven, it is essential that we perceive Jesus as the model of each of these character traits. It is Jesus to whom we are joined in the true marriage covenant, and it is He who gives full expression to each of the Beatitudes. Therefore, to embrace the Beatitudes as our lifestyle is to cooperate with the process of conformity to His image, which is our destiny.

It is a compelling thing to consider that in the person of Jesus, God gave full expression of His desires for mankind through this one true Man. As a man full of the Holy Spirit, Jesus knew the heart of His Father, and He lived His life in complete agreement with His Father's will. This truth helps us to comprehend one of the more startling events in Jesus' life, recorded in the Gospel of John:

> *Now the Passover of the Jews was at hand, and Jesus went up to Jerusalem. And He found in the temple those who sold oxen and sheep and doves, and the money changers doing business. When He had made a whip of cords, He drove them all out of the temple, with the sheep and the oxen, and poured out the changers' money and overturned the tables. And He said to those who sold doves, "Take these things away! Do not make My Father's house a house of merchandise!" Then His disciples remembered that it was written, "Zeal for Your house has eaten Me up." (John 2:13-17)*

Jesus went to Jerusalem with an understanding from His Father, one that was achieved in a place of intimate communion and prayer. He was fully aligned with the Father's character and therefore saw all things from the Father's perspective. He knew what the Father had in mind when He called the nation of Israel into existence. He knew that the true identity of this people could only be realized in conformity to the Father's vision for them. Jesus had chosen His disciples based on the Father's leading, seeing in them the destiny of apostolic authority, even while they were immature and carnal. Jesus understood that the temple was intended to be a prophetic window into God's desire to have a dwelling place with His people. It was to be a place of communion and intimacy, with full access to all who would come, a place of mercy and grace where people would be invited into the empowering presence of God.

The spiritual leaders of the day, however, had turned the temple into a religious bastion, a stronghold of legalism and oppression that served more to separate the people from God than to open the way to Him. The presence of the moneychangers in the courtyard revealed a pollution at the core of the system. When Jesus encountered the situation, He was blasted with the discrepancy between what was in His

Father's heart and what was being expressed by those who were placed to reveal the Father to the people. The temple had been so overrun with empty ritual that God had long before withdrawn His presence from it.

The text in John 2 says that Jesus was consumed by zeal for His Father's house. A deep passion burned in Jesus' heart for God's people to realize their destiny as kings and priests in the kingdom of God.[11] He yearned to see intimacy between His Father and His people, to see the power of God released upon the nation in the way His Father had intended from the beginning. So when Jesus encountered a religious system that produced the very opposite, He was enraged. He experienced what can truly be called "righteous indignation," where His anger was rooted in His passion to see everything conformed to His Father's image.

In our day, most religious systems find themselves on the other side of the spectrum. Rather than being overly concerned with external behavior at the expense of heart reality, the religious systems of our day shy away from any call to righteousness. We prefer to speak about a sappy version of love that makes no demands, issues no call to radical living, and leaves us in our unrighteous mess. The Christian Church today is filled with all sorts of compromise and greed, with broken marriages and open resistance to the will of God as revealed in the Scriptures. For fear of scaring people away from the institution, we have dumbed down the gospel to the point of impotence, and then we wonder why twenty-four million believers have left the institutional church to seek an encounter with God that will actually bring change to their lives.[12]

But impotence is not only the scourge of the mainstream, seeker-oriented institution. The churches that claim the power of God are just as devoid of anything beyond bells, whistles, and the occasional testimony. Once again I want to quote Bob Sorge:

> *We live in an hour where there is a huge gap between the Gospel we preach and the level of our experience in the Kingdom. We preach a Gospel of power, of healing, of miracles, of signs and wonders, of the resurrection power of Jesus Christ; but what we actually experience falls woefully short of the*

---

11 See Exodus 19:6
12 See George Barna's disturbing and exhilarating book *Revolution* (Wheaton, Ill.: Tyndale House Publishers), 2005.

fullness we proclaim. The demonized come to our meetings and leave with their demons; the handicapped come in their wheelchairs and leave in their wheelchairs; they come to the meeting blind and leave blind; they come deaf and leave deaf. The lack of power in the Church, at least in America, has us living under a great shroud of reproach. [13]

This caricature of New Testament Christianity is appalling to Jesus in our day even as it was during His time on earth. He longs to come and encounter His people in power, to bring cleansing and purity, and to release the authority of His kingdom to His people in unprecedented ways. When Jesus cleansed the temple, the result of the cleansing was that "the blind and the lame came to Him in the temple, and He healed them" (Matthew 21:14). Oh, how we need a breakthrough of the righteousness of Jesus in His Church today!

Righteousness as the Source of Gladness

Another dimension of Jesus' commitment to righteousness is revealed in Psalm 45. The writer of this beautiful poem is singing a hymn of praise to the King, a love song that finds its ultimate fulfillment in the person of Jesus. Under the leading of the Holy Spirit, the writer makes this declaration about Jesus that points with boldness and clarity to the benefits of loving righteousness:

Your throne, O God, is forever and ever;
A scepter of righteousness is the scepter of Your kingdom.
You love righteousness and hate wickedness;
Therefore God, Your God, has anointed You
With the oil of gladness more than Your companions.
(Psalm 45:6-7)

The rulership of God through His Son Jesus is revealed here as eternal. Jesus' authority is rooted in righteousness, and every decision He makes as king will be made in line with God's view of reality. Now here's the wondrous point: because Jesus loves righteousness and hates wickedness, God has anointed Him with the anointing of gladness more than any other man.

---

13   Sorge, *Unrelenting Prayer,* 135.

Do we get this? There is a direct correlation between the passionate pursuit of righteousness and the realization of gladness in our lives! To the degree that righteousness becomes our passion, we will live in the experience of joy. Do we see that righteousness cannot mean a suffocating system of external practices that are superimposed upon an uncooperative human nature? Rather, righteousness can only mean a deep conformity to the reality of how things are in God's heart. As we are transformed by the love of Jesus and become like Him by the power of the Holy Spirit, loving and pursuing righteousness and hating the perversion of it, we will find ourselves being flooded with gladness "more than our companions."

This is why Jesus says we must hunger and thirst after this condition. The pursuit of righteousness must become the fundamental passion of our lives if we truly desire to reach our power potential. A story from the history of Israel serves to illustrate the intensity of hunger and thirst when it really gets serious. Consider this section from the book of Isaiah:

> *Through the wrath of the LORD of host the land is burned up,*
> *And the people shall be as fuel for the fire;*
> *No man shall spare his brother.*
> *And he shall snatch on the right hand and be hungry;*
> *He shall devour on the left hand and not be satisfied;*
> *Every man shall eat the flesh of his own arm.*
> *(Isaiah 9:19-20)*

This text was written as a warning to the nation that judgment was coming from God; because of the people's disobedience, they would experience extreme hunger. Their hunger would be so severe that they would eat the flesh off their own arm to survive. That's serious hunger!

Interestingly, in the Sermon on the Mount, just a few phrases after He has spoken the Beatitudes, Jesus uses language of similar intensity:

> *If your right eye causes you to sin, pluck it out and cast it*
> *from you; for it is more profitable for you that one of your*
> *members perish, than for your whole body to be cast into hell.*
> *And if your right hand causes you to sin, cut it off and cast*
> *it from you; for it is more profitable for you that one of your*

members perish, than for your whole body to be cast into hell. (Matthew 5:29-30)

Jesus is saying here that nothing matters as much as doing what it takes to be conformed to God's character. So what if we lose something that seems really important now? In the end we get it all back and more. Sometimes we count the cost of obedience and feel distress over what we will miss if we really get serious about God and His kingdom. But Jesus is inviting us to consider what we will miss if we *don't* get serious about what He is saying here. God is offering us full blessing and happiness, more power and authority than we will know what to do with, and we're worried that we might miss out on some silly temporal pleasure. We forfeit an unimaginable and eternal inheritance of power and authority for the sake of something that is ultimately worthless! We must get hold of this truth deep in our hearts.

The Motivation of Seeking Righteousness

Why is this pursuit of righteousness so important in our lives? Because it simply means that we can become everything God intended us to be. I appreciate the Armed Forces of the United States, and it is with due respect that I say they cannot fulfill their promise to their recruits to "Become all that you can be." The power to make us all that we can be rests with God alone and is released only to those who find their craving for righteousness satisfied in God.

This goes back to this most basic thing. God has a design for each of us that is perfect and that will fit in perfect harmony with His design for the rest of His creation. Our happiness, the full realization of God's blessing in our lives, is dependent upon that craving being satisfied. The release of power to bring healing, deliverance, and salvation to the people we love and to the nations of the earth depends upon His righteousness being formed in us. To try to find our fulfillment apart from that design is to live frustrated, empty, and unfulfilled.

As we close this chapter, we want to repeat the wonderful list of promises from Psalm 112, which speaks to the quality of life reserved for those who are found to be righteous. Consider these things that God says concerning the righteous (taken from Psalm 112:6-9, New Living Translation):

- They will be long remembered.
- They do not fear bad news.
- They confidently trust the Lord to take care of them.
- They are confident and fearless and can face their foes triumphantly.
- They share freely and give generously to those in need.
- Their good deeds will be remembered forever.
- They will have influence and honor.

The wicked will see this and be infuriated. They will grind their teeth in anger; they will slink away, their hopes thwarted (112:10).

The amazing reality is that these things are promised by God to those who hunger and thirst for all things to be conformed to the reality of His character. They will be fully satisfied, satiated with righteousness! They will see all things become as they should be, and that reality will literally last forever. Marie and I have decided that we want to be part of this group. Our hope is that you do as well.

POWER POINT OF THIS CHAPTER:

The most important issue of our lives is to have our character totally in alignment with the character of God so that the power of God's kingdom may be released through us.

FOR DISCUSSION AND REFLECTION:

1. In your personal journal, write down your old perceptions of righteousness and how you have attempted to live righteously.

2. Now write some situations in your life that need the raw power of God to be released to bring healing, deliverance, and restoration.

3. Add to your list some ways that righteousness and power could be expressed in your life now as you gain understanding of how Jesus lived as a righteous man.

4. Think of some things that may be stumbling blocks to righteousness in your life. Your list might include such things as materialism, resentment, jealousy, skewed priorities, unforgiveness, and prejudice.

5. Ask the Lord Jesus to forgive you for these things and to bring your character into line with His.

6. Share these things with your small group of friends, and ask them to pray with you for the power of the Holy Spirit to bring you to true righteousness.

CHAPTER SEVEN:

POWERFUL PEOPLE ARE MERCIFUL

*Blessed are the merciful, for they
shall obtain mercy. (Matthew 5:7)*

Marie

Recently, as I struggled to write about mercy, I had a wonderful revelation from the Lord. It happened during a period of time in which I had been asking the Lord to reveal to Gary and me why signs and wonders are largely absent in our western Church today. The Lord began to show me that you cannot have mercy without love, because mercy flows out of love. And the opposite is true also. It is impossible to show love without the presence of mercy. We could fake it, but then we end up feeling like a fake and others sense the counterfeit. As I was reading Francis MacNutt's recent book *The Nearly Perfect Crime*, I came to a powerful understanding of why we are not seeing signs and wonders in our Church today. McNutt writes: "God seems to pour out His power to heal the sick for two basic reasons: (1) it shows His love and compassion for His sick children, and (2) miraculous healing also serves as a witness to the truth. *Love and truth are both involved in miraculous healing.*"[1]

---

1   Francis MacNutt, *The Nearly Perfect Crime* (Grand Rapids: Chosen Books, 2005), 97. Emphasis mine

As you read on and understand that mercy flows out of love, ask the Lord to give you His love and mercy so that you can have power and authority not only to ascend His holy hill to minister to the Lord but also to lay hands on the sick and see them healed. Then you will be doing what Jesus does. Read on for more exciting understanding of this very important Beatitude.

This particular Beatitude was difficult for me because over the years I had become tough in order to survive. The walls I had built around myself for protection could be named "selfish" and "self-centered." They were high and they were thick. My thoughts and goals were focused on how I could make myself the most happy, comfortable, and successful in the eyes of the world. Hardly anyone could penetrate my walls. I never understood or encountered the sheer mercy of God, or so I thought, until every possession that I owned and the people I cared about were taken from my life over a period of two years. I found myself in a place of desperation and despair. In that place of utter destruction, I began to understand the mercy of the Lord when I did not deserve anything. Here is a story that happened to me in the midst of losing my beautiful home and selling over half of my belongings.

After being unemployed for nine months and not being eligible for unemployment compensation, I received my first job offer as a fundraiser at a nonprofit Christian organization named Northwest Medical Teams International. After a few months of training, my supervisor sent me to Romania to observe the children's home and orphanages that they support there. The Lord began to show me the things that grieve His heart. I believe this trip was the first seeding of His mercy in my heart and soul.

Before I had left on this trip I had a moving sale and had packed most of my possessions in preparation for the movers to come upon my return from Romania. This was one of the most heartbreaking moments of my life because I was being forced to turn over the proceeds of the sale of my home to my past business partner. I was in my bedroom doing final packing when I remembered some money—$6,000—I had hidden in my closet from the moving sale. When I went to find it, I discovered it was missing. I frantically looked everywhere, but it was gone! The next day the movers came, and I asked them to be looking in case the money had fallen behind something. They didn't find it. I went into prayer, begging the Lord to have mercy on me and reveal where the money was.

Two weeks later, going from riches to rags, I found myself living in a bedroom of a home belonging to an acquaintance. I was sitting at my desk, trying to pay bills with the little money I had left. I began to cry out to the Lord to have mercy on me and tell me where the money was. Just then I heard a voice in my head say, "Telephone bill." I quickly retrieved the phone bill out of the stack on my desk and ripped it open. I scanned down the page at all the dates and numbers I had dialed, only to realize that calls were made from my home while I was in Romania. No one had a key, and no one had permission to enter my home while I was gone.

I went deeper into prayer and petition, asking the Lord to reveal whom these numbers belonged to. I heard that same voice say, "City of Bellevue." I grabbed the telephone directory and flipped to the City of Bellevue section, and about three-quarters down the page were the same numbers that were on my telephone bill. It listed the number as a home probation office. Instantly I knew that someone who was on probation had broken into my home and needed to call into this office as a probation order. The next morning I called my friend who was the Chief of Police for the City of Bellevue, and he confirmed my suspicions. My real estate broker was involved in a scam with this man, and they had probably duplicated my key. Because the Lord had mercy on me and heard my cries of desperation, He answered my prayers. We were able to file a police report and file a claim with insurance. I was able to retrieve most of my money. In addition, the Lord placed it in the hearts of my friends to take up a collection, and the money turned out to be the difference between the $6,000 and what the insurance paid. The Lord had also shown mercy to me through the generosity of my friends. He had begun to show how His mercy works when we really do not deserve it.

Mercy is having a tender and compassionate love for those who are not deserving or those who are having great difficulties in their lives. Mercy understands and identifies with the sufferings of those in misery. The following story illustrates in another way how God's mercy has changed me. His mercy has played a major role in my journey of learning how to be holy and righteous so that, as Psalm 24 describes, I can ascend the holy hill of the Lord and dwell in His presence.

Two years after moving out of my home, I was a different person.

I looked at people who had financial loss and hurts in their lives with different eyes. Mercy was growing rapidly in my heart and soul. While shopping in my local grocery store, I came across two young teens asking for donations to Northwest Harvest, a food bank in the Seattle area. The girls handed me a list of food items that were desperately needed because of the downturn in the economy and the thousands in our community who were unemployed.

I put the list into my basket, and then the Lord reminded me of His mercy over me. I felt His love for those that needed provision, and I could actually feel the compassion He had for those suffering without food. In the past I would have thrown the information sheet away and not given it another thought, content on getting my own grocery list filled. But I felt God's mercy as I thought about the baby food and formula that was being requested on the list. It seemed like the more groceries I put into the cart for this donation to the food bank, the greater the sense of mercy grew in my heart.

My purchases filled four bags, and the cashier was almost embarrassingly grateful to me. When I went out of the door and put the four bags into the grocery cart of the teens who were collecting the donations, they said, "Oh, this is the most we have received all day." I felt so sad when I heard that, and then I thought how the Lord must be grieving because we have hardened our hearts to others and have forgotten how to demonstrate the Lord's mercy.

I had help from a young man who carried my groceries out to the car. I explained to him my sadness that so many people had walked by those young girls without any donations of food. He said that he understood how I felt and then went on to explain that the local football team had raised a great deal of money for themselves at this grocery store just recently. But, he said, people did not seem to want to make a donation for the poor.

What has happened to us that we would show mercy to the football team and not to the children that are going hungry?

Think about this carefully: "Blessed are the merciful because they will be shown mercy" (NIV). The Lord Jesus pours more of His mercy on the merciful—a spiritual act that comes through His love for us. When we take that first step of obedience in being kind, merciful, and loving, He in turn will pour even more of His mercy upon us. That's what Jesus means when he says in Matthew 6:10, "In this manner therefore pray: ...Your Kingdom come, Your will be done on earth as it is in heaven." His will in heaven is that we be merciful on earth and then that mercy will be shown to us.

The most important thing to remember is that Jesus searches our hearts for our motives. If our motive in carrying out an act of mercy is solely to earn or gain something for ourselves, it will be discounted in the Lord's eyes. However, if we are motivated by holiness because God is holy, then the Lord will fill us with more of Himself, His holiness and His mercy. What an incredible blessing!

As I left the parking lot of the grocery store that day, I looked back and saw the girls waving at me, big smiles on their faces. I know that they will remember that the Lord Jesus told me to buy those groceries.

Prepared in Advance for Acts of Mercy

Please consider this passage from the book of Ephesians:

> *But because of His great love for us, God, who is rich in mercy, made us alive with Christ even when we were dead in transgressions. It is by grace you have been saved. And God raised us up with Christ and seated us with him in the heavenly realms in Jesus Christ, in order that in the coming age he might show the incomparable riches of his grace, expressed in his kindness to us in Christ Jesus. For it is by grace you have been saved, through faith—and this not from yourselves, it is the gift of God—not by works, so that no one can boast. For we are God's workmanship, created in Christ Jesus to do good works, which God prepared in advance for us to do. (Ephesians 2:4-10, NIV)*

When my heat was turned off in the middle of a Minnesota winter, and I came home to find my twin toddlers and their nanny shivering in their snowsuits, my nanny showed me great mercy. Out of her mercy for me, she did not call me home early from work because she knew that we desperately needed the money. She had clothed both herself and the babies in their snowsuits for many hours to keep warm. That day in the grocery store, many years later, the Lord brought back to my memory what it is like to feel alone in the world with no one to care. But Jesus cares, and He is in the business of providing for our needs because of His great mercy. The Scriptures clearly show us that we cannot do anything apart from God. The process of becoming merciful must begin with God in order for us to have the kind of mercy that He extends to us every day. Luke 1:49-50 says, "For He who is mighty has done great things for me, and Holy is His name. And His mercy is on those who fear Him from generation to generation."

Some time ago I was at my favorite department store purchasing some cosmetics. I looked up to see a woman of about fifty approaching. I noticed that she had a wool scarf wrapped entirely around her head so that none of her hair was visible. She was devoid of any makeup, and she had a very bad bruise on her forehead and nose. Her arm was in a cast. I immediately experienced an outpouring of mercy, and sorrow from the Holy Spirit came over me. I felt a nudge from the Lord to approach her. For a moment I thought that I couldn't just go up to a stranger and talk to her. Silently I prayed, "Lord, You will have to help me."

I proceeded into the hosiery department and was paying my bill when I noticed her again a short distance away. The Lord said, "Tell her about Me." I called out to her, and she looked up, surprised. I asked her how she had hurt her arm, and she said that she had fallen in the street, onto her arm and face. She said it might have had something to do with the brain surgery she had recently undergone for a malignant tumor. You can imagine my surprise when I discovered why God wanted me to speak to her and show her mercy. I found out her name was Louise.

Louise willingly told me her story. She had been raised Catholic, had not been in church for years, and had never read the Bible. She told me that a man with beautiful grey hair had approached her a few weeks previously and said that he wanted to tell her about Jesus. He told her that he was a Baptist and attended a church that turned out to be only a few blocks from her home. He told her that he wanted her to know how much Jesus loved her, and then he just disappeared. The following Sunday she walked to the church, looking for this man, but no one seemed to know him. She told me that she believed he was an angel.

This was a confirmation that God had been speaking to me. I told her all about Jesus and how much He loves her—so much that He wants her in heaven with Him. I gave her some cash to buy a Bible and directed her to a Christian bookstore just a couple of blocks away.

That evening she called me to tell me that her husband had found out about what had occurred and was furious with her for accepting money from a stranger. He told her that she did not need church and was to return the money immediately. I prayed with her and asked God to soften his heart and also heal her cancer. The next day she called again to tell me that the doctor was very happy because her tests had come back negative. She was free of cancer. And her husband came home from work and said that he was sorry he had treated her so badly, and was going to try hard to be kinder to her. Praise God for His mercy and answered prayer!

The episode had an even wider impact. The staff at the bookstore heard the whole story from her, and as a result they committed themselves to pray for her. As a result, Louise has a Christian sister who has been praying for her daily.

Mercy is a gift from God that expresses itself in love for one another. It changes you and how you view the world. The blessed gift of mercy brings real life and a love for others into your world. If you feel that you are not a merciful person, ask God to change your heart. In Greek, the word *mercy* means compassion—to sympathize or feel what others feel.

Mercy is not simply a wave of pity for someone. It is sometimes difficult to feel someone's pain or suffering because we are so absorbed in our own feelings, schedules, and responsibilities. Or we might be gripped with fear that the other person's circumstances could happen to us, so we run in the other direction in order not to have mirrored back to us how vulnerable we are. We must always be merciful, because we can never know when our circumstances might change drastically and we ourselves might be in need of mercy. In the encounter with Louise, if I had been self-absorbed in my own problems at work and home, I would have missed a great blessing and testimony for God as well as the honor of telling Louise about God's love for her.

An Attitude of Mercy

God created us in His image because He loves us and wants a relationship with us. But what if we have no point of reference for a God that is tender and loving, merciful and kind, because of the way we were raised or the painful experiences we have had in our lives? Ask God to change your heart to be gentle and merciful. Ask God to put people into your life to help you and pray for you. Ask God to show you through His Word how merciful Jesus was and how much He loved the lost.

I was with my granddaughter Amanda on an outing in Port Orchard, Washington, one sunny day. She was about twelve at the time. I spotted a man who was homeless eating berries off of a blackberry bush. He was obviously hungry by the way he was shoving the berries into his mouth. I immediately felt so sad because we have so much, so I suggested to Amanda that we go to the corner grocery store and buy him some food. We were very careful of our choices and purposefully chose foods that would be healthy for the man, such as fruit, cheese, milk, and bread.

When we went back to that spot to find him he was gone. Amanda was disappointed, so I decided to keep looking for him. Sure enough, we found him just down the street sitting on the ground and looking very sad. I left the car to deliver the food, and his expression of glee made my heart leap with mercy for this stranger. But the bigger blessing came when Amanda and I were back in the car together and she quoted a verse from the Bible. It was so precious to me to hear Amanda say, "Grandma, we really did this for Jesus when we fed this man that had nothing, because it says that in the Bible." I was so blessed to hear her words of mercy. Jesus tells us clearly that when we do acts of mercy to "the least of these My brethren, you did it to Me." (Matthew 25:40)

Philippians 2:5 says, "Your attitude should be the same as that of Christ Jesus" (NIV). In other words, we should take on the disposition and temperament of Jesus. The Bible puts a greater emphasis on our attitude than on our actions, which is because we will act out our attitude. Our attitude reflects the way we think, and as we think, so we are.[2]

Mercy in Forgiveness

Mercy means extending a favor or kindness to one who doesn't deserve it and can never earn it. God's mercy is totally free. Mercy is the forgiveness of God toward us when we do not deserve it. When we forgive others, we are being merciful even as He is merciful.

2   See Proverbs 23:7

Forgiveness plays a major part in our being capable of extending mercy toward others. If we are harboring a bitter root that grew because we were unwilling to forgive, not only will our prayers be affected, but it will also be difficult to show mercy toward others.

One day as I was praying, I asked God how it is possible to honor your mother and father when they have been physically, sexually, or emotionally abusive. In the commandments in Exodus 20:12, it clearly says, "Honor your father and your mother, so that you may live long in the land the LORD your God is giving you" (NIV). In Ephesians 6:1-3 the Bible says, "Children, obey your parents in the Lord, for this is right. 'Honor your father and mother—which is the first commandment with a promise—'that it may go well with you and that you may enjoy long life on the earth.'"

As I tried to relate this commandment to my own life as a child, the Holy Spirit began to help me understand that God had intended my parents to be kind and loving. However, Satan took a stand in their lives, and my parents, in their free will, chose to sin. God gives each of us free will. The Lord showed me that if I would show mercy to my parents with forgiveness, I would really be doing it for Him. That made my decision so easy!

After praying about this for many days, I decided that I needed to fly back to the Midwest and ask my father, whom I had not seen for twenty years, for forgiveness. You may ask why I should ask him for forgiveness—after all, he abused me as a child. Something was happening to my heart. I was submitting my will to the Lord and trusting, in faith, that God will see me through. I wanted the promise that comes after His commandment, which says that we will enjoy a long and happy time here on earth. Forgiveness is the act of sending away; it means to cancel, to grant free pardon for, or remission of, an offense or debt. It means to give up all claim to, to give up hold of, to cease to feel resentment against, to set free. When I asked my father for forgiveness for my responses and actions toward him, this act of mercy released me into an area of peace and serenity that was supernatural.

Does that mean that what the other person has done does not matter or that there will not be consequences for their actions? No, of course not. Forgiveness resulting in mercy is a process that comes by prayer of relinquishment. Mercy is an act of kindness that demonstrates your love for Jesus. God gave me His mercy and the strength to call my father and tell him that I would like to see him.

My father met me in a restaurant, and when he walked through the door, I was surprised to see a very old man—someone I may not have recognized had I passed him on the street. There was kindness between us that was merciful on both our parts. All thoughts of revenge, anger, and shame were abandoned.

On one level, my father had every reason to be furious with me. Only seven years previously, on *Good Morning America* and other shows, I publicly revealed my childhood abuse. I had also, much more recently, threatened to file a lawsuit against him in order to restrain him from traveling to the northwest and visiting his grandchildren. Only by the mercies of God was I was able to thank him for the things he had taught me. We talked about all the great times we'd had horseback riding. I invited him over to my sister's house the next day for a dinner that I prepared. How excited my sister and I were for the opportunity to tell him about Jesus! We did have fun, and we took lots of photographs. We knew that we were truly honoring our Father God through this act of forgiveness and mercy.

I flew back home, and the following week attended my home fellowship Bible study. I was so happy to see that, because of my obedience, others there had gone to their own fathers and asked for forgiveness. What a blessing I received from God! The ultimate blessing was that I felt a freedom I had never experienced before. I had been released from a bondage that had been holding me captive for years. I realized that my father is God's responsibility, not mine.

Can you see that the order in which Jesus put the Beatitudes is perfect, and is designed for our healing and as a path to holiness and righteousness? How could we possibly be merciful if we are not first poor in spirit, acknowledging our sins, our pain, and our dashed hopes, and then confessing them? Then we must mourn those losses, sins and broken dreams. This brings us to a meekness that will generate friends and bring loved ones closer. You will begin to hear the Lord's voice more clearly.

Soon you will hunger and thirst for more.

Gary:

You've had the experience before. Unexpectedly, completely out of the blue, you've found yourself facing a situation in which the well-being of another person is entirely in your hands. You can turn the circumstance any way you choose, but the choice you make will affect the person before you in a profound way.

Maybe it's something as commonplace as a casual conversation in a group of acquaintances, and someone makes a comment that leaves them wide open for being made the butt of a sarcastic joke. Do you take the opportunity and stab them with your wit, so that you will be seen as clever and gain an advantage? Oh, it may leave that person embarrassed and exposed, but what the heck, it's all in fun, right? Or do you make the merciful choice and let them off the hook, choosing instead to hold their interest above your own?

Perhaps it's a more substantial situation. You're on your way to an important meeting, or maybe just headed home after an arduous day at the office, and you pass a car on the side of the road that has a flat tire. The single mom is staring helplessly at it while the kids are crying in the back seat, and you have a choice to make. Common thought would suggest that she probably has a cell phone and will get help on her own; and besides, you never know when it's a trap to hook you and harm you somehow. Do you make the choice for self-preservation, to not disturb your routine with the needs of that person, or do you make the merciful decision and stop to help?

Jesus found Himself in that kind of situation one day, and it's recorded in John's Gospel:

Now early in the morning He came again into the temple, and all the people came to Him; and He sat down and taught them. Then the scribes and Pharisees brought to Him a woman caught in adultery. And when they had set her in the midst, they said to Him, "Teacher, this woman was caught in adultery, in the very act. Now Moses, in the law, commanded us that such should be stoned. But what do You say?" This they said, testing Him, that they might have something of which to accuse Him. But Jesus stooped down and wrote on the ground with His finger, as though He did not hear. (John 8:2-6)

It's hard to imagine a more dramatic scene in which the well-being of an individual is so completely in the hands of another. Jesus has the power of life and death over this woman, who is brought to Him forcibly and without mercy. She has been caught in the act of adultery, torn from the arms of an illicit lover so that the religious leaders could make a point at her expense.

A lot is hanging in the balance of Jesus' response. The scribes and Pharisees are trying to catch Jesus in a mistake so they can accuse Him and discount the mounting evidence that He really is the Son of God. They care nothing about the woman; she is merely a prop in their theatrics, a throwaway nobody whose life means nothing to them.

But her life means something to Jesus. He responds to their challenge in a fascinating way—by stooping down and tracing in the dirt with His finger. I have read many opinions of what He was doing in that gesture, but my own belief is that He was tuning into His Father's voice, waiting for the wisdom that comes to those who ask. How could He be merciful and still uphold the Law of Moses? Make no mistake: she is really guilty, and by the demands of the Law that Jesus Himself authored, she must die. However, if He agreed that she should summarily be executed, He would be really no different from the legalists, and His followers would be staggeringly disappointed and stunned. If He refused to uphold the Law, He could be easily dismissed as just another liberal with an antireligious bias and humanistic agenda.

As the scribes and Pharisees continued to press Him for a response, the understanding from the Father's heart was revealed to Jesus. As the crowd waited in the tension of the moment, Jesus spoke with the amazingly balanced understanding that is characteristic of godly wisdom:

> *So when they continued asking Him, He raised Himself up and said to them, "He who is without sin among you, let him throw a stone at her first." And again He stooped down and wrote on the ground. Then those who heard it, being convicted by their conscience, went out one by one, beginning with the oldest even to the last. And Jesus was left alone, and the woman standing in the midst. (John 8:7-9)*

There is not only incredible genius in Jesus' response to the situation; there is amazing mercy shown to one who is in an absolutely powerless place. Jesus' answer satisfied every demand of every heart present. He upheld the rightness of the Law, acknowledging that the standards of God are clear and strong. But He also took the focus off the woman, who had been singled out as the only transgressor, and put it back on the accusers, pointing the same judgment at them that they wanted to impose upon her. Without compromising the standards, Jesus took the stones out of the accusers' hands and at the same time brought conviction to their hearts of their own lack of righteousness.

When we begin to emerge into the righteousness for which we hunger and thirst, one of the great dangers we face is becoming *self*-righteous, proud of our achievements, thankful that we have moved significantly into the character of Jesus, perhaps more than many others. We have experienced some success in cutting off the desires of our old nature, and we rightly abhor the values and practices of the world system that we have rejected.

God's intention is that we would be so very conscious of how graciously He has received us and healed us of our addictions to the ways of death. God intends for us to always be aware that Jesus Himself bore the pain of our condemnation, giving us mercy when we deserved death. But instead we can begin to give ourselves credit for our growth, and before long we find ourselves looking down on those who are less righteous. When this happens, we are well on our way to becoming Pharisees, blocking the way to God by erecting monuments to our own righteousness.

This is why the character trait of mercy immediately follows the pursuit of righteousness. Only those who begin to develop a lifestyle of mercy show evidence that the righteousness that has emerged in their lives is truly the work of the Holy Spirit. Jesus was well aware that He was calling His disciples to a state of being and a practice of life that was beyond the ability of mere self-discipline. He knew that He was calling them to true humanity, a life of partnership with God through the Holy Spirit. So the reality He was exhibiting in the encounter with the woman in the street was a model of what it means to be truly human—merciful in the strength of the Father.

But the street drama was not yet complete. One person in the crowd *was* without sin and could therefore rightly and justly put this woman to death. He had correctly reserved judgment for Himself, and the whole crowd of witnesses waited breathlessly for His verdict. It came in the most tender way imaginable:

> *When Jesus had raised Himself up and saw no one but the woman, He said to her, "Woman, where are those accusers of yours? Has no one condemned you?" She said, "No one, Lord." And Jesus said to her, "Neither do I condemn you; go and sin no more." (John 8:10-11)*

At first glance, this response from Jesus seems to only satisfy half of the needs of the moment. Mercy is granted, but what about righteousness? Doesn't He just let her off the hook, basically saying to her, "Hey, it's no big deal. Nobody's perfect, and you've had a tough life. God bless you, and have a nice day."

Nothing could be further from the truth. This is no unrighteous sentimentalism at work here, but rather a stunning example of God's mercy and grace to redeem a life, snatching it from the jaws of death.

First of all, Jesus didn't see this woman as the Pharisees saw her—a pawn for their use, a cipher that could be discarded once their point was made. Jesus saw one that had been fashioned in the heart of His Father before the foundations of the world, one destined for greatness. She was the object of God's affection; and because Jesus was about to present Himself as the sacrifice for sin, she was no longer the focus of God's wrath. She was born to be a lover of God, and only the combination of His mercy and grace could release her from the prison of her sin into the glorious liberty for which she was created.

In the fourth chapter of the New Testament letter to the Hebrews, we are given an amazing insight into the ways of the kingdom of God. A powerful instruction in mercy outlines the principles behind Jesus' encounter with the adulterous woman:

> *Seeing then that we have a great High Priest who has passed through the heavens, Jesus the Son of God, let us hold fast our confession. For we do not have a High Priest who cannot sympathize with our weaknesses, but was in all points tempted as we are, yet without sin. Let us therefore come boldly to the throne of grace, that we may obtain mercy and find grace to help in time of need. (Hebrews 4:14-16)*

According to this text, Jesus has taken the role of High Priest in the presence of God. He has been qualified for this position because He lived as a man in all the pressures of human existence and yet never one time failed to live up to the demands of the Law. He was not a legalist, yet He was perfect in all His ways, living out His life in intimate friendship with His Father. Because He experienced everything we experience, His heart is tender and compassionate to the struggles we have. Since He lived as a man but never sinned, He is now the standard for true human existence and is qualified to stand as judge.

But His judgments are not harsh; they are merciful. In the Hebrews passage we are invited to come boldly into His presence. The word *boldly* means to come in the freedom of full self-disclosure, knowing that we will be received with mercy and not wrath. Like the woman in the street, we find ourselves naked before the One who has all the power, and we are at His mercy. And wonder of wonders, mercy is what we receive! Compassion, understanding, tenderness—all these merciful things flow to us from the heart of Him who knows everything about us and is sympathetic to our situations.

But here is the awesome and surprising twist: Though we are given mercy, we are not left dangling in our brokenness. God's mercy is not mere softness, not the sort of deadly tolerance that seems to receive people without judgment but really just leaves them in their lost and broken condition. God's mercy is strong and filled with remedy for the sickness that pervades our lives. That remedy is called "grace."

Grace is an empowering word. Grace is an endowment of strength, the ability to live in the holiness and righteousness of God. We come to Him in brokenness and in poverty of spirit to receive the mercy we need. It is given to us in abundance, and then we are infused with what is essential—the grace to step out of our broken condition and be formed into the likeness of the true Man whose death and resurrection purchased our lives for God.

That's what Jesus did for the woman in the street. He showed her mercy by not condemning her, but then infused her with grace when He said "go and sin no more." He was not merely challenging her to change her behavior. He was speaking a word of empowering grace, infusing into her the ability to change her way of life and begin to live as He created her to live.

Psalm 45:2 tells us that the King is "fairer than the sons of men; grace is poured upon [His] lips." This verse, which speaks prophetically of Jesus, lets us know that when Jesus speaks to us, there is an inherent power to do what He asks us to do. Inherent in His command is the ability to obey the command. So like the woman in the street, we are shown mercy in our place of need, but then we are called forth into a new kind of existence, given the ability to reach our power potential.

It is the same kind of thing that happened when Jesus came to the disciples in the middle of the night, walking on the waters of the Sea of Galilee as they fought for their lives in a terrible storm.[3] Remember, Jesus did everything He did as a man empowered by the grace of God through the Holy Spirit. Here He is demonstrating the authority that God intended humankind to have over the created elements. Seeing Jesus and hearing Him say *"It is I,"* Peter has a moment of intense and unimaginable revelation. There is a *man* standing on the water! Not a ghost, not an apparition—a *man*! Suddenly all the rules have changed, all the boundaries of human experience have been exploded. In an instant, Peter sees that whole new realms of activity have been opened up to him. He is captivated by the power demonstrated by Jesus and staggered in the implications that this event has for him. His mind is overloaded, but his spirit is pulsating with the wildness of his potential in a way he has never known. Peter therefore makes a wild request: "Lord, if it is You, command me to come to You on the water!"

It's a stunning appeal, but Jesus simply says, "Come." He doesn't gloat in His ability that exceeds Peter's grasp. He doesn't belittle Peter for being afraid. Rather, He sees in Peter someone who longs to reach his power potential, desiring to come to the fullness of what it means to be a human being. So Jesus speaks a command, which is really a word of grace, and Peter is given what he needs to obey. It is mercy at its best—an embracing of a man in his weakness, with a word of grace that comes to empower him to become what he was intended to be.

The Rewards of Mercy

The wondrous promise that is made to those who are merciful is that they will be shown mercy. I, for one, need and desire all the mercy I can get. In my own silliness and brokenness, I find that situations emerge

3   See Matthew 14:25-33

with frightening frequency in which I need mercy both from God and from those around me. So the promise of God in this particular Beatitude is that if I am a merciful man, He will see to it that mercy is my portion.

Jesus gives us a helpful insight in Luke's version of this sermon:

> *But if you love those who love you, what credit is that to you? For even sinners love those who love them. And if you do good to those who do good to you, what credit is that to you? For even sinners do the same. And if you lend to those from whom you hope to receive back, what credit is that to you? For even sinners lend to sinners to receive as much back. But love your enemies, do good, and lend, hoping for nothing in return; and your reward will be great, and you will be sons of the Most High. For He is kind to the unthankful and evil. Therefore be merciful, just as your Father also is merciful.*

> *Judge not, and you shall not be judged. Condemn not, and you shall not be condemned. Forgive, and you will be forgiven. Give, and it will be given to you: good measure, pressed down, shaken together, and running over will be put into your bosom. For with the same measure that you use, it will be measured back to you. (Luke 6:32-38)*

Here Jesus is saying something deeply meaningful to us. *If we will do good even to those who are our enemies, we are taking the character of our Father God, and we begin to be His sons and daughters.* We are to become like our Father and then act like He does in specific situations. As we do this, we find that the payback principle of heaven begins to operate in our lives. Whatever we give away comes back to us in multiplied measure. If we give mercy and forgiveness, speaking with grace and temperance even to those who wound us, we become receivers of mercy *"pressed down, shaken together, and running over."* I don't know about you, but I want that kind of payback operating in my life!

Marie:

This next story is how the Lord rewarded me with power and authority after I responded with His mercy to the children in Romania and Moldova.

On the plane, returning home from Romania, my heart was grieved. I had never seen such poverty and had never experienced such a roller coaster of emotions. I realized that this is what the Lord must feel for these children. I asked the Lord what I could do, and the Lord clearly said to me, "Teach my people about poverty." I wept and responded, "Lord, I do not know how to do that, but I am Your servant and Your daughter and I will do whatever You want."

A couple of days later I called a friend who owned an event company back in the Midwest. She had known hardship and heartache, so her heart was moved as I told her about the orphanages. Then, as we prayed together, the Lord began to impart a vision to us. I went to my colleagues and began to lay out a plan.

I started to envision a multisensory museum. I was later told that the concept is similar to that of the Holocaust Museum, which I have never seen. Forming a team, we began to plan how each vignette that our guests experience would touch their hearts. We wanted them to experience the crying of the sad and lonely children and the smells of their urine-soaked beds. They would see the anguish in the children's eyes. As they negotiated the museum floors, they would be walking the dumps in Mexico where the children live, eat, and sleep. Similarly, they would experience the war refugee camps in Kosovo.

Included in our vision was the idea of hosting this event at a venue with plenty of space for not only the museum but also an auction and dinner. The Lord led us to Sand Point Naval Base in Seattle. The base had been sold to the city, and we were able to rent an airplane hangar and the brig for a very low price. The facility was perfect, and it would hold the number of guests we had envisioned.

The budget went to six figures, and it seemed a huge risk. However, I had confirmation after confirmation that this was of the Lord. He provided the donated audio-visual equipment. We received corporate sponsorships that underwrote the start-up costs. Graphics for the invitations and auction books were donated, and the auction items began to pour in. God provided a team of committed volunteers. We named the event "The City of Hope and Light."

Finally the big day arrived. Two television stations sent reporters and film crews, and we were featured on the news. None of us had any idea whether the auction, dinner, and museum visit would flow progressively and in a timely fashion, but we should have known: the Lord had given us a peace, and we were seeing His mercy and grace on everything we touched. It seemed that the power of God was upon us!

We had a major international business figure and a high-profile politician, Phil Condit, and congresswoman, Jennifer Dunn, sharing the podium as our keynote speakers. Like many of our guests, both had tears in their eyes as they toured the museum. By the time people left the museum to enter the airplane hangar for the dinner auction, the Lord had touched their hearts with His sorrow and mercy.

The auction raised a record amount of money. The auctioneer said that he had never seen an auction go so smoothly or known a first-time auction to produce that much money. The concept of The City of Hope and Light has continued since that time, though it has changed in its scope and style. The most miraculous thing, however, was that God showed people His pain for the broken and abandoned in the world. How miraculous and exciting to see God's purposes fulfilled in our lives and to hear His voice saying, "This is the way, follow Me."

POWER POINT OF THIS CHAPTER:

Showing mercy to those around us is a true indication that we are touching our inheritance as the children of God.

FOR DISCUSSION AND REFLECTION:

1. Write in your journal a number of ways that the Lord has shown mercy to you, not treating you as you deserved, but according to His mercy.

2. Reflect on some ways that your journey into righteousness would tempt you to be proud, seeing others as less spiritual than yourself. Ask the Lord to forgive you for any of these attitudes.

3. Think of several ways that God would have you show mercy to people in your sphere of influence. Write down these things, and make a plan to do these acts of undeserved kindness.

4. Share these ideas with your group of friends, and pray together that the Lord's mercy would become a trait of your character.

CHAPTER EIGHT:

POWERFUL PEOPLE
ARE PURE IN HEART

Blessed are the pure in heart, for
they shall see God. (Matthew 5:8)

Marie:

In this chapter we are going to look at three dimensions of purity of heart: (1) truthfulness in thought, (2) pure love for God, and (3) purity in actions.

In Psalm 51:6 we are told that God desires "truth in the inward parts." What strikes me the most about this verse is that, if the Scripture's meaning was accurately understood, everything else regarding purity would follow.

Recently Fox News had this caption on their Internet headline news: "Americans are Liars." A national survey revealed that most Americans lie in order to elevate themselves or make themselves feel better. Feelings of powerlessness and insignificance drive them to lie. We lie on resumes, at job interviews, on taxes, to our spouses, and sometimes we just plain exaggerate a story. We all are liars, and we have come to think it is okay. It is not okay because the Lord is calling us to purity so that we may see Him. You cannot lie and have a pure heart.

Just think about it: when we lie we go to prison, when we lie we feel guilty, when we lie we separate ourselves from people and from God. For so long I thought that purity of heart meant to be sexually pure or referred to those who lived life with pure motives. I began to pray about this when I heard a prophetic friend say that while she was on a twenty-one day fast, the Lord spoke to her about one of the things He was going to judge the hardest, and that was lying. We think a little lie is going to hurt no one.

I came upon a book written by Art Katz titled *The Spirit of Truth*.[1] I was startled to read what the Scriptures said about speaking the truth. Gary and I began to do an inventory of ourselves, and we soon discovered how easily and often we stretch the truth or just plain lie to avoid confrontation. We prayed about this and asked the Lord to help correct us the second it happened. He has been faithful to correct us almost immediately, although the process has been painful at times.

We recently had someone in our home who had gotten fired from her job. She told us in a confession that she "sort of lied." I stopped the conversation to say, "Wait a minute, I think it is important to say that you lied and that you have been guilty of this in the past." This person acknowledged the truth, and we were able to pray for deliverance with success. A couple of days later we were at the home of a relative, and I was discussing the subject of lying. She said, "Oh yes, I am a liar also. In fact, it comes so easily sometimes." I think we are all capable of this when it suits us because we get caught in an uncomfortable situation or we want to do something to which the rules say "no." We exaggerate and say it is not lying; we hide our emotions and say it is not lying; we do things that we know are not morally or ethically right and we say it is not lying; we build ourselves up and say it is not lying. I personally think that one of the worst things wrong with our society today is lying. How can we ever trust someone who lies, and yet we lie so casually?

God desires truth in the inward parts of our heart. Purity of heart in the arena of truth-telling is essential if we want to see God, the One who is Truth, and if we want to speak the truth in such a way that power will accompany the declaration of it. It will not work any other way.

Gary:

The powerful dynamic of truth in the inward parts is that it involves

---

1   Art Katz, *The Spirit of Truth* (Burning Bush Press). See www.benisrael.org.

a complete formation into the character of Jesus. Truth must also be directly related to love, because Jesus is truth and He is also love. In order to walk in truth, one must also walk in love, which requires purity of heart.

Someone asked Jesus one day, "What's the most important thing God ever commanded people to do?" (my paraphrase). Jesus didn't even hesitate—*"Love the LORD your God with all your heart, with all your soul, with all your mind, and with all your strength."*[2] Jesus was underscoring the clear and repeated teaching of the Old Testament that from God's perspective the most important thing about His relationship with His people *was not perfect behavior but whole-hearted love!* Over and over again, as the great leader of Israel and the one who brought them God's Law, Moses exhorted the people to *"love the LORD your God."* Nine times in the book of Deuteronomy alone he urges them to set the full affections of their hearts on the Lord, often with the promise of amazing blessing attached to the keeping of that commandment.[3] Please understand that we are not in any way minimizing the importance of correct doctrinal understanding, or spirit-empowered ministry activity. They are both vitally important. However, they must take their proper place behind loving God, for without love, all the thinking and all the activity is just so much noise.[4]

When Joshua took over the leadership of the nation after Moses' death, leading the people into the land the Lord God had promised them, he continued the entreaty that was so central to Moses' teaching:

> *But take careful heed to do the commandment and the law which Moses the servant of the LORD commanded you,* **to love the LORD your God,** *to walk in all His ways, to keep His commandments, to hold fast to Him, and* **to serve Him with all your heart and with all your soul.**" *(Joshua 22:5, emphasis mine)*

Two things out of this verse need to be emphasized. First, we must see that God's primary desire is that we love Him. He is first and foremost a "heart-God," not a "mind-God." It will not do to merely think about God, even if we think deeply and correctly. As important as deep

---

2   See Mark 12:30
3   See Deuteronomy 6:5; 11:1, 13, 22; 13:3; 19:9; 30:6, 16, 20
4   See 1 Corinthians 13

and correct thinking is, God's primary target in the whole affair of relationship with human beings is the heart, not the mind. For it is the heart that is the center of all human reality, the core of being that gives direction and focus to our thoughts and actions. If our hearts are not in touch with Him, our thinking and our behavior will become dry, stilted, and ultimately lifeless.

Love from the heart is also the great equalizer of human beings. If God valued the mind most highly, an unfair distinction would be made between those who are mentally gifted and astute and those less able to connect the synapses in their grey matter. If God put the highest emphasis on activity, then those with able bodies and much energy would be valued more highly than the weak.

However, God does not put primary value on thinking or doing. He puts primary value on the motions of the heart. Paul the apostle says it this way:

> *Though I speak with the tongues of men and of angels, but have not love, I have become sounding brass or a clanging cymbal. And though I have the gift of prophecy, and understand all mysteries and all knowledge, and though I have all faith, so that I could remove mountains, but have not love, I am nothing. And though I bestow all my goods to feed the poor, and though I give my body to be burned, but have not love, it profits me nothing. (1 Corinthians 13:1-3)*

If our lives are not first about loving God and second about loving those around us, then we have no real basis for grasping the reality of our existence, no possibility of reaching any potential for power and authority in our lives.

I have a young friend who lives in Wisconsin whose name is Jared. In his early twenties, Jared is a Downs syndrome child whose strength lies squarely in the center of his chest, rather than in his brain or his muscles. For some reason that can only be attributed to God's kindness to me, Jared has decided that I'm his friend and that he needs to pray for me. On the occasions when I am around him, he sits with me and prays for me nonstop, often with weeping, always with great fervor.

Jared will never be a scholar. He will never be an athlete. But he is today and always will be a great lover of God and a prayer partner in the work God has given Marie and me to do. Jared is a heart guy through and through, and I would not dare to offend God by minimizing Jared's place of authority and power in the kingdom of God. There is a purity of heart in him that cannot be measured this side of eternity, and I can't wait to know him once he is fully transformed in the presence of the Lord. I am certain I will be tempted to kneel in his presence.

A second thing must be seen in the phrase that is in focus here: we are to love God *with all of our heart.* Love for God cannot be a part-time occupation relegated to the "spiritual slice" of our well-compartmentalized lives. Love for God is to be the full focus of our entire heart, with no competitors lined up desiring to usurp our affections. Wholehearted affection, love for God without compromise, is the way to life, the way to power and authority, the way to all things. For you see, wholehearted love for God is inevitably expressed in the full range of our will and emotions, in the fully developed processes of the mind, and in the fully enabled strength of our bodies to serve Him and His purposes among people.

The Motivation for Wholehearted Love

The language that Jesus used for this wholehearted love is "purity of heart." "Blessed are the pure in heart," He said, "for they shall see God." The right reward of a lover is the self-disclosure, the revelation of the Beloved. When love is wholehearted—with no compromise or self-centered motives—the revelation can be complete. Therefore the whole motivation of the lover of God is given to us in four short little words: *"They shall see God."* The lover's longing will be satisfied, for the revelation of the Beloved will be full and complete.

The foundational driving force in humankind's entire existence is to see God. The person of God is the wondrous reality we were created to enjoy. He has placed in our hearts the capacity and the longing for wonder and amazement, and we will not be content without it. Add to that wonder the dimension of love, and the promise of God's self-revelation becomes overwhelming to our frail human systems. Even those who claim to deny His existence are motivated by this longing for wonder, for they strive with all their being to fashion some sort of god that they may gaze upon and be in awe of. Whether the focus of their energy be their own accomplishments, their own wisdom, or their infatuation with sensuality or wealth, human beings were created with the desire to be dazzled, the longing to be wowed by something stupendous. We crave it; we travel the world looking for it. There is a reason why the "Seven Wonders of the World" are not called the "Seven Curiosities." We yearn to gaze and be dumbfounded by beauty and majesty.

It is precisely this issue that focuses for me the dismal failure of contemporary expressions of "Christianity," especially in the Western world. God has become small in the eyes of American Christians, having been relegated to the ever-shrinking "spiritual" compartment of our lives. Instead of seeing Him as the worthy object of our affections, stunning in His beauty and awesome in His ways, we have reduced Him to the lowly status of being the facilitator of our comfort. We want Him merely to help us feel better. In our craving for exhilaration, we simply have too much access to other things that have a more appealing "cool factor," things that are quickly and easily accessible, that don't mind being one of a thousand little icons clamoring for the affections of our hearts. The technology available now is so fascinating, so varied, and so inexpensive that it seems impossible to exhaust the options. We can watch movies on our iPods, download thousands of songs on our phones and wristwatches, find out everything about anything via Google, interact with the full range of the knowledge of good and evil on our high definition TVs, and do all of it whenever we want. Who has time to sit before the God of heaven and earth whose timetable for self-revelation seems far too slow for our helter-skelter lives? Who wants to wait before the presence of the Lord while His Spirit works in us the character necessary to bear the weight of signs and wonders? We can just go to the Cineplex and flip out over the latest special effects that give us the illusion of power much more easily than we can cultivate the real thing.

It is to this group of scrambled people that Jesus says these simple but shattering words: "Blessed are the pure in heart, for they shall see God." The question then becomes, "What do I really want?" Do you really want the shallow, short-term buzz that accompanies a gadget that will be obsolete before the warranty runs out? Or do you want to see God? Do you want the temporary pleasure of sin that sizzles for a minute but leaves you ashamed, violated, isolated, and probably infected? Or do you want to see God? What do you want?

If you want to see God, you must begin to love Him with all your heart and get rid of the other stuff that stands in the way.

So Where Do I Start?

If you have had the fortitude to get to this point in this book, my guess is that you are already experiencing the wooing of the Holy Spirit to go deeper in the understanding of God's love for you and His purpose for your existence. Jesus said that no one could come to Him unless they had been drawn by the Father, and so even the desire to pursue the knowledge of God is something that is given to you by Him in the first place.[5]

Misty Edwards, an intercessory missionary in the International House of Prayer in Kansas City, has written a song that perfectly describes the process of tapping into increased revelation. She says it this way:

I'll take my cold, cold heart, I'll take my unrenewed mind,
I'll take Your Word in my hand, and then I'll give You time
  To come and melt me.
I can't even love You unless You call my name,
I can't even worship unless You anoint my heart, God.
I can't even want You unless You want me first,
Come fan the flame! Oh, come fan flame!
Do what only You can do—come fan the flame!
Just let my heart be alive, let me be livin' deep,
  deep on the inside.
Come fan the flame! Hey! Hey, yeah, come fan the flame![6]

The reality of the Beatitudes is profound as one follows the progression of this journey toward power potential, since the way we begin the journey is the way we carry on throughout the journey. In other words, the thing that draws us into the journey in the first place—a sense of need and poverty before the presence of God—is the very thing that carries us through to the end of it. At the beginning of this book we looked at the perfection and beauty of the man Christ Jesus, coming to see that He is the normal human being and that He has all the power

5   See John 6:37, 65
6   Misty Edwards, "What Only You Can Do", *Always On His Mind*, Forerunner Music, 2005. Used by permission.

that we desire. That understanding faced us with our poverty of spirit and brought us to a deep sense of mourning and grief over our condition. Following that understanding came the revelation of our meekness, both the sense of who we are and who we are not in the presence of this mighty One.

As we began to realize that there really is a hope of realizing the power and authority that Jesus has for those who love Him, we began to hunger and thirst for that reality to be established in our lives. The longing for congruity and conformity to His image gripped us, and we began the process of stripping away every competing thing. As we did this, we found out how much we need the mercy of God to help us in our need and found that if we become merciful people, His mercy will be released to us all the more.

The activation of God's mercy in our lives brings us then to purity of heart—the desire for a single focus to our internal motivations and longings. Only He will be enough for us. Only His character will release to us what we really want. As he wrote Psalm 17, King David had the understanding in a clear way:

As for me, I will see Your face in righteousness;
I shall be satisfied when I awake in Your likeness.
(Psalm 17:15)

Implications for Holy Living

As purity of heart begins to become our priority, there are inevitable implications for how we live our lives. We simply cannot have pure hearts and continue to give ourselves to behavior that is contradictory to the character of God. Jesus said that all evil things that defile people proceed out of an impure heart. Vile behavior, such as evil thoughts, murder, adultery, fornication, theft, false witness, lying and blaspheming, comes straight out of the polluted heart.[7] There is no compartmentalizing of life in the kingdom of God. What you are on the inside gets expressed on the outside sooner or later, and the only way to deal with the externals is to deal with the internal realities of the heart.

We've all heard people give the excuse for their behavior that sounds something like this: "Well, I'm under a lot of pressure, and I'm

7   See Matthew 15:19

just not myself today." The fact is that the pressure situations in our lives reveal the true self. We can live the lie when there is no pressure. We can maintain the façade, play the games, put the best face forward, and prop up the illusion. But when the pressure is on, we find out what's really inside.

And so God gives us the pressures of relationships, of stress at work, of economic instability, of physical distress—all for the purpose of letting us see deep into our own hearts. Here we come face to face with the realities that need to change in order for us to reach our power potential. The person whose heart is pure is the same under pressure as they are when the pressure is off. When the work of the Holy Spirit has been allowed to have its effect in one's heart, the character of Jesus is what emerges. When God finds someone whose heart is pure, He can then release power and authority without fear that it will be misused.

There is a marvelous story in the Old Testament book of Daniel that gives us insight into this reality. The setting is this: the nation of Israel had been brought into slavery by King Nebuchadnezzar of Babylon because of the people's sinfulness and disobedience. But a number of the Jews had maintained righteous lives even in the face of this national disaster. Daniel and three of his friends—Hananiah, Mishael, and Azariah—determined to keep themselves holy unto the Lord even in the context of being trained for leadership in the Babylonian court. The text of Daniel 1:8 says that Daniel "purposed in his heart" not to defile himself with the delicacies of the king's table. He and his friends determined to keep their hearts pure, and the blessing of the Lord came upon them because of this purity of heart.

Then in chapter three of the story, Daniel's three friends were arrested because they made behavioral decisions out of the posture of their hearts. The king had demanded that everyone bow before a statue of himself that had been erected in the city. The three Hebrews could not obey this command because their hearts were set on the worship of the true God, not on the expediency of self-protection. When the king discovered their decision, his pride was offended to the point of rage, and he ordered that the three be thrown alive into a blazing furnace as punishment.

Just before they were thrown into the fire, legend tells us that Azariah stood and prayed one of the most profound prayers I have ever encountered. Under the pressure of a life and death choice, the purity of his heart was revealed:

> *Master, we have been diminished more*
> *than any other nation,*
> *and we are this day the most lowly in all the world*
> *because of our sins.*
> *At this time we have no ruler or prophet or leader*
> *or whole burnt offering or sacrifice or offering*
> *or gift of incense*
> *or place to make an offering before you and to find mercy.*
> *Nonetheless, **may we with broken heart and***
> ***humble spirit be accepted***
> ***as though with whole burnt offerings of rams and bulls,***
> ***and as though with myriads of fat lambs.***
> *In this way let our sacrifice appear before you today.*
> ***And may we follow you wholeheartedly,***
> ***for those who trust in you will know no shame.***
> ***Now we are following you with all our heart, fearing you***
> ***and seeking your face.*** *Do not put us to shame,*
> *but deal with us according to your gentleness*
> *and according to the magnitude of your mercy.*
> *Deliver us according to your wondrous works,*
> *and bring glory to your name, O Lord.*[8]

One must notice the positions of the heart that are referenced here. The prayer is that they, with broken heart and humble spirit, would be accepted; that they would follow the ways of God wholeheartedly, giving themselves with all their heart, fearing God and seeking His face. You see, choices for how we live are made out of the posture of our hearts, and when purity of heart is in place, we can make the choices of life that are the most difficult, knowing that glory, mercy, and deliverance will be our portion.

When the crucial moment came, the three were thrown into the flames but not devoured by them. By living out of a whole heart, they were able to bear the weight of the glory of God's presence with them,

---

8   The Prayer of Azariah, a second-century BC addition to the Book of Daniel, normally inserted between Daniel 3:23 and 24, but excluded from Protestant Bibles. Taken from www.bible.org/netbible/pra1.htm. Emphasis mine.

and they were set free. An astonished King Nebuchadnezzar saw a fourth man with them in the holocaust,[9] *one "like the Son of God."* He commanded that they be set free, and made a decree honoring the God of Israel. Purity of heart won the day, and the glory of the Lord was revealed upon three young adults who dared to live out of their hearts' posture before the Lord.

Marie:

After I accepted Jesus Christ into my life in the early 80s, God placed on my heart the need to be healed of my wounds. All the negative messages still played and replayed in my head: I will never amount to anything; I have a lousy personality; no one really loves me and no one ever will. No matter how successful I became or how many clothes I bought, those messages kept running.

God built into us an automatic radar system that allows us to detect when something is not right. This "radar system" is often referred to as a conscience, or you might hear people mention the word discernment. When Jesus ascended into heaven to be with our Father, God sent the Holy Spirit to be with us to guide and direct our lives. An example of this happened with a prophetic friend of mine who stopped at our home to visit. After each of us recounted some personal events from our past lives, I told her that I was going to share something that I had never told anyone before. The Holy Spirit quickly nudged me, and I said to her, "That was not the truth. The fact is I have told that story to at least three others." As I have thought this event through, I am beginning to see that the Lord is working in my life on the purity of my thoughts. Instead of not thinking much of this "little white lie" or a slight exaggeration that might not hurt anyone, the fact is that when I exaggerate, it is a lie. But the good news is I was able to ask for forgiveness immediately from her and from the Lord. I realized I experienced a purification of my spirit. What a wonderful revelation!

At this point in the book it is crucial that you stop and ask yourself and God if you are a liar. If you tell any lies at all or exaggerate, you must call it as it is or you will not see God in the power you have desired.

---

9   The central meaning of *holocaust* is a burnt offering. I have used that term intentionally here to connect the sufferings of God's people through the centuries with those of the biblical record.

For the sake of finding and experiencing God's presence and the power He wants to impart to you, the time has come to be honest with God, friends, family, and yourself. Do the inventory and ask God to reveal those places of deception. The reward is hearing and seeing God!

In order to understand being pure in heart, we must first examine the two words, *purity* and *heart*.

The meaning of *purity* includes: "cleansed, not soiled, unmixed substances, and extreme sincerity." *Heart* refers to "true character" and "inward life that drives our thoughts and emotions." Our heart has been described as the temple of our emotions. Fear, love, courage, anger, joy, sorrow, and hatred all relate directly to the heart. Purity does not always relate to our sexual lives. If we are harboring hatred toward another person, we have soiled our thoughts, and we are not sincere about forgiveness. This will separate us from seeing God and experiencing His power.

Purity stems from love for Jesus Christ. According to Billy Graham, this purity of heart comes as an act of God after one has renounced sin and received Christ.[10] The pure substance of our hearts is composed of love, peace, joy, kindness, goodness, self-control, gentleness, faithfulness and patience. Think about lust, anger, jealousy, envy, idolatry, lying, and hatred. Can such things live in harmony within you without giving you impure thoughts? They certainly do not mix with the fruits of the Holy Spirit.

I know a woman who is now separated from her husband of thirty years. In many ways she is a kind and caring person. However, she harbors so much hatred and anger toward him because he had an affair with his secretary that it shows in her face, her actions, and the words she speaks. She is having great difficulty expressing love toward others, because she does not have it in her heart. Instead, her heart is filled with bitterness, anger, fear, and revenge. What a horrible way to live life. Unless she repents and comes to purity of heart, she will never receive the fullness of what the Lord has for her.

If a creek has impurities in it from people dumping trash or chemicals into the water, you will not be able to see clearly to the bottom. In the same way, if we pollute our hearts with unclean thoughts, we will not be able to see or hear the Lord clearly. We may look clean and beau-

10   Billy Graham, *The Secret of Happiness,* (W Publishing Group, 2002).

tiful on the outside, but by harboring feelings of hatred, fear and sorrow we muddy our relationship with God.

Four Areas of Purity

We must face four issues if we desire to stand before God with a pure heart that is prepared to receive deeper revelation of the nature and character of God.

1. Spiritual Purity

To be spiritually pure means to be undefiled or uncontaminated. Because we are sinners, we need continual cleansing. In Psalm 51, David says, "Create in me a pure heart, O God, and renew a steadfast spirit within me" (51:10). There is an exercise that I did almost daily as the Holy Spirit was healing my heart through the Beatitudes. I recommend that everyone pray and declare Psalm 51 over yourself by inserting your name to make it personal. When we do this it is music to Jesus' ears and something supernatural begins to happen inside us. It awakens our hearts and souls, and opens our eyes. I know for myself that praying this Psalm changed my life.

When we receive Jesus as our personal Savior, He forgives all our sins and continues to forgive us, to wash us daily when we confess our sins to Him and ask His forgiveness. We give Him permission to purify our motives and to conform our actions to His character.

To be spiritually pure, it is essential to continually fill our minds and hearts with things that are pure and to eliminate the entrance of spiritual pollutants. It also means living in an ongoing relationship of intimacy with Jesus and accountability with other believers. If we are spiritually pure, it will show in our actions. Gary and I, for example, have had to say "no" to most movies and television shows simply because they pollute our hearts and minds, inhibiting the free flow of intimacy with God that we desire.

One of the Psalms helps us understand the importance of the Word of God in this matter:

How can a young man keep his way spotless? By keeping your
words. With all my heart I seek you, do not let me stray from
your commandments. In my heart I treasure your promises,
to avoid sinning against you. (Psalm 119:9-11, NJB)

I know of a wonderful, funny, talented man with a wife and two children. He had an addiction to pornography. He was caught once, and his
wife threatened to leave him, but he promised never to view porn again,
and he joined a support group. Then, all of a sudden, he had a tremen-
dous workload that kept him late at the office, sometimes until 2:00 AM.
He was finally caught using the company computers to satisfy his porn
addiction. He lost his wife and children. Though this seems like a high
price to pay, the real cost of impurity to us is that our eyes are blinded
to the true beauty of God, which we were created to behold. That is the
real tragedy of giving ourselves to impurity.

2. Mental Purity

We keep the mind clean by not tempting it with pornographic material, drugs and alcohol, and lust for things or other people. Entertaining
these temptations can alter our mental state and drive us right into sin.
Jesus tells us to think on those things that are "true, noble, right, pure,
lovely, admirable, excellent and praiseworthy" (see Philippians 4:8).
Don't clutter your mind with bitterness, revenge, or hatred. Be mindful
of the books you read, the movies you see, and the television you watch.

I remember listening to Dr. James Dobson on *Focus on the Family*
one day. He talked about how shocked he was when he first reviewed
the pornography that was being distributed, and was confronted with
the sexual activities of kids today, involving multiple sex partners. I remember him saying that after a while it ceased to shock even him.

This is the danger for all of us: we become desensitized to television, movies, and magazines in which the content is predominantly
sexual. Today, many among the younger generation don't even know the
difference because they have never experienced the wholesome family
shows that were prevalent forty or fifty years ago.

3. Emotional Purity

When we face the reality of our feelings, especially when those feelings are destructive and hurtful, we can begin to process them and sort

out the truth concerning them. Feelings cannot always be trusted. For example, there may be times when you feel fearful even though you are perfectly safe. Or there may be times when you feel angry at a perceived wrong against you. Perhaps you sense something concerning someone else, but you never see the manifestation of what you sensed.

Feelings are not bad—God created us to be emotional beings. Sometimes, however, emotions can't be trusted to tell us the truth about a given situation. Feelings are neither good nor bad, except when they are destructive to our health emotionally, physically or spiritually. Then we need to do something about them. We need to ask God to help us understand His Word, which brings a true perspective to our hearts and minds. As we meditate on the Word of God, we are empowered to develop self-control so that our feelings do not control us.

I have previously related part of my experience at the treatment center in London, Ohio. Here is the rest of the story...

The counselors finally encouraged me to tell my story to the group. Then, without telling me what they were going to do, they very cleverly performed a role-play of my parents' behavior toward me. They stalked around me, disguised in clothes similar to what my parents would have worn. They whispered softly in my ear the messages I had received as a child, while the group sat on the floor and watched. "You'll never amount to much," they hissed. "Why don't you have a great sense of humor like your sister?"

All of a sudden the dam of pent-up emotion from years of negative messages broke. It took two counselors to hold me when the anger finally came. Afterward, the relief was so great that my legs were weak, as if they would no longer bear my weight. I am convinced that the reason I have no major health problems today is because I was able to express all this pain from the early stages of my adulthood.

It is sad for me to look back and think about the lives of the people who were with me in the treatment center. One beautiful young woman was dying of AIDS and did not know whether her new baby would escape or survive the disease. Her husband had had numerous affairs and had passed HIV to her. Besides the baby, they had two other children who would eventually become orphans.

Another woman had been so brutally sexually abused by her father and brother that she had turned to other women for love and comfort because of her fear of men.

Do you see why "Blessed are the pure in heart, for they shall see God" is so important? Put simply and plainly, if we are not pure and holy, we ruin our own lives and the lives of others, and we will be accountable one day before God.

4. Physical Purity

One day as I was praying about all the sexual impurity around us, my heart was grieving for our youth today. I was in prayer, asking the Lord what I could do, and He led me to Joel 1:2-7, which says:

> *Hear this, you elders; listen, all who live in the land. Has anything like this ever happened in your days or in the days of your forefathers? Tell it to your children, and let your children tell it to their children, and their children to the next generation. What the locust swarm has left the great locusts have eaten; what the great locusts have left the young locusts have eaten; what the young locusts have left other locusts have eaten. Wake up, you drunkards, and weep! Wail, all you drinkers of wine; wail because of the new wine, for it has been snatched from your lips. A nation has invaded my land, powerful and without number; it has the teeth of a lion, the fangs of a lioness. It has laid waste my vines and ruined my fig trees. (NIV)*

The Life Application Bible, New International Version, provides this commentary about this passage: "The people's physical and moral senses were dulled, making them oblivious to sin. Joel called them to awaken from their complacency and admit their sins before it is too late."

In the last couple of years, I have had the pleasure of meeting Dr. Joe McIlhaney, founder and president of the Medical Institute For Sexual Health in Austin, Texas. He is often a guest on *Focus on the Family,* he sits on President Bush's advisory board regarding the sexual health of America, and is an advisor to the Center for Disease Control in Washington DC. I have been shocked to find out from him the truth concerning the sexual promiscuity of our youth today. Do you know that over 90 percent of cervical cancer is caused from a sexually transmitted disease called HPV (Human Papilloma Virus)?

Also, it is reported in the Arlington Institute newsletter (among others) that HIV/AIDS is becoming increasingly resistant to drugs. Some sexually transmitted diseases (STDs) are rendering our young girls infertile. Our young adults dress provocatively, and if we comment on this, we are considered prudish. Many of our movies are nothing less than soft porn, and our video games are violent. Parents must be careful what their children watch on television, because programs are so sexually saturated—but what parent can police this 24/7?

Tell me that we have not drifted far from being pure in heart! What a risk we are taking of the possibility of not seeing God! Today we have an STD epidemic because so many people, young and old, have multiple sexual partners. Young adults today do not think that oral sex is sex and therefore is not sin. The national apathy toward President Clinton's involvement with Monica Lewinsky demonstrated this. Divorce has played a large role in this too. Kids tell me that they do not feel loved at home and are seeking love and acceptance through their peers.

When the Lord gave me the Scripture from Joel 1, I decided to gather a group of girls between the ages of fifteen and seventeen at my house to speak the truth about their sexual activity. One girl, beautiful both physically and spiritually, told me that she was a strong Christian and so were her parents. She told me that she had dated only one young man, but that he was away at school. I asked her whether she was sexually active with him, and she said yes, but her parents did not know and think she is still a virgin. She told me that her boyfriend attends a college out of state, so I asked her what happens when he is gone and she misses the proms and other social events. She said that two other young men take her to the events. I asked her whether they ever placed sexual demands on her, and she said no—that the only thing they ever wanted was oral sex. When I told her that she had now had sex with three men, she burst into tears. I prayed with her, and she seemed to feel better. However, the important thing is not that she feels better but that her sorrow leads to repentance and a change of behavior to maintaining purity. We are held accountable once we know the truth.

When these girls again met at my home at a later date, I asked them why they dressed so provocatively and gave in to boys so easily. They said that it made them feel powerful and in control. What is missing in their lives?

Another girl told me that she had experimented with same-gender sex and group sex. She has had multiple sexual partners since the age of thirteen. In her case, her parents were divorced and seemed to have blurred boundaries on what was age-appropriate. This girl's father was deep into pornography, and this daughter had walked in on him during one of those times.

Through my research I discovered that parents are feeling so guilty about their divorces, multiple sexual partners, pornography, and everything in between that they do not set clear boundaries for their children out of guilt and fear. What we *should* be fearing and respecting is God. Somehow we do not think anything is going to happen to us. Don't we realize that we are going to face Him some day? Why has God become so distant to us? We behave as though we are going to live forever without accountability. But life on earth is only training for our life with Christ in eternity.

God tells us in the Song of Solomon how to treat each other sexually. The Bible makes it clear that sexual intimacy is reserved for, and is to take place within, the context of marriage. God has created sex to be beautiful and something to be desired. However, through our strong will, rebellion against God, and desire for instant gratification, we have corrupted what God intended for good. Sex is a deeply intimate act of love between one man and one woman in the context of marriage. It is an act that honors your mate with a gift from God intended for our pleasure. When we violate God's order for sexual relationship within the confines of marriage, we reap the consequences in both body and spirit of guilt, disease, and childbirth out of wedlock. And it separates us from the Lord. This step into purity is profoundly important in order to see and hear the Lord, and all we have to do is say, "Yes, help me Lord."

Gary:

Purity of heart and the resulting purity of lifestyle are essential if we want to live in the presence of God. He will only release full power to those whose hearts are like His, devoted to Him in love. Hearts like this will be the fountainhead of right living, the wellspring of decisions that are righteous and that produce fruit in keeping with God's character.

If our clean living isn't rooted in purity of heart, we will sooner or later succumb to self-righteousness, condemning those around us whose behavior does not conform to what we think it should be. In order to please God and receive authority from heaven, all our activity must proceed from a heart that has been fully captivated by love for Jesus.

By the same token, if our actions are not characterized by purity, it is clear that our hearts are out of line. The Scripture is clear—it is out of the heart that all activity proceeds, and only a pure heart can give rise to a lifestyle that conforms to the ways of Jesus. Only people with a pure heart will see God, and only those who see God can reach their power potential, for it is by seeing Him that we become like Him. May the Spirit of God encourage you with His strength to make purity of heart the goal of your life.

POWER POINT FOR THIS CHAPTER:

Wholehearted love for God eliminates all the barriers to seeing Him as He is.

FOR DISCUSSION AND REFLECTION:

1. Reflect on what the Holy Spirit has said to you about being wholehearted in your love for Jesus and your pursuit of His plan for your life. Write in your journal any areas of compromise and double-mindedness that have come to your attention.

2. Ask the Lord to forgive you for these things, and for the strength to pursue Him with all of your heart.

3. Make a list of actions in your life that have arisen out of impurity in your heart.

4. Ask the Holy Spirit to clean the filter of your mind so that His Word may flow to you in its purity and holiness.

5. Share these things with your group of friends and pray together for the Lord's healing in your life.

CHAPTER NINE:

POWERFUL PEOPLE ARE PEACEMAKERS

*Blessed are the peacemakers, for they
shall be called sons of God. (Matthew 5:9)*

Marie:

Do you think that you can be a peacemaker if you are not at peace? What about those people who would do anything to keep the peace, out of fear of someone or something? What about those who keep peace at any cost because they are torn by feelings of insecurity and want people to like them? This is not the kind of peacemaking Jesus is talking about. The word for peace in Hebrew is *shalom,* and it means all things which will make for a person's highest greatness. In the NIV Exhaustive Concordance the Hebrew word for *peace* is defined with words such as *"prosperity, goodwill, triumph, good health, safety, security, and blessing."*

In Bill Johnson's and Kris Valloton's book *The Supernatural Ways of Royalty,* Bill suggests that "We will only have authority over the storms in which we have peace." This statement has changed so many things for me. For us to be peacemakers, we must be at peace. If we do not have the security of a calm interior, our peacemaking will just be false.

In November of 2004, I led a group of people who came to Kona, Hawaii, for a teaching on "The Father Heart of God." A man whom I'll call John received a strong word of direction from God. John had a major position in his church and was very successful in business. He was stressed on all fronts because of his time constraints and commitments. His wife longed to go away with him to this teaching, but it had been some time since she was able to pry him away from his work schedule. After getting a leading from the Lord, I called him and spoke to him about some "downtime" with his wife. A couple of days later he returned the call and agreed to come to Kona.

About three days into the teaching John began to wonder why he was there. Then the Lord began to speak to him. John had a business partner that was not seeing God's perspective the way John did. As a result, their relationship became more and more strained. During the teaching God asked John to give the business to Him. Then He asked John to physically give the business to his partner. Can you even imagine John's surprise when God asked him to give this amount of assets and money away to a partner with whom he was having serious tension?

For months John had neglected to face the problem of his strained relationship with his partner. There are many of us who think we are following God and are loving peace but instead are stacking up trouble for the future because we fail to face these situations and to take action. The peace in the Bible that is called "blessed" does not come from evading issues; it comes from seeking wisdom from the Lord.

When John went back to his home, he prayed about the issue some more. He made an appointment with his partner and asked all of us to pray. John explained to his partner that he felt they saw being a Christian from very different perspectives and that this made a division between them. He went on to say how sorry he was for the way he had treated him and asked for forgiveness. Then he said something that will impact this man for life. He told him about his trip to Kona and the teaching he had just received. He told him that God had spoken to him, and he said, "God told me to give the business to you." He had already explained that he had given the business to God, because everything he had was His anyway. John told his partner that he was not asking for any cash reimbursement. He explained that his relationship with God, his family, and church were more important to him than business. John's business partner's jaw dropped open, and he said he could not agree with John's decision. He said, "I am going to give my half to you, and now we have all of it on the table. I would rather have your friendship than this business, so if you want to sell it, close the doors, or you just take it over. It is up to you." He also said that he didn't totally understand all that went on with John, but he did know that the man that left for the teaching and the man that came back and sat across from him was not the same man. Later John told me that God healed him of pride and showed him humility in Kona, which led him to be a peacemaker.

As we write this chapter a year and a half later, the situation progressed to where John actually bought out his partner in a peaceable way. Their friendship remains strong, and the blessing of God's prosperity is more fully released to John and his family.

Gary:

The story that Marie has just told beautifully illustrates the issues of peacemaking that we encounter in our lives on a frequent, if not daily, basis. Most people in our time, especially those who have a strong drive to power, know the tension produced by the difference between how we want things to be and how they actually are. Almost invariably these tensions are traceable to conflicts between people. One person or group is convinced that things should be one way, and the other person or group is just as convinced that *their* perspective is the correct one. We might develop all sorts of rationale about why our position is the right one, but the other guys do the same thing, and we end up filled with tension, mired in a situation where peace is nowhere to be found.

As much as we hate to admit it, the tensions often arise because we are determined to be sovereign in our own sphere of influence, however great or small it may be. We want the authority and power, and we want others to recognize that we have it. It may not be in a business situation. It may be such a common thing as a long-standing disagreement between husband and wife about where they should live or how they should discipline their children. The tension could take the form of a disagreement surrounding a political issue or a religious position. Any situation that threatens our sense of well-being or leaves us feeling that we're not safe or that we will not be protected can result in a lack of peace and build tension in our lives.

Again, we are convinced that almost all of these situations boil down to a real or perceived tension between people who each want to have their own way. The letter of James, who was the brother of Jesus, speaks to these issues in a most straightforward fashion:

> *Where do wars and fights come from among you? Do they not come from your desires for pleasure that war in your members? You lust and do not have. You murder and covet and cannot obtain. You fight and war. Yet you do not have because you do not ask. You ask and do not receive, because you ask amiss, that you may spend it on your pleasures. (James 4:1-3)*

How do we suppose that we can deal with situations like these in the character of Jesus? If it is His desire to give us real power and authority, how do we exercise that power with wisdom and grace, expressing our strength in such a way that everyone involved is built up and is empowered to become more like this Man whom we love?

I believe that we must begin with a consideration of who Jesus is as peacemaker *par excellence*. He is the model for all aspects of our lives, and it is nowhere more true than in the arena of making peace.

Jesus as the Essential Peacemaker

Consider this passage from Paul's letter to the believers in Ephesus, especially the part that is emphasized:

> *Do not forget, then, that there was a time when you who were gentiles by physical descent, termed "the uncircumcised" by those who speak of themselves as "the circumcised" by reason of a physical operation, do not forget, I say, that you were at that time separate from Christ and excluded from membership of Israel, aliens with no part in the covenants of the Promise, limited to this world, without hope and without God. But now in Christ Jesus, you that used to be so far off have been brought close, by the blood of Christ. For he is the peace between us, and has made the two into one entity and broken down the barrier which used to keep them apart, by destroying in his own person the hostility, that is, the Law of commandments with its*

decrees. His purpose in this was, by restoring peace, to create a single New Man out of the two of them, and through the cross, to reconcile them both to God in one Body; in his own person he killed the hostility. He came to bring the good news of peace to you who were far off and peace to those who were near. Through him, then, we both in the one Spirit have free access to the Father. (Ephesians 2:11-18, NJB)

I love the phrase in verse 14 that asserts that Jesus "is the peace between us." Paul is saying here that the only hope for reconciliation between Gentiles and Jews is in the physical person of Jesus, who through His sacrificial death and resurrection made peace between God and people, and then between the races. Let me illustrate this in a homely sort of way.

I remember a time when my family and I lived in Aurora, Colorado, where I was the pastor of a Vineyard Church. We had two pets in our house, a feisty little miniature Schnauzer named Sam and a neurotic cat named Mitzi. Sam was the newcomer to the household, while Mitzi had been in place for years, ruling the roost in her scornful and detached elegance. She had long been undisturbed in her place of favor, but when Sam joined the party, everything changed. Suffice it to say that they did not get along well. It was very interesting, however, that both animals liked and trusted me, and as I would sit on the floor from time to time and play with each of them, they would become calm and settled.

One day as I was in that posture stroking Mitzi's fur and enjoying her purring, Sam came bounding into the room. I could feel the tension in Mitzi's body, but she did not flee the situation. She remained next to me, with my hand resting on her back. With my other hand, I drew Sam to the other side of my body and began to pet him as well. Soon both animals were at rest and quiet. I decided to try what turned out to be a fascinating experiment.

I took my hands off both animals and began inching them toward my lap. As I moved my hands, I scratched the carpet, and both pets followed my hands until I was stroking them again. As I drew my hands closer to my lap, the animals continued to come nearer and nearer to each other. Before long these two antagonists were nose to nose, with their heads resting on my lap, focused on my affections, but inches from each other. Because of their affection for and trust in me, Sam and Mitzi could face each other in a peaceful way.

If we ever hope to live in peace ourselves, we must have Jesus as the peace between us. When Marie and I were married in January of 2005, we designed my wedding ring to reflect this understanding. From some pieces of jewelry that Marie already had, we took two small diamonds and a lovely ruby. We had our jeweler friend mount the ruby between the diamonds, symbolizing the blood of Jesus between us that ties us together in unity. It's a lovely ring and an all-important statement of where our peace, unity, and harmony with each other finds its source.

But we are called to something greater than just living in personal peace. We ourselves are called to be peacemakers, reproducing the ministry of Jesus that brings reconciliation to the lives of those around us. So, it is important to come to some measure of understanding of what Jesus did to make peace. The text in Ephesians 2 says that Jesus broke down the barrier of separation and abolished *in His own person, in His flesh,* the enmity or hostility between the Gentiles and the Jews. Let me try to explain what this means.

The barrier that is mentioned here was a literal wall in the Jewish Temple that separated the Court of the Gentiles from the place where the Jews could go to worship God. By His own sovereign choice, God designated the Jews as His own people and declared that only by embracing the Jewish Law could Gentiles know God at all. This literal wall symbolized the spiritual separation between the Jews as God's chosen people and everyone else. But when Jesus came on the scene, He came as the full expression of all humanity, not just the Jewish version. In His identity as a Jew, but also as the fullness of the Gentile races, He fulfilled all God's requirements for all humanity by His perfect obedience to the Father's will. He loved the Father with all His heart, soul, mind, and strength. When Jesus gave Himself to be crucified as the payment for our sin, He was qualified to be the Savior of all races of men. By His sacrifice He broke down the wall of separation between God and the human race and between the different races.

The point of this is that in a relationship of intimacy with Jesus, every individual from every race of people can find the potential of reaching their full destiny and identity. I no longer have to be jealous of you, because Jesus will reveal my true identity and destiny to me. He will also ensure that I will reach that destiny, so I can live at peace with myself and with you.

God has made marvelous promises to every race of people as well as to every individual who will turn to Him and listen for what those promises are. Because of what Jesus has done, every one of us can be confident that God will keep His promises to us.[1] When you can stand in the confidence that God will keep all His promises to you, you can live at peace with those who have their own promises to be fulfilled. Jealousy and strife no longer has to be an issue between us because Jesus has brought us together and has assured us that all God's promises will be kept.

As I stated in chapter one, when Jesus became a man, He became the sole definition of humanity, the total expression of what it means to be human. This reality includes both Jew and Gentile. There is no true humanity outside of relationship with Him. Those who are arrogant may resist this fact, but it does not change the truth of it. So, when Jesus lived His life as a man on the earth, He was setting the template for how true humanity lives in the situations of life. How did Jesus do this? By embodying the Beatitudes! Let's look at this statement in summary fashion:

- Jesus was poor in spirit. He never asserted His humanity above His relationship with His Father. He never insisted on His own way, but did only what He saw the Father doing, spoke only what He heard the Father saying.

- Jesus mourned over the condition of humanity. He knew how things were intended to be in the Father's heart. He knew the joy that God intended for the people if they would follow His ways, and the brokenness of people around Him caused Him to grieve over their situations. When He took our sins into His own body and was crucified, He mourned in an ultimate way as the bearer of all iniquity.

- Jesus was meek. He knew who He was from the Father's perspective, and He knew the authority that had been given to Him. He therefore never used other people for His own benefit. He never had to protect or defend Himself, but entrusted His own life fully into the Father's hands.

---

1   See 2 Corinthians 1:20

- Jesus was passionate about righteousness. He loves the reality of how God intends for things to be and hates the perversion of that reality. He therefore is fully committed to do whatever it takes for you and me to fully realize our identity and destiny. There is a day yet coming when Jesus will be fully satisfied with us!

- Jesus was merciful. Because He endured everything that we go through and yet never failed to live according to the truth, He fully understands our weakness and our struggles. He has mercy on the broken, restoring them gently to a place of blessing.

- Jesus was the epitome of those who are pure in heart. His one motivation was to love His Father and to present Himself blameless before God so that by His sacrifice the people God loves could be redeemed from the penalty of sin and death. He never set His eyes on anything that was impure, nor did He give in to the lies of the enemy.

- Jesus was the one persecuted for righteousness' sake, as we shall see in the chapter that follows.

He lived it all! Every demand of God's holiness was met in Jesus Christ as the true High Priest, the representative of all humanity before God. So, when Jesus presented Himself to the Father as the offering for sin, the payment for the redemption of all humanity, God's demands were satisfied by this perfect sacrifice. Therefore all who would put their trust in Him would be reconciled to God and would receive the power and authority to actually live like Jesus did.[2]

The key to peace with God now is not being Jewish or keeping the Law but living in intimate friendship with Jesus. Peace is made possible for me as I accept the fact that He has bought my life with His blood and that from now on I do not belong to myself but to Him. In the language of Ephesians 2, Jesus "brought me close." By His perfect life and the sacrifice of His body, Jesus broke the barrier between God and humanity and made peace *in Himself* between us and God.

In exactly the same act, He brought peace between us as human beings. He broke the barrier that separated us from each other. The age-old conflict between Jew and Arab has to do with inheritance. The Jews insist that the inheritance comes through Isaac, Abraham's son by his wife Sarah. The Arabic peoples insist that the inheritance

2   See John 1:12-13; also 1 John 2:6

comes through Ishmael, Abraham's son by the handmaid Hagar. Jesus, however, dispels the argument on both sides! Since He is the literal firstborn, the only begotten Son of God, Jesus is the sole heir of all of God's kingdom. But when He came as a man and lived in the flesh as the prototype human being, He reconciled all humanity with God. Jesus became the fulfillment of every promise made to every people group. In this way, every human being was invited to share in Jesus' inheritance simply by believing in Him and giving his or her life to Him. In His physical body, Jesus is the full expression of everything God intended Isaac's descendents to be. He is also the full expression of what God intended Ishmael's descendents to be.

Jesus is the prototype human being, the completion of what it means to be human—male or female, Gentile or Jew, slave or free. When Jesus died, all the divisions between humanity and God and between human beings and each other died with Him. When He rose from the dead, He was raised to a new kind of humanity, one in which there are no longer any barriers. When we embrace Jesus by responding to His invitation to relationship, we too become descendants of Abraham through faith in Jesus. We are brought into the family of faith and are made one with God and one with each other *in the person of Jesus Christ.*

Since the inheritance comes through Him alone, every individual must become reconciled to God through Christ Jesus. There is no other name, no other person in heaven or on the earth sufficient to break down the barriers.[3] When we come to Jesus and submit to His Lordship, we become joint-heirs with the firstborn Son of God, Jesus Christ. We all get the inheritance! There are no longer any second-class people. We are all before God in equal standing with His perfect Son.[4] We all get the power and authority! No one who comes to God through Jesus Christ is left out! We can all have what we really want.

How We Become Peacemakers

Marie:

Let's take a look at how you can have peace and, as a result, be a peacemaker. The Scriptures say that peacemakers will be known as "sons of God." You will be called a child of God. The most important

3   See Acts 4:12
4   See Galatians 3:28

point to remember as we go through this seventh Beatitude is that the peace that Jesus is talking about is a gift from God and is supernatural. You will not find long-lasting peace by seeking it through money, love, gifts, homes, or vacations. Those are all short-term and can be taken away in an instant. If the goal to living here on earth is to become holy and take on the character of Jesus so that we will know Him in eternity, we must think about what He was like when He walked the earth as a man filled with the Holy Spirit. If someone touched His robe because they wanted to be healed or called out to Him because they wanted Him to heal their children, He peacefully and willingly did that. Do you remember when His disciples would tell the people not to bother Him and to leave Him alone? Jesus rebuked them and insisted that the children and the needy ones be allowed to come to Him, because He wanted to bless them as well.

It is important to study the character of Jesus, because He was a peacemaker, and yet when the time came He threw the moneychangers out of the temple because it was a place of worship. We must not get peacemaking confused with passivity, and we must realize that being a peacemaker leaves room for righteous anger. Peacemakers are committed to seeing the righteousness of God established on earth as it is in heaven, no matter what the cost.

One of the most significant Scriptures in the Bible is John 14:27—"Peace I leave with you, my peace I give to you." One important key to this peace, which results in your being a peacemaker, is prayer. A former pastor said one time that for many of us today, our prayer life is a "prayer snack." In other words, we nibble at prayer when we feel like it, or when we need something. We do not think of prayer as being vital to sustaining us, and therefore we don't understand why we go through life feeling anxious much of the time.

When my son Dan went off to the war in Afghanistan, I was fearful that something was going to happen to him. I went to prayer—as did many of my friends—and had a supernatural peace most of the time. Every once in a while I would slip back into my old behavior, and then I would remember that I had Jesus to talk to, and I believed what He said to me. James 3:17-18 is a powerful Scripture:

But the wisdom that comes from heaven is first of all pure. It is also peace loving, gentle at all times, and willing to yield to others. It is full of mercy and good deeds. It shows no partiality and is always sincere. And those who are peacemakers will plant seeds of peace and reap a harvest of goodness. (NLT)

Peacemaking and Conflict

This Beatitude is intriguing, because one would think that "peacemaker" refers to those who love the absence of conflict. Instead, it means not evading issues for the sake of a false peace but facing them straight on so that everyone involved can experience God's full blessing for their lives and come to true peace. This path may lead us through a valley or struggle that we don't understand, but the important thing to do is to stand up for God's purposes to be established. As an example, in the beginning of my marriage to Gary I was introduced to Rachel, my new daughter, who was sixteen at the time. Many major issues arose in our relationship, one being Rachel's depression because of her mom's death from cancer just a few months prior. It would have been easier to ignore all the signs and walk away for the sake of the absence of conflict. But, instinctively, I knew that God had a purpose for her and had sent me into this family quickly to bring true peace. Rachel and I had many unpleasant confrontations, but they were healthy, prayerful confrontations and today only a short time later the Lord has blessed me with an awesome new daughter who I love to be around. I received the biggest blessing a few weeks ago when she was in Seattle visiting with my family and we were out to dinner with my grandchildren. Rachel said, "I love my life." WOW! It is important to note that with peace comes a true sense of love and security.

There are really two parts to this Beatitude that need to be studied: the first is that we must not avoid an issue for the sake of false peace; the second is to have a presence that radiates peace and serenity.

In Hebrew, the word for "peace" is *shalom*. If someone says *shalom* to you, he means that he wishes you the absence of evil and bad things, and the presence of all good things. If we take a look at all the discord in the family, church, and world, we will see that unless the heart is changed, there will never be peace. Remember, the heart is the seat of our emotions. Out of the heart come our will, mind and personality. That is the reason many will say, "Out of the words of your mouth is the state of your heart and soul."

The following are examples of a few actions and emotions that will steal our peace. Again, I have referenced examples from my own life, having experienced how impossible it is to be a peacemaker if these are present in your life.

Pride Proud people think of themselves as better or more success-ful than others. They may stir up strife or perhaps not tell the truth. Prideful people boast and take what may not belong to them. They will take credit that is not due them. They will dominate a conversation and not let others speak. Remember the story I told earlier about John, who gave away his business? He told me that pride crept into his life and humility disappeared as he became more successful in the eyes of the world. I know of a man who is very successful according to the common measurements of our culture. He owns a highly profitable company and lives in a large home. He has children who by all appearances are very successful and devoted to Christ. The sad part about this man is that he frequently boasts about the people he meets or invites to his home. He is always telling others how much money he gives away and how people do not appreciate the gift. He makes promises he does not keep, disappoints many, and divides Christians. His wife looks tired and worn down. Is he a peacemaker? My conclusion is that he must be a very unhappy and insecure man inwardly and that his heart and soul are crying out.

Self-focused love Looking at the way young women dress today and how teens are having multiple sex partners tells us a great deal about how self-focused and selfish the current culture has become. We divorce when things do not go our way, and we leave our children in daycare so that we can have a bigger home or another new car. We have affairs, watch pornography, and live with partners outside of marriage.

I remember when a woman in my Bible study group was dying of cancer. She was so ill that she was taking large doses of morphine to subdue the pain. One day we asked her if she would sit in the middle of the rooms that we could pray for her healing. The Lord healed her miraculously. She lived for many years after that, but lived in utter pov-erty. Another woman and her husband, who were very wealthy, would pray for her and encourage her, but they never gave her any money to help her out. They would spend money on cars, vacations, jewelry, and their home, but would not give anything to her. I remember a pastor who, speaking on the radio one day, said that if you want to see where someone's heart is, just take a look at his or her checkbook.

Meanwhile, this poor, suffering woman was in her late fifties and living with her abusive father because she could not afford to live anywhere else. She was found in her bedroom after being missing for a couple of days, dead of a heart attack. I feel sad when I think about the loneliness and turmoil of her death. I suspect that out of our lack of compassion for her dire financial situation she died without peace, because many in her circle of friends did not feel conviction about the true meaning of being a peacemaker. Or maybe they did not understand the word *peace* as Jesus meant it. But now because of Jesus' precious Beatitudes we can ask God today to bless us with being peacemakers.

Jealousy and envy Envy can cause division among friends. It can bring strife and competitiveness to your workplace. People can get into terrible financial trouble if their neighbors purchase a new car or boat, and they become jealous of that item. How can you possibly have peace or be a peacemaker with that kind of feeling inside of you?

While working in the nonprofit world of fundraising, I met some pretty wonderful and generous people. I came into contact with some of them frequently at dinners, luncheons, and meetings. I met others who volunteered at regional events. Many of these people became friends, and I began to witness the style in which they lived. Because of their generous hearts, I was invited to their homes, to their clubs, and to go boating on their yachts. I was invited to many of their parties and was included with their families on special holidays. I was greatly blessed by the experience of their love toward me and my family.

However, envy—a true enemy of peace—began to grow in my heart. I began to try desperately to keep up appearances in terms of my clothing—some of which I could not afford. Then I went on a couple of trips that were not included in my budget. I remember when I started to think, *Oh, I wish I could live like them and not have to work so hard!* I remember getting very sad when they would take extravagant vacations together as couples; I of course could not afford the five-star hotel and the first-class airfare.

The envy was very subtle as it began to take over some of my thoughts. I began to express my feelings of being left out. The old stuff that Satan whispers began playing in my head once more. The feelings of low self-esteem returned, along with the thought that I was not in the same class as my new friends. These were the old messages that I had heard in my childhood. I was in sin, out of God's will, and my peace was being stolen. Debt was mounting up on my charge cards, and I was moving away from God and losing my peace.

Then something happened that caused division between one of the women and me, and I was out of the group. The wonderful thing is that it was God who either allowed this to happen or caused it to come about in order to get me back on track. I had to confess my sin and ask the Lord to forgive me. I also had to lay down my rights and go in a humble spirit to my friend who had wounded me deeply by the things she had said to me. Looking back at her words, I now acknowledge that her words were the truth and that she had expressed them in her confusion over my behavior. In my confession to her the Lord had commanded me to be a peacemaker, and I could only do it by His grace, forgiveness and love.

There can be no real peace in the world unless we have peace with, and trust in, God. Being a peacemaker does not mean being passive. It means promoting unity and harmony at the deepest levels of the heart, both in relationship with God and with one another. In order to be a peacemaker, you need both self-control and self-respect in order to be pure in heart and in motive. Gossip cannot be a part of a peacemaker's life. It is a horrible tool of Satan that destroys peace and stirs up dissension in relationships.

The Bible says that it is out of the heart that murder, pride, adultery, jealousy, gossip, selfish ambition and anger come. As long as we remain in a "heart-diseased" state, there can be no peacemaking. It is only as we are filled with a greater measure of God that we can become peacemakers. Being a peacemaker results in our bearing the fruit of the Holy Spirit. The book of Proverbs contains profound wisdom on peace: "There is deceit in the hearts of those who plot evil, but joy for those who promote peace" (Proverbs 12:20).

The best part of this Beatitude is God's promise at the end: "they shall be called children of God." Can you imagine the privilege of being recognized as a child of God? When you have gone through the process of healing as contained in these Beatitudes, and then desire to be a peacemaker, you become a very special, privileged child of God. If you have supernatural peace, you can hear God's voice more clearly.

Many people have asked me how I hear the voice of the Lord so clearly. Things that the Lord has told me have come about exactly as He has said, including healings from disease. At times when I have been witnessing to someone and talking to them about accepting Jesus into their lives, I have clearly heard the Lord saying, "Bring them to Me, they are ready." When I have obeyed, the person has always accepted Christ as their Savior. What a thrill to hear His voice.

When you are called a "child of God" as a result of being a peacemaker, you will also have a more effective prayer life. The Lord will protect and guide you in an even greater way. All you have to do is ask God to help you be a peacemaker. You must be willing to set down your rights and walk humbly through the briar patch of your life. The Lord will show you the way as His precious child.

Gary:

Since Jesus is the model of what it is to be a peacemaker and enjoys the supremely powerful designation as "the Son of God," it is essential that we seek to make peace even as He did. I want to suggest several components of peacemaking that will bring to us the full rewards of sonship.

First, we must learn to see individuals as God sees them. We must begin to know them as they exist in the mind of God, not just as we see them in their natural condition. In Paul's second letter to the believers in Corinth, he wrote profoundly about this process:

For the love of Christ compels us, because we judge thus: that if One died for all, then all died; and He died for all, that those who live should live no longer for themselves, but for Him who died for them and rose again. Therefore, from now on, we regard no one according to the flesh. Even though we have known Christ according to the flesh, yet now we know Him thus no longer. Therefore, if anyone is in Christ, he is a new creation; old things have passed away; behold, all things

have become new. Now all things are of God, who has recon-
ciled us to Himself through Jesus Christ, and has given us the
ministry of reconciliation, that is, that God was in Christ rec-
onciling the world to Himself, not imputing their trespasses
to them, and has committed to us the word of reconciliation.
(2 Corinthians 5:14-19)

Those who live in the power of being sons or daughters of God are compelled by the love of Christ, living out of the desire to please Him and not themselves. One of the primary expressions of this love is to see people as God sees them, as new creations. Our goal as peacemakers is to help people become aligned with the truth of God's definition of their lives. This does not come by imposing our opinions on them. It means that we lay down all our opinions and seek God for the revelation of His wisdom concerning them, for God knows every individual perfectly and has a perfect plan for their maximum joy and fulfillment. If we will seek after God's wisdom in this way, He will reveal His heart and speak to us about these people and their situations. He knows all things and is eager to reveal His ways to those who ask Him.

Once we have some sense of God's perspectives, we intercede for others in prayer, allowing the compassion of the Father to fill our hearts. We feel the pain of their hurts and bear the burdens of their difficulties together with them. We gently and tenderly speak to them of how God sees them, how He loves them perfectly, and how He will give them the power to become all they were created to be. We lead them into encounters with the person of Jesus, inviting them to receive His mercy and grace for their lives. We help them see that only in relationship with Jesus can they come to any hope of fulfillment and power.

We confront sinful patterns in their lives in a spirit of humility, knowing that we are weak ourselves and subject to the same kinds of problems.[5] We walk alongside them, encouraging them with patient love until the truth gets settled in their hearts and they can live out of their own growing faith in Christ. In Proverbs 25:15 we have a beautiful state-ment about the power of patient and gentle peacemaking:

By long forbearance [patience] a ruler is persuaded,
And a gentle tongue breaks a bone.

---

5   See Galatians 6:1-5

We make ourselves available to stand between two people who are in disagreement, drawing them to the person of Jesus that their points of disunity might be settled. We do not settle for mere tolerance, which claims to accept people as they are but in reality leaves them in their broken and condemned existence. Peacemaking in the Spirit of Christ has nothing to do with tolerance as it is defined in contemporary culture. The biblical peacemaker is one whose passion is first to see people reconciled to God and His definitions of reality. Only then can we realistically hope for peace between people as brothers and sisters in Christ.

Those who give themselves to this kind of living are called "sons of God." They reflect the character of Jesus and show by their lives that the Holy Spirit has had His way in their hearts. God's pleasure is upon them, and He will make all His resources available to them that they might have maximum power to do what He has given them to do.

POWER POINT FOR THIS CHAPTER:

Reconciling people to God and to one another establishes us in our identity as God's sons and daughters.

FOR DISCUSSION AND REFLECTION:

1. Consider the reality that in His own physical body Jesus reconciled the entire human race to His Father. Write down several ideas that are implications of this truth in terms of your relationship with God and with other people.

2. Write a list of several things in your life that keep you from peace with God and from being a peacemaker in your relationships with others.

3. Think of several people you know who need to come to peace with God or come to peace with someone else. Ask the Holy Spirit how you can partner with Jesus in being a peacemaker in these situations.

CHAPTER TEN:

POWERFUL PEOPLE ARE PERSECUTED FOR RIGHTEOUSNESS' SAKE

Blessed are those who are persecuted for righteousness' sake,
for theirs is the kingdom of Heaven. (Matthew 5:10)

Marie:

Doesn't it seem ironic that after all the praying, and when every desire of your heart is to please God and conform to the ways of Christ, you should come under persecution? Don't God's ways seem so right and clear that others should be able to see this also? Yet 2 Timothy 3:12 says, "In fact, everyone who wants to live a godly life in Christ Jesus will be persecuted" (NIV).

If we see the Beatitudes as an absolute teaching of Jesus' character as a man filled with the Holy Spirit, and not simply as something subject to interpretation relative to society today, we will find that they represent an outlook radically different from the world's point of view. Who would ever have thought of the possibility of the Ten Commandments being removed from our city halls and courtrooms? Who would ever have thought that homosexual marriage would be an acceptable ceremony, recognized by our laws? Who would ever have thought that a pro-life Supreme Court judge nominee would be blocked from being elected? Who would ever have thought that pornography would be accessible from our homes and that our children would be able to view it on television, on the computer, or at the library? Most shocking of all, who would ever have imagined that someone in this world would try to clone a human being?

The world praises pride, not humility. The world endorses sin, especially if you can get away with it. And when we as Christians stand up against what is not right, we are persecuted. Recently, in talking with a pastor, I suggested that most churches do not stand up and fight against the gay rights movement because they are afraid they may lose their tax exemption status by getting into political issues. He replied, "No, I don't agree with that. It is because the gay rights people are so violent and radical, and people fear for their churches and lives." A pastor that Gary and I have met recently is hearing a great calling from the Lord to start a House of Prayer. But he is beginning to get so much opposition from the church where he is employed. The group that is being called to prayer and intercession is now confused, and the fact of the matter is, they are touching on the edges of persecution. The pastor may lose his job, and now faces the question of whether he will follow Jesus' leading in his life, or choose to preserve his job.

A close friend of ours, Andy Comiskey, leads Desert Stream Ministries, an international organization whose ministry is focused on setting people free from gender confusion and the gay lifestyle.[1] He told us about a conference his organization sponsored in Boston, where many in the gay lifestyle were set free by encountering the man Christ Jesus and the power of His Cross. Andy reported, however, that the reaction of the gay community was vicious and nearly violent. Hundreds of gay activists gathered outside the seminar location and screamed in hatred at Andy, his team, and those attending the conference. The person of Jesus and His call to righteousness will not be popular among many in our day. We will know the reality of being hated for His name's sake.

This is the challenge: if you have a "high calling" from God, a calling to live in righteousness and in the power of intimate friendship with Jesus, you *will* be persecuted. Are you ready?

In his book *The Purpose Driven Life* Rick Warren says,

> *Since God intends to make you like Jesus, he will take you through the same experiences Jesus went through. That*

1   See www.desertstream.org for more information concerning this significant ministry

includes loneliness, temptation, stress, criticism, rejection, and many other problems. The Bible says Jesus "learned obedience through suffering" and "was made perfect through suffering." Why would God exempt us from what he allowed his own Son to experience? Paul said, "We go through exactly what Christ goes through. If we go through the hard times with him, then we're certainly going to go through the good times with him!"[2]

After going through this teaching on the Beatitudes, you should now have a better understanding of the character of Jesus. Jesus was righteous, living in exact harmony with the character and will of God. Out of that obedient lifestyle, He was broken for us. He mourns for us. He is meek and humble. He is righteous and merciful. He is pure in His motives, actions, aspirations, and thoughts. He is a peacemaker. And for all of this He was persecuted literally to the death.

Not long ago I had a life-changing experience in which I encountered persecution. Sometimes when we are confronted with certain kinds of situations we do not immediately recognize it as persecution for righteousness, because it can be so subtle and deceptive. This particular incident hurt many people, including me. However, when I recognized that my motives had been pure and that I had been trying to do the work for the Lord, I confided in a very wise mentor friend. She told me to go back to the people involved, but this time in the opposite spirit. I did not understand what she meant, so she told me to purchase Loren Cunningham's book *Making Jesus Lord: The Dynamic Power of Laying Down Your Rights.*[3] I discovered how to respond in difficult situations with humility instead of arrogance, with kindness instead of anger. This book changed my behavior and reactions, and I realized that the Lord was teaching me something about the character of Jesus. Having released my own feelings and choosing His style instead of mine, I went back in love to some of the people involved in this experience. James 1:2-3 made a profound impact on me—"Consider it pure joy, my brothers, whenever you face trials of many kinds, because you know that the testing of your faith develops perseverance." God wanted me to learn this so that I could teach others. If God has called you to be like

2   Rick Warren, *The Purpose Driven Life* (Grand Rapids: Zondervan, 2002), 197.
3   YWAM Publishing, 1989

Jesus, He will draw you to a life that calls for self-sacrifice, humility, and obedience.

I have another story that illustrates persecution in a time of my life when I desperately needed a job. It happened shortly after I had lost my company and everything else I have mentioned earlier in this book. With the help of a friend, I had developed my first resume, which I sent out to several companies. I received a call from the president of a coffee company to come for an interview because they were looking for a branch manager. After going through numerous interviews with this company, I was encouraged to have my last one with the president once again. I was positive that the interview went well and the job was going to be mine until he asked a question of me. He said, "My men and I go out and drink after the day is over, and sometimes we curse and drink a little too much. Is that going to bother you? Because we think you will be a fit for the position." I told him that I was a Christian, I do not curse, and I would not be joining them for the drinking, but I would do a wonderful job for them otherwise. I never heard from him again even though I had all the credentials and had made it to the final interview being told I was the number-one candidate.

Other forms of persecution are more blatant. These originate with those who hate the godly. These people will fight through the legal system, or even resist physically, for things like keeping abortion legal or pornography in our libraries, keeping Christian books out of public schools, and retaining teaching on the acceptability of homosexuality.

We each have a choice as to how we respond to such persecution or attack. Though I have not experienced such overt persecution, my desire is that my personal choice would be to respond as Jesus taught in the Beatitudes—a response that manifests the fruits of the Holy Spirit. I pray that I would choose to suffer with cheerfulness, patience, self-control, gentleness, kindness, and love, bringing about peace and joy. The blessing of trying circumstances is that they expose the reality that is in our hearts, allowing us to see places where growth into the character of Jesus is necessary. It becomes easy to understand why this Beatitude follows "blessed are the peacemakers"—because as Christians who will be persecuted for following Jesus, we must continue to function as peacemakers, with patience, love, kindness, and self-control.

Two Necessary Things

There are two parts to this Beatitude that are essential to understand. The first is persecution and the second is righteousness. The persecution that Jesus is speaking of here is measured by the experience of the prophets through the centuries who were murdered for their commitment to obey God. It is not merely having to endure snide comments or being snubbed at a social event. We have so little experience of persecution in our culture that it is difficult for us to understand what Jesus is saying here. But as we consider what the Bible says, we will come to a very sober understanding of what is being declared over those who choose to live in righteousness.

A righteous person is one who, by the power of the Holy Spirit, makes the character of God the plumb line of his or her everyday life, first internally, and then externally.

The NIV Life Application Bible says that persecution can be good because:

1. It takes our eyes off earthly rewards
2. It strips away superficial belief
3. It strengthens the faith of those who endure
4. Our attitude through it serves as an example to others who follow

If we blend in with everyone else and do not stand out as Christians, probably no one will ever want what we have. Chances are, we have settled for life as usual, and complacency has become our way of life.

Somewhere along the line I decided that there must be more to my life as a believer in Jesus, because if our current experience is all we can hope for, then verses like John 14:12 haunt us:

I assure you, most solemnly I tell you, if anyone steadfastly believes in Me, he will himself be able to do the things that I do; and he will do even greater things than these, because I go to the Father. (John 14:12, AMP)

What in the world did Jesus mean when He said that we would do greater things than these? This statement has really provoked me into a place of wanting authority and power from the Lord. I am no longer satisfied to do business as usual. I have discovered through the Beatitudes that we were born for greater things.

When I began work on this book, I had been single for many years. On occasion I would write out an extensive list of the qualities that I would like my "dream man" to have. I prayed over this list. One time, after reading my list, a pastor said to me, "Oh, I see! You want Jesus himself!" Finally I decided to tear it up and let God decide what He wanted for my life.

During this time an acquaintance introduced me to a wealthy, attractive man with whom I went to dinner. It did not take long to discover that he did not even pass the first three qualities on my list. He wanted to pursue the relationship, so I gently tried to tell him that I am a dedicated Christian, with Jesus at the center of my life and values. It later got back to me, via my acquaintance, that this man had said that I was "too Christian." What a wonderful compliment! Has anyone ever commented to you that they can see Jesus in you, or that you shine with His light, or that you always seem happy? Those are the signs of being a Christian. We will all have trouble in this life, but it is how we respond in these situations that makes the difference. Expect to be criticized and persecuted for Jesus' sake.

The New Living Translation of the Bible is vivid and just a bit sarcastic in its language in 1 Corinthians 4:10-14:

Our dedication to Christ makes us look like fools, but you are so wise! We are weak, but you are so powerful! You are well thought of, but we are laughed at. To this very hour we go hungry and thirsty, without enough clothes to keep us warm. We have endured many beatings, and we have not homes of our own. We have worked wearily with our own hands to earn our living. We bless those who curse us. We are patient with those who abuse us. We respond gently when evil things are said about us. Yet we are treated like the world's garbage, like everybody's trash—right up to the present moment.

This is a very sobering statement. It made me think of an incident when I experienced hostility and rejection in circumstances in which I was trying to carry out the will of the Lord to bring souls into the kingdom of God and send them out into the world as missionaries. Instead of bitterness, anger or shame, however, the Lord showed me to pray for blessings for those who had hurt me. He showed me that, in the midst of and in spite of my circumstances, I was to call on Him for my peace, joy and contentment. During times of loneliness the Lord said to me, "I am sufficient for all your needs."

Very recently, I participated in an online survey in which the question was asked, "Do you think people in our country are abandoning God?" I voted "yes," as did over 65 percent of those who participated—in spite of the fact that over 50% of our population attends church. This, combined with the fact that statistically Christians don't take a stand against the movement to remove God from public places for fear of a militant, abusive minority, made sense to me. Don't you think that this is persecution against Christians in our own country?

I feel violated when I see my grandchildren watching violent shows on television and hear them say, "It doesn't bother us." I feel the threat of persecution growing closer when God's precious Ten Commandments are removed from public places. The court system is changing moral law that has been at the foundation of our country for decades. Do you not feel the growing menace of persecution when the liberal movement takes away the definition of marriage as a covenant between a man and a woman? Or do you say, "Oh well, there's nothing I can do about it!"? Well, you can do something—you can pray as the Lord moves your heart with compassion and love.

2 Timothy 3:12 says,

In fact, everyone who wants to live a godly life in Christ Jesus will be persecuted, while evil men and imposters will go from bad to worse, deceiving and being deceived. (NIV)

The passage that follows this is critical for your growth and walk with Jesus:

But as for you, continue in what you have learned and have become convinced of, because you know those from whom you learned it, and how from infancy you have known the holy

Scriptures, which are able to make you wise for salvation through faith in Christ Jesus. All Scripture is God-breathed and is useful for teaching, rebuking, correcting and training in righteousness, so that the man of God may be thoroughly equipped for every good work. (2 Timothy 3:14-16, NIV).

I know that many of us feel helpless in the face of the unrighteousness all around us. After all, we have been taught to have a Christlike spirit, and that we will be known by our fruits: kindness, gentleness, self-control, love, peace, patience, joy, faithfulness, and goodness. But what about the righteous anger that Jesus expressed when He threw the moneychangers out of the temple? Have we become too complacent and desensitized to sin to act when we should? Or is it that we think we are powerless to do anything?

I was up at 2:00 AM one night in need of pain medication. I decided to watch TV while I waited for the medication to take effect. Flipping through the channels, I was enraged to come across a hard porn site—the first time I had seen anything like this, and it was right in my bedroom! I decided to take action, so I complained to the property managers about the choice of channels available on residents' televisions. I was very concerned that when my grandchildren came to stay, they would happen upon a channel like this. Thankfully, only a short time later, I realized that the property managers had indeed remedied the situation. Though I was not persecuted in that situation, I believe there comes a time when we must be willing to risk being persecuted for the sake of righteousness being established.

"Blessed are those who are persecuted for righteousness sake, for theirs is the kingdom of heaven." In other words, the rule and reign of God in your life will be real, both in this age and in the age to come. Do you really believe that? Your reward is that you will be given God's kingdom as your inheritance and the authority to pray for the sick and see them healed.

I remember when I was building my restaurant and discovered that my contractor, an elder at my church, was double-billing me, my landlord and our church for bogus charges. I carefully gathered all the evidence and documented it with the help of two friends who also attended our church. I presented the evidence to the senior and assistant pastors. They appeared shocked and called a board meeting the very next week. I then presented the evidence to the board, with the elder concerned present. I was called a liar and an emotional female. I was humiliated and treated very badly. I walked out defeated.

Next, the two friends who had helped me said that they would again take this evidence and confront the elders. The board, however, would only allow one of the men to appear before them. The other had to sit in the waiting room. My friend was told that he was a traitor and that he needed to repent and apologize to the board. He, too, came out of his meeting defeated. It seemed useless to fight for righteousness because of the persecution that resulted. I questioned God, saying, "Where are You, God? I thought You had asked me to do this. Why did you leave me to the wolves?"

But Jesus was faithful. Just a few weeks later, the owner of a very large construction company and his wife were having breakfast in my restaurant. He had experienced the same sort of double-billing as the contractor for our church. He knew the truth but was concerned that if he came forward, he would lose the job, which involved millions of dollars.

So I decided to ignore this couple, because I was so disappointed that they would not back me with hard testimony. As I walked past their table, he said, "Marie, are you angry with me?"

I said "Yes." I told him that I thought that he was a coward to not come forward with the truth—all for the sake of money. His wife then said to him, "See, I told you that you should come forward and tell the truth."

I decided to sit down and listen to what they had to say. They then told me everything that was going on. Again I called my two friends, and they met me at their offices within thirty minutes. We recorded the whole story on tape, since it was so fresh in my memory. My friend then distributed copies of the tape to every board member and elder in the church. Within a couple of days the owner of the construction company was called in to verify my testimony, and the truth was exposed. However, the strange thing was that when the board announced at church on Sunday that the elder concerned was resigning, they commented on what a wonderful man he was, and how much he had done for the church. The church body was never told the truth, and I sat listening, shocked.

I soon got over my feelings of persecution and focused on the Lord, because I knew that He had chosen me to reveal the truth because of my tenacity and fortitude. I had to refuse to take the matter personally. A book by Dr. William Barclay, *The Gospel of Matthew*, helped put things in perspective for me. In it he explicitly describes the physical and mental torture to which Christians were subjected in the days of the Roman emperor, Nero. For instance, Christians were covered in pitch and set alight, to act as living torches to light his garden parties.[4]

In this country it has been unlikely that we would die or suffer physical torture for standing up for Christian standards, though I believe the day is fast approaching when harsher forms of persecution will become commonplace. However, even now we will be made fun of, hassled and worn down. Remember that life in this age is simply a testing and preparation for eternity. Your purpose in life is to pass the test, become like Jesus and prepare to meet the Lord.

Gary:

Every day, all around the world, people give their lives for the sake of the name of Jesus. The Barna Group, a Christian research organization headed by George Barna, has reported that every day more than 460 people die precisely because they are associated with the name of Jesus Christ.[5]

One such situation occurred November 21, 2002, just outside of Beirut, Lebanon, in the Mediterranean coastal city of Sidon. Bonnie Witherall had come to work that morning at the childcare center in which she served the Arabic community around Sidon. Because of the love that Jesus had poured out in her heart, Bonnie and her husband, Gary, had dedicated their lives to serving the Arabic population of southern Lebanon. Their hope was that through loving service these children of Abraham would be drawn to the heart of Jesus.

At shortly after eight o'clock in the morning, the front doorbell of the childcare center rang, and Bonnie went to see who was there. Anticipating that it would be a Lebanese mother dropping off her child, Bonnie was instead greeted by a member of a radical Islamic group who

---

4   William Barclay, *The Gospel of Matthew*, (Louisville, Ky.: Westminster John Knox, 2001), 129.

5   www.barna.org

pointed a pistol at her head and shot her between the eyes. Over the next weeks and months, Gary Witherall, along with the believers and the missionary community in that area who knew Bonnie, struggled to find some basis for comprehending this vicious and senseless murder. It was only through the ministry of the Holy Spirit that understanding came over time: there is a sharing in the sufferings of Jesus, a communion of sorrows that is precious to God, and that He promises to those who love and serve Him.

Some of the passages in the New Testament that are the most difficult to reconcile with the common worldview of the body of Christ in America today are texts that speak of persecution. Much of the approach of contemporary churches is about tolerance, unconditional acceptance, and the importance of being "seeker friendly." The common idea is that because God is kind and good, and since Jesus would never turn anyone away from relationship with Himself, the church must never insist on radical change in a person's life. While I agree that the Church exists to embrace people as they are, and that accepting people in their broken condition is at the center of Jesus' strategy, in many settings today there is a call to "tolerance," which in its current expression takes a totally non-biblical perspective. Tolerance today means a willingness to leave people where they are, avoiding at all costs any call to repentance and change. We fear that we might communicate second-class status to those who have chosen "alternative" lifestyles. The call is, *"Come one, come all! You are loved, therefore you can stay just as you are!"*

I recently watched an interview with an openly gay actor who had taken the role of a Christian in a Hollywood movie released early in 2006. This actor also claimed to be a believer in Jesus. The interviewer was questioning the actor about any tension between being a follower of Jesus and being gay. The actor's response was that he had searched his own heart and was very comfortable that his orientation and lifestyle was in no way conflicting with his relationship with God. Many church groups and leaders in our time would agree, and there has been much controversy throughout the Anglican/Episcopalian, Methodist, and Lutheran communities on issues like this, or on other issues such as abortion and women's rights.

The difficulty with these arguments is that while sounding right they are fundamentally opposed to the truth of God as revealed in the

Scriptures. There is just enough truth in these positions to lead us into horrible error if we are not in tune with what God says in His Word concerning such matters. It is absolutely true that Jesus embraces whoever will come to Him, loving them as they are. But it is absolutely untrue that Jesus will allow us to continue in unrighteousness as a lifestyle. His Word to the woman caught in adultery was powerful and pointed: "I do not condemn you. Now go, and leave your life of sin" (John 8:11, paraphrase mine). There is merciful receptivity to anyone in any condition who will come to the feet of Jesus, but there is also power to change our way of living so that we are conformed to His character and nature. Holiness is not an option: it is essential if we want to see God, if we desire to walk in the power and authority that He created us to have.[6] The grace of God that is available to change us must not be ignored or refused, or else on the day of His appearing we will find ourselves on the outside looking in.

While some leaders of congregations have no doubt heard the voice of the Lord in structuring their programs to be maximally accessible to the unbeliever, my guess is that for many other leaders it's a different thing. I'm guessing that for many the motivation is to make it easy for people to come in, give their money, hear an encouraging message and leave without being provoked in any way that would give them a reason to not return. We want the favor and the good wishes of the community. We want political correctness and tolerance as our first priority, and if those things impinge on biblical standards—well, surely gentle Jesus will understand.

To Follow Jesus Is to Pursue Righteousness

Flying right in the face of that approach to religion are the statements of Jesus about the importance of righteousness and the necessity of being conformed to His character and nature. Then, in the final Beatitude, Jesus takes it to another level and begins to speak about being persecuted for the sake of righteousness, about being hated by the world for the sake of His name. The promise of persecution because of identification with the name of Jesus is unequivocal. It is strong stuff, promised as a certain reality and not merely suggested as a possibility. If we are going to be followers of Jesus, it means that we will be those

6   See Hebrews 12:14-15

who proclaim and embody a message of righteousness. As those who make that choice, we will be in for the kind of violent resistance that has dogged the trail of truly prophetic people for millennia.

You see, it is the person, the name, and the character of Jesus that is the issue in our day. Everyone is glad to talk about God because we have redefined Him in our image. We turn to the "higher power," however we may think of Him (or Her!), and make sure that our holidays include people of all faiths. We have done away with the absolutes of the historical Christian faith, assuring ourselves that a God of kindness would surely not eliminate anyone from His presence. We use the flawed reasoning that emerges in a postmodern, relativistic society to assert that as long as people are sincere, God will embrace them at the end of the day.

When one begins to speak of the Jesus of the Bible, however, the atmosphere changes. Jesus, after all, makes claims of exclusivity. He calls people to radical discipleship, saying things like "I am the way, the truth, and the life. No one comes to the Father except through Me." (John 14:6) He makes statements that blow away the possibility of considering Him to be merely a "good teacher," insisting that He is of one essence with the Father.[7] He boldly asserted that Abraham, the historic father of faith, saw Jesus' day and rejoiced in it. When the Jewish leaders reacted with anger to this statement, Jesus invoked the secret name of God, applying it to Himself and declaring, *"Before Abraham was, I AM!"*[8] He informed His opponents that there would come a day when they would witness His return to the earth in power and glory, coming with the angelic armies of heaven to defeat His enemies and establish His righteous kingdom on the earth.[9]

These are not statements that engender positive feelings in people of other religious systems. These are exclusive statements, statements by *a man* who is also the God of the universe, claiming that one day He will descend from heaven in supernatural power to institute a literal kingdom and govern the entire planet! The assertions Jesus makes are offensive to all those who have chosen another way, for He is declaring that He alone will be supreme at the end of the day. These are the asser-

---

7   See John 10:30 and 17:22
8   See John 8:56-58
9   See Mark 13:26

tions that got Him killed, and those who follow Him and are conformed by the Holy Spirit to His image and character will receive the same reactions that He received.

In 2004, when Mel Gibson released his stunning depiction of the sacrifice of Jesus entitled *The Passion of the Christ*, the controversy was not fundamentally about anti-Semitism or too much violence. The core of the controversy was that the person of Jesus was being lifted up and exhibited in glory and power, and the world's system HATES that! When Jesus is exalted, the devils tremble and darkness is shaken.

When C. S. Lewis's beloved story *The Chronicles of Narnia: The Lion, The Witch and the Wardrobe* came to the theaters in 2005, there was again a point of controversy. Although there was much less noise than with Gibson's portrayal, the critics were once again aghast that a presentation of Jesus in the allegorical character of Aslan should be so blatant.

The name of Jesus is hated by the world today, as it has always been. And it is not only hated in faraway places inhabited by "savages" and the "unenlightened." Hatred for the name and person of Jesus is alive and flourishing in America as well. One only has to recall the tragedy of the Columbine High School massacre on April 20, 1999, in Littleton, Colorado, to realize that this is so. Two angry young boys, Eric Harris and Dylan Klebold, came to school that day armed with automatic weapons, seeking to vent their rage. Two of their victims, Cassie Bernall and Rachel Scott, were asked if they believed in Jesus. When they responded "yes," they were summarily executed. Perhaps they would have been killed regardless of the answer, but the fact remains that for these two girls and their murderers the issue was the name of Jesus.

The person of Jesus is the essential matter. The centrality of His life, death, resurrection, and soon return is paramount in our day, as it has always been. The call to righteousness empowered by the Spirit of Christ is essential, but it will not be received well by those whose hearts are turned away from God. Jesus is the issue; He always has been and always will be the issue. The simple and unshakable fact is that all those who are committed to following Him in a radical way and to declaring His call to righteousness will be hated even as He is. When you sign up to follow Him, be sure to read the fine print.

Jesus Is Just so Right!

Jesus is not only objectionable to people because He makes audacious claims concerning Himself. He is hated because He is *so right*, so holy, so uncompromising, and yet so kind and good. We could tolerate Him better if He was kind and good and had some quirks in His behavior, some chinks in His armor. If He had some hidden issues that He struggled with, we wouldn't have to wrestle with our own sense of shame and inadequacy whenever we look upon Him. The problem is that He is so perfectly *righteous* that His presence brings us to an immediate awareness that we are not. And for this He is hated.

You see, we hate anyone who breaks the curve. Remember the "curve" grading system in school? Grades are awarded according to one's standing in relation to the rest of the class. We can look pretty good as long as no one in the class really stands out above the rest. Mediocrity is acceptable as long as excellence is kept out of the picture. But when some kid shows up in school who is really smart, he or she breaks the curve, exposing the rest of us for the average students we are. Therefore, we hate that kid, even though we envy him or her.

That's what Jesus did. He broke the curve. He came and showed what true humanity was to be like—filled with humility and gentleness but with an uncompromising righteousness that was far beyond anything that could be produced by religious zeal. He lived from day to day in a vibrant and intimate relationship with God that exposed and shamed the religious leaders, and they hated Him for it. He modeled the love of God for the broken and throwaway people of the earth, exposing and angering those whose religious principles kept them at a haughty distance from those who needed God's mercy the most. He invited the "whosoevers" to come to Him and receive mercy from Him, and then to find the gracious power they needed to become like Him!

But it wasn't just the religious elite who were angered by the righteousness of Jesus. The masses who initially responded to Him with great enthusiasm eventually turned on Him as well. It became obvious that the crowds had their own agenda for Him, but He resolutely refused to do anything according to the timetable of popular opinion. When the people wanted to make Him king, He avoided them and went into hiding.[10] He understood that He had an intercessory work that had

10   See John 6:15

to be done first. He had to live perfectly by the power of the Holy Spirit, doing everything—*everything!*—according to the will and timing of the Father. He had to relinquish control of His own life and die sacrificially, atoning for the sins of all humanity. He had to be raised from the dead by the power of God into a whole new kind of human existence. He had to impart His Holy Spirit to His followers, ascend into heaven, and wait in the Father's presence until the time was right for Him to return and lay claim to His inheritance.

This insistence on waiting for the Father's timing to establish His earthly kingdom angered the common people even as His teachings, character, and power angered the leadership. The populace wanted a king *now* who would overthrow the Roman invaders, bring peace to the region, meet their physical and material needs, and generally make their life easier. They wanted a Messiah according to their felt needs, not according to the will of the Father. When Jesus refused to acquiesce to their expectations, choosing instead to wait for the Father to release all authority to Him in the fullness of time, the people turned on Him, and vented their hatred by agreeing to His murder.

Jesus was persecuted and killed because of His commitment to righteousness—the ways and purposes of God acted out in real life regardless of the short term consequences. His promise to us is that as we are conformed to His image, as the Beatitudes become the description of our lifestyle, we will experience the same kind of persecution that He endured. We will stand in the long line of prophetic people through the ages who have counted their own lives as nothing in view of the surpassing value of knowing Him and the power of His presence.

As we face the reality of this Beatitude staring at us from the pages of Scripture, we will have to wrestle with the stark contrast it presents to our cultural orientation. We have long had a belief in the body of Christ that Jesus should be made attractive. We want Him to be marketable, and if we do a good job of presenting Him as a non-offensive, tolerant servant whose main function is to bless us, the crowds will flock to our meetings and support our programs. And frankly, there is much truth to this thought *at the beginning stages of relationship with Jesus.*

Jesus comes on the scene wooing people with compassion, acts of mercy, and powerful deliverance. He is kind to the broken, and accessible to those eliminated from the religious circles of the day. He makes friends with tax collectors and sinners, and prostitutes are comfortable in His presence. Even though His words are strong and uncompromising, people can avoid dealing with the implications of His teachings because the pressure is not yet on them. But when Jesus insists that we must really live like He speaks, He gets into trouble. When it becomes clear that He means to open His kingdom exclusively to those who respond to His invitations to intimate friendship leading to character transformation, He begins to be provocative and controversial.

It disturbs us when Jesus tells us that we will be persecuted if we identify with Him, choosing righteousness as the real goal of our lifestyle and character. In Matthew 24:9, Jesus is even more overt, insisting that at the time of the end of the age "they will deliver you up to tribulation and kill you, and you will be hated by all nations for My name's sake." This is going to happen to us, in our day, in the "normal" circumstances of our lives, to the degree that we are conformed to the image of Jesus and His character of righteousness. The very thing for which we hunger and thirst, the pathway to power and authority on earth as it is in heaven, is going to get some of us killed!

We may well ask this question: "*If this righteousness thing is going to get me killed, how can it be the pathway to my power potential? What good is power going to do me if I'm dead?*" The answer is simple and profound: Your life does not end with what happens to you in this time frame. Jesus' kingdom is not *primarily* of this present age, and the power and authority for which we long and yearn is not going to be exercised *primarily* before He returns to the earth. There will be a partial fulfillment of the promise, but the fullness of what we're after will only be ours in the age to come, in the kingdom that Jesus establishes on the earth. Then it will be ours forever. The fundamental choice that faces us is this: will we opt for the pursuit of real power and authority that will be expressed in the ages of eternity, or will we settle for the radically inferior power that comes by the assertion of our strength and only endures for this present, evil moment?

Jesus was clear in His teachings. He told parables of kings and masters that entrusted monetary means to servants to see what kind of stewards they were. When the servants did well with what they had been given, they were promised great power and authority *in the age to come.[11]* Jesus is always looking forward to the reality of His eternal kingdom, never measuring things in the short term. He intends to be King over all things, and He intends to share His authority with a Bride who is like Him. The more we pursue Him and are made to be like Him, the less palatable we will be to the people of a worldly system that has totally different values and goals.

So What Does the Bible Say about Persecution?

Nave's Topical Bible, a well-respected resource for Bible students, lists over seventy-five different chapters in the Scripture that speak of the persecution of the righteous. I want to list some of these passages, with a short comment attached to each one.

Psalm 11:2 states that *"the wicked . . . make ready their arrow on the string, that they may shoot secretly at the upright in heart."* There is a hatred at the heart of wickedness, and the focus of that hatred is righteousness and those who live in it.

Psalm 37:32 asserts that *"the wicked watches the righteous, and seeks to slay him."* The truth about tolerance is that the righteous will not be tolerated by the wicked of the earth.

Proverbs 29:10 tells us that *"the bloodthirsty hate the blameless,"* and Isaiah 29:20 reports that *"all who watch for iniquity are cut off."* Those who are unrighteous are driven by the rage of Satan, and their anger is focused on those who have the character of God.

In Isaiah 59:15 the prophet declares that *"he who departs from evil makes himself a prey,"* while Jeremiah 2:30 informs us that the sword of those who resist the Word of God *"devoured the prophets like a destroying lion."*

The prophet Amos adds his understanding in Amos 5:10 by saying, *"They hate the one who rebukes in the gate, and they abhor the one who speaks uprightly,"* and Habakkuk closes out the Old Testament record by asking the people of God why they stay silent *"when the wicked devours a person more righteous than he?"*

Moving into the New Testament record, we hear the resounding of Jesus' words to the disciples in Matthew 10:22—*"You will be hated by all for My name's sake. But he who endures to the end will be saved."*

11   See Matthew 25:21,23

More than twenty times in the Gospels Jesus warns His disciples that if they follow Him and declare His teachings, they will be physically persecuted, beaten and killed for the sake of His name.

The book of Acts carries on this theme in chapter 5, verse 41, where we are told that the disciples, having been beaten for preaching the truth about Jesus, were *"rejoicing that they were counted worthy to suffer His name."* Acts 7:52 asks a penetrating question: *"Which of the prophets did your fathers not persecute? And they killed those who foretold the coming of the Just One."*

Beloved, *we* are the ones who are foretelling the coming of the Just One! It is this same Jesus who is returning to establish His kingdom on the earth, and the world is no more excited to hear about it this time than they were the first time He came. Even as they persecuted the prophets, so they will persecute all who seek to live according to righteousness and for the sake of the name of Jesus.

The apostle Paul carries on the litany in his second letter to the Corinthians, where he gives this description of the life of an apostle:

> *We are hard-pressed on every side, yet not crushed; we are perplexed, but not in despair; persecuted, but not forsaken; struck down, but not destroyed – always carrying about in the body the dying of the Lord Jesus, that the life of Jesus also may be manifested in our body. For we who live are always delivered to death for Jesus' sake, that the life of Jesus also may be manifested in our mortal flesh. So then death is working in us, but life in you. (2 Corinthians 4:8-12)*

More than twenty times Paul gives voice to the reality of persecution in his life as a follower of Jesus and a preacher of righteousness. It's a far cry from the privileged life of the so-called "apostles" of our day whose path is garnished with favor and honor, recognition and prosperity. Admittedly, I like favor and prosperity as much as anyone, but I'm forced to give way to the weight of Jesus' words that if I am truly given over to His character and the message of His kingdom, I am going to be persecuted. As a matter of fact, the presence or absence of persecution in one's life seems to be a biblical barometer for righteousness. The more that righteousness is the focus of our message and the practice of our lives, the more we will live under the scourge of persecution.

The epistle of James speaks of this, as do the letters of Peter, the letters of John, the letter to the Hebrews, and the book of Revelation. It is everywhere in the Scripture, and we cannot avoid the message that if we follow Jesus closely, if we experience the transforming power of the Holy Spirit, if we love His Word and His ways, we will be persecuted by those whose hearts are captivated by the distortions of the spirit of this age.

So, What's the Payoff?

There has to be some sort of reward for this, right? A blessing statement has been attached to each of the Beatitudes, and we need to be certain that a blessing is coming to those who endure the difficulties promised here. And indeed, there is the promise of great reward in the age to come. Doesn't that pique your interest? What could Jesus mean when He speaks of "great reward in heaven?" It is the reward of joy that comes to those who are numbered with the prophets of old, those who have laid down their lives for the sake of Jesus and for His message of righteousness and truth.

The kingdom of God belongs to those who by the transforming power of the Holy Spirit are made into the likeness of Jesus. His presence, His rule, and His reign over all that exists will be the reward that is given to those who are persecuted for the sake of righteousness. We cannot begin to comprehend the wonder and glory of that reward. All we can say is that a very real day is coming when everything will be fully conformed to the way God designed it to be. There will be no sickness, no death, no war, no disagreement between family members. There will be no confusion of identity, no lack, no hunger, no crime, no perversion. There will only be righteousness—everything functioning in the way it was created to function, with the fullness of God's blessing all around every day. The kingdom of heaven is coming to the earth! That's the reward I want, and it's the reward that will come to those whose hearts are captured by this glorious Man.

Jesus, make me to be just like You.

POWER POINT FOR THIS CHAPTER:

As we make the character and power of Jesus the goal of our lives, we set ourselves up for harsh and evil resistance from those who do not love Him.

FOR DISCUSSION AND REFLECTION:

1. Since being persecuted for the sake of Jesus' name is still mostly unthinkable in our American culture, consider some things for which you might experience resistance for standing up for what is right. Write these things in your personal journal.

2. List any pressures you feel that would keep you from taking a stand on issues of righteousness.

3. As you consider situations like the Columbine massacre, how would you prepare yourself to answer the question, "Do you believe in Jesus?" if you knew the answer could cost you your life?

4. Begin to write a list of situations and issues concerning which you are determined to stand up for the sake of righteousness, for the sake of the name of Jesus.

5. Share this list with your group of friends, and pray over one another for the grace to stand in coming times of persecution.

OUR STORY TODAY—REACHING FOR OUR POWER POTENTIAL

Marie:

As I write this, Gary and I find ourselves in Maui, Hawaii, celebrating our first anniversary and teaching at the Youth With A Mission base with twenty-six students in a Discipleship Training School. It is hard to believe that we have been married a year already.

The other day I was thinking back on what God had spoken to me at the beginning of 2005. It was clear that we were to take a year to blend the new family, and then after that year God would birth the ministry He had for us. The Lord was faithful to His word this week. The story goes like this.

During the first year of our marriage, the Lord began to tell Gary and me that we must align ourselves spiritually and mentally with Him. That meant that the inside of our home, our thoughts, and our behavior must line up with our teaching. He was beginning to impress on us the urgency of righteousness in our teaching, and He was insistent on our living that way. It was clear to us that the Lord wanted to blend the message of what Gary has taught for years on intimacy with Jesus together with my understanding of the Beatitudes in Matthew 5, in the Sermon on the Mount. I had studied them for many years, had written a manuscript, and had witnessed several people—including me—being healed through the Beatitudes.

Our relationship with each other began in November of 2004, when Gary was our speaker at an event that I was involved with called "The Kona Encounter." I was on contract with YWAM's University of the Nations in Kona, Hawaii, raising money for the university. The Kona Encounters was an event to familiarize potential donors with the university while teaching on the "Father Heart of God."

Gary had lost his wife to cancer the previous summer, and I had been single for about fifteen years. I yearned inside to be married to a man who chased after intimacy with Jesus and had a deep compassion for people whom the Lord wanted to heal. My heart burned for the broken and the lost. I was beginning to lose hope that I would ever have my prayers answered. But in the weeks prior to the Encounter, a friend named Mindy had called to tell me that she had heard that Gary was to be our speaker. She believed that God was sending him to me as His choice to be my husband.

It was Saturday, November 6, 2004, when I picked up our speaker, Gary, and his friend Dave at the airport. Our event would begin with a reception at the Orchid Hotel that evening.

The first time I set eyes on Gary I knew that he was the person for me. Funny feelings began to take place in my spirit and through my whole person. That evening at the reception I had difficulty concentrating. The next day, when he began to teach, my heart melted because of the love he had for the Lord and his teaching about intimacy with Christ. Later in the week many of the people attending the encounter, including staff, began to tell me they had a feeling that the timing was right for me to meet the man that the Lord had chosen for me. I even asked two of the couples if they could pray specifically for Gary to come into my life, and they said they already had been. They, too, felt that Gary was the person God had chosen for me.

During the week and through the teaching the Lord began to work on my heart regarding my shame secret that I had carried for years— the fact that I had been married several times. Through a story that Gary was telling about a man that was deep into pornography and then tried to commit suicide because of his shame, I had an encounter with God that sent me into deep pain, physically and spiritually. The Lord wanted to heal me so that he could bring Gary into my life. He had an enormous purpose for my life, but I needed to be healed from shame first, as it would always hold me back from being transparent and telling the truth about God's mercy and grace.

Toward the end of the week many people had their lives transformed, and I was delivered from my shame as I shared my dark secrets with a group of friends from the Encounter. Following that, my friend Julie walked me through a deliverance of confession and prayer. It was the end of the week, and Gary had already left to teach in Denmark. He had never even really noticed me, even though we were in several of the same social settings throughout the week.

I was convinced that everyone, including me, had misheard God about this new romance. How could I have been so silly, behaving so like a teenager that week? How could my friend Mindy have misheard God when she said, "I know that God told me that Gary is the man for you."

I returned to Seattle, and a couple of days later I received a call from Mindy asking me how things turned out for Gary and me. I reported that nothing happened and nothing ever would. She informed me that she was certain that she heard the Lord and was going to send Gary an e-mail about the issue. I replied that this would not be a good idea. She insisted, and I relented with the stipulation that I see the note before she sent it. She sent the e-mail to Gary in Denmark, but did not send it to me first. In fact, I never read the e-mail until a couple of months later.

It was shocking! She had titled the e-mail "Your future wife." In the e-mail she told him that I was in love with him and that I was the perfect woman for him. She embellished my attributes to a degree of embarrassment. But the e-mail did get his attention.

Gary:

Shortly after Mary's death in June of 2004, I began to receive prophetic words about marriage from people I knew and trusted. One young man gave me a book on marriage, reporting that he had felt led by the Holy Spirit to give it to me. Another good friend shared that he had been impressed that God was going to sideswipe me with romance and knock me off my feet. Two women that are part of the leadership team at the International House of Prayer in Kansas City had similar dreams in which they saw a tall, blonde woman approach me and sweep me off my feet, and then we went off together.

So I began to ask the Lord about these things, because frankly, I would be in a mess as a single man. I needed a wife then, and I need one now! My teenage daughter Rachel needed someone to step into the void in her life left by her mom's death, and so I was in a receptive mode.

When I got to Kona for the Encounter week, Marie met my friend Dave Gerry and me at the airport. I assumed she was an assistant of some sort, and in my arrogance I really didn't pay much attention to her. I didn't realize at all the kind of highly gifted and called woman she is! I had no idea of the feelings and conversations that were happening in the background, and I was oblivious to the whole dynamic that was emerging. In fact, when my friend Dave encouraged me halfway through the week to consider Marie as a focus of interest, I blew off his suggestion in a rather flippant way.

The week progressed, and while I was impressed at her boldness and strength, no signals were going off in my spirit that anything was going to come of this new acquaintance. So when the week ended and we said our farewells, I felt no sense of disappointment or letdown, since I had not been aware of anything during the week.

The following week I was in Denmark teaching at a Bible college when Mindy's e-mail came. The subject line slapped me in the face, and I instantly knew who it was Mindy was referring to. The e-mail was bold to the point of outrageous, with Mindy offering to serve as a matchmaker between us, even though I didn't yet know for certain the identity of this woman of my dreams. I wrote back and asked Mindy to tell me the woman's name, saying that I would pray about the matter and take any steps I felt the Holy Spirit wanted me to take.

Mindy sent me another e-mail with Marie's name in it, and I realized that I had known in my spirit from the moment I received the first note that this was something the Lord was doing. I felt very cautious and uncertain, but strangely excited. I had no contact information—no e-mail address or phone number—and so I simply prayed and told the Lord that if He opened the door, I would walk through it.

The next day I got an e-mail from Marie. She had sent out a note to all those who attended the Encounter telling some of the stories of what God had done. One story was particularly compelling. And now I had an e-mail address. I decided to knock on the door ever so slightly and see if it would open.

I responded to Marie's note in very general terms, acknowledging that I had enjoyed the week, that the stories were delightful, and that it would be nice to do this again sometime. Who knows, I said, maybe we would play golf together and become friends. Click "send."

I got a response in mere minutes. Marie's next note said that she would like to become friends, and perhaps it would be best if I would take the lead on that. She also said that she was going to include one of the stories she told in a book she was writing.

My heart began to beat faster as I realized that perhaps God was doing something here. I wrote back once again, mentioning that I had written a couple of books and that I'd be interested in reading hers. By this time a few days passed. I returned from Denmark and headed to my friend Dave's home in Wisconsin, where I was when Marie sent the manuscript that was the foundation for the book you are reading.

Marie:

Gary and I began to correspond via e-mail for about two weeks. In the first week I made reference in our conversation to the fact that I had written a manuscript surrounding the Sermon on the Mount with an emphasis on the Beatitudes. He asked me to send it to him. Fear gripped my heart, because over the previous couple of years I had inserted my life story into the manuscript. You see, the journey that I had taken in my life toward healing was the same journey that was spelled out in the Beatitudes. The Lord had purposely put the Beatitudes in that order that broken people might be led through a healing process.

Now the test was before me. Would I truly trust the Lord that He has taken away my shame through His death on the cross and that Gary would accept me just as I am—forgiven and cleansed? I took that step of faith and pushed the send button on my computer because the Lord had spoken to me and said "Send it imperfect as you are imperfect." I went to bed a couple of hours later knowing that if Gary was the man that the Lord had sent to me, he would accept me with the same love that Jesus has for me.

Gary:

When I received the manuscript I spent the entire next night reading through it. I must say I was unnerved by the devastating nature of the situations that Marie had endured, and by her frankness in telling the stories. My mind had not been prepared for what God was doing, and I felt myself trembling a bit at the prospect that was before me.

The Lord's response to me was immediate and stern. I was suddenly aware that I was reacting out of a spirit of religious pride, and God was not pleased. I sensed His word coming to me in my mind and spirit, saying: "Gary, if you withdraw from Marie because of these issues in her history, you are a fraud. You will never again preach the Bridal Paradigm with integrity or with power."

Needless to say, I was stunned with the quickness and finality of the Holy Spirit's word to me. I knew that it was true and that God was bringing me into this relationship for His own purposes. You see, the whole gospel reality is that Jesus gave Himself for a weak and broken Bride, to love her into wholeness and establish her as His perfect counterpart and eternal partner in authority and power. God wanted this relationship to reflect His story and to illustrate the gospel in a flesh-and-blood way.

I responded to the Lord, saying that if He was doing this in my life, then I wanted His love for Marie to be poured out in my heart. Within minutes I began to feel the surge of His love filling me, and my heart began to pound with anticipation of this new romance that was being released.

Marie:

Gary tells me that he stayed up all night reading the manuscript. He said that he was surprised and saddened at the same time by my story. I can well imagine the shock he had when he read about the many extraordinary events of my life. Sometimes it is hard for even me to believe the extreme highs and lows in my life.

The next day when Gary called me and told me the Lord was giving him *His* love for me, I knew that Gary was my gift from the Lord for which I had prayed for many years. I knew that even though I had failed the Lord in areas of obedience, when He spoke to me I was forgiven because I never turned my back on Him or blamed Him for my troubles. Gary was my prize.

We were married three months from when we met. We had a beautiful wedding in Kona during a time when Gary was teaching another Kona Encounter. We had the honor of having Loren Cunningham, founder of Youth With A Mission, perform the ceremony. He saw the Lord merging two people with ministry mandates from the Lord.

I had to move to Kansas City, Missouri, leaving all my children, grandchildren, and friends behind. I had just purchased my home in Seattle, Washington, eight months prior. It had an English garden that I dearly loved and a view of Puget Sound. It was a home in which I felt so safe, in which the Holy Spirit had done much restoration in my life. And now I was moving to a state where the summers were so hot and humid and many people did not welcome me because of their love for Gary's deceased wife. What in the world was God doing now? But I sensed I was in for another huge assignment from the Lord and this one was going to be very exciting. A dear friend had shared with me years earlier that she had a dream in which she had a "knowing" that I was going to be speaking to thousands of people and that through the pain and restoration of my life God was going to heal them.

Gary:

As Marie and I began our relationship, it became clear that part of God's plan for us was to model the Bridal Paradigm in our ministry together. If the plan of God is to reveal the romance in His heart toward His Bride, it made sense to us that He would want to exhibit that reality through our lives as we minister to His people. Right from the beginning we knew that we would be teaching side by side, giving voice and expression to His purposes.

This reality was a huge answer to a long-standing question I had of the Lord. Through the course of my life in ministry, I had received in the neighborhood of twenty-five prophetic statements that my wife and I would be standing side by side, teaching and ministering together. I had always taken that literally, but because of Mary's personality and gift mix, that promise had never materialized.

When Mary died, that question loomed large in my mind: *Lord, what about the promise of teaching with my wife? What was that all about?* You can imagine my surprise when the Holy Spirit spoke to my heart and said that the promise was still good. I realize now that in the mystery of God's sovereignty, He had known all of this and was now releasing that prophecy in the context of my new marriage to Marie.

Marie:

In the first part of our marriage the Lord spoke to us about His insistence that we be the same on the inside of our home as we are on the outside. The Lord began to show us that the way to His divine power was through righteousness. Gary's involvement in leadership at the International House of Prayer in Kansas City allowed me the privilege of spending hours in the prayer room seeking the Lord on what that meant to Him. I cried out for many days to the Lord to give me deeper understanding and revelation regarding His heart and sufferings.

One time Gary and I were teaching in New Mexico, and I was awakened at 1:00 AM to the Lord's voice saying "In the courtyard you will have understanding." When Gary awoke in the morning I asked him what that meant. He explained that outside the temple in biblical times there was a courtyard where the people worshiped the Lord. We believed God was telling me to keep pressing into worship in the prayer room because I would receive understanding there.

My heart broke with sadness and longing every time I would go to the prayer room and hear the singers crying out for Jesus to come in His power. I saw the wonderful young adults praying for healings, and yet not much power was coming from the Lord. Yes, there were healings here and there but not in the abundance of divine power that we were praying for. Then Gary began to receive from the Lord a poverty of spirit as he realized that he grieved the loss of healing anointing that he had known some years before, but that had been forfeited through his pride and arrogance. He began to ask the Lord to forgive him and restore the gift that he knows the Lord did not take away. We saw that the Lord was waiting for both of us to come to that place of repentance and righteousness as forerunners in what God desires to do in the Church, His Bride.

So we pressed into repentance and proceeded to get pretty beat up in the process. We knew in a way that the Lord was spanking us, but the reward was going to be great as we came into obedience and alignment with Him. One day in the prayer room the Lord showed me that we would see the deaf hear, the paralyzed walk, and the blind see. He gave me a Scripture on which to meditate concerning Peter's restoration in John 21. The Lord commanded Peter to "throw your net on the right side of the boat." When Peter obeyed, there was an astonishing catch of fish, and that day Peter was restored to his calling and destiny. I knew through a revelation that the Lord was saying, "If you throw yourselves into righteousness, you will be restored and you will see the miracles that you are crying out for."

Along the way the Lord was really pressing hard into Gary for change, and I was feeling a bit smug about myself. God had not yet spoken to me about the evil in my heart, until one day I heard Him say, "This is what I hold against you." He brought back to my mind the year 1991, when I had just recently moved to Seattle. I still had a lot of money at that time, and I was sitting at my kitchen table asking the Lord how much money I should send to my sister Denise and her two children for Christmas. She was a single mom with two small children. I had previously helped her start a cookie store at the University of Minnesota campus, and she had done quite well until the IRS made a serious mistake. As I prayed about the amount to send her, I thought that $500 would be sufficient, but I heard what I thought was God telling me to send her $3,000. I was a bit stunned at the amount and then went about arguing with the Lord, until I became convinced it was Him. So I wrote the check for $3,000 and set it on the kitchen table. Two weeks later I received a frantic call from her. She was crying because the IRS had frozen her meager checking account and her children's $700 savings account. She told me her house payment was going to bounce along with her other bill payments. My sister had never asked me for any money, so when I asked her the amount it did not come as a surprise to me when she said she needed $2,500. Yes, you guessed it! The $500 that I was going to give her plus the $2,500 amounted to the $3,000.

I picked up the check and put it in the mail, and it became a great testimony on hearing the voice of the Lord. But this is what the Lord held against me. My heart was evil because I made her pay it back as soon as the IRS found her innocent and returned the money. The Lord spoke to me again making it clear that His intent was for that money to be a gift and not a loan.

Recently I told Gary what the Lord had told me and that I must now return to my sister the $2,500 and ask for forgiveness. Gary responded that he sensed I was to double it and give her $5,000. In my heart I knew he was right. So a couple of days later we were in Minneapolis, and I gave her the check. She told me that the night before I had called she had been crying out to the Lord about her finances. She asked the Lord if he would increase their income because they had been faithful, and the next day she received my call. What a blessing it was to me to be able to hand over the $5,000 and see my sister's face.

At the same time, the Lord was speaking to Gary about getting affirmation from the wrong sources. He was showing him how broken he was in this place. Gary went to the very difficult place of repentance and then mourning for his sin. These times really affected me; however, the fruit of those times are worth it now.

Another image that was shown to me came in January of 2006. It was the picture we have previously described of a house shaking with power that is bursting from the roof. I saw that "Righteousness" was the address, and then I had the impression that the Beatitudes are the roadmap to the address. What a startling and remarkable word picture! God was giving us more insight into how we can have righteousness formed in our lives.

A Token of Coming Power

In January of 2006, Gary and I traveled to Paia, Maui, to teach at the YWAM base. Paia is a spiritually dark place with much Buddhist and New Age influence. There are many who live on the streets or in broken down cars, and I thought I had stepped back into the 1970s hippie days. It was not at all how I had envisioned Maui. But Gary and I were very grateful to the Lord for providing this trip for us as we were able to celebrate our first wedding anniversary in Hawaii, in close proximity to where we had gotten married. We had a sweet anniversary present from the Lord for which we are very thankful.

On the way over to Maui I was praying and asking the Lord to give us a divine power encounter with Him indicating that we were on the right track with the message of righteousness and the Beatitudes. I actually asked God to show us a real miracle. When we arrived at the airport and were picked up by the staff, we found out there would be twenty-six students. We discovered later that one of the young men, Steven, was twenty-three years old and a deaf mute. He had been born prematurely, weighing two pounds at birth. He had never been able to hear or to speak plainly.

The first day of class began on a Monday morning with Gary and I telling about our lives. I noticed soon after we had started teaching that Steven was in the front row with his interpreter sitting parallel to us. The Lord almost immediately started to impress on me His sorrow for Steven's deafness. Steven could barely be understood when he spoke, so I was quite surprised when I saw him the next day on stage with a microphone telling everyone about the Lord and how he suffered on the cross for our sins. It was so difficult for me to understand him, and I felt pain for this young man because I realized he had the gifting of a preacher.

That is the day the Lord infused into my heart to pray for Steven's healing. All through the week Gary and I taught on intimacy with Jesus and His soon coming as a Bridegroom King for His Bride, the Church. Through the week there was lots of prayer and repentance with kids coming to a place of forgiveness and mercy in their hearts as they began to receive the message of God's love for them. Gary taught them how to prophecy over their own lives from the Word of God, singing the Psalms out loud with a microphone. It was so precious especially to see the self-conscious young men sing with voices that sounded lovely only in heaven. Their hearts had been changed—and oh, how the Lord must have rejoiced with their sweet melodies as they raised their voices to heaven!

The next Monday Gary and I knew that we had to begin to teach on the Beatitudes, leading the students to righteousness. We taught for the first day on the nature of Jesus as the normal human being, Who is for us the model of life in the power of the Holy Spirit. Much animated discussion took place as the students' traditional perceptions of Jesus were challenged by the teaching of the Word.

On Tuesday we began to teach the Beatitudes. At the morning break that day, Steven came up to us and told us that he knew the day had come, that he had the faith for his healing. He said that he had a feeling in his stomach that God was going to heal him. So we decided to interrupt the teaching session for a time of prayer. I quickly went over to summon the school's leader and asked him to come quickly. We all gathered around Steven, but before we prayed for him, we asked the Lord to show us our sins and asked for a cleansing. Some of the students confessed sin to each other in repentance. What a beautiful sight that was!

For the next three hours we worshiped the Lord and prayed for Steven, asking the Lord to clear his ear canals, restore his damaged nerves, and empower his speech. Many of the girls were praying with a true intercessor's heart, like that of Mary of Bethany, weeping over Steven's brokenness.[1] Many of the students broke off from time to time to begin praying the Scriptures over him. For myself, I have never prayed like that before, and I could not stop crying for this precious young man that has endured so many challenges in his life.

About halfway through, Gary stopped everyone and asked the interpreter to sign to Steven. Gary asked her to find out from Steven if there had been any changes. Steven said that he could hear the keyboard, the girls singing, and a baby crying. We were all so encouraged, so we decided to all fast through lunch and pray until we felt the Lord's release. Gary and I left about 2:00 PM, and the rest left shortly after.

That night I could not sleep, and I prayed for Steven until almost 3:00 AM. We found out later that four of the girls had been awake most of the night in a terrific spiritual battle. They finally went to sleep with their Bibles on their chests, hugging them tightly.

The next morning after we taught until noon, Steven approached Gary and me and told us he had pain behind both of his ears all night, and they were continuing to pop. Also, a staff leader came and told me about heat she had felt in her hands when she laid them on Steven's ears the day before. Steven had also felt the heat. I knew then that the Lord was giving her the faith to step forward for healing prayer to be answered. So I asked her to join us right then to pray again for Steven's healing. The four of us sat down on the floor and prayed that what healing had been done would be completed.

Gary and I then left for lunch and returned to our place to take a rest. Three of the students were waiting for us in the driveway. They approached Gary, demanding that we come with them for a surprise they had. Gary and I hurried to the women's residence to find about

1   See her story in Luke 10:38-42, and in John 11:1-44.

fifteen students gathered in a circle. When they saw us, they all yelled out in unison, "Steven!" and he came out of the house with a huge grin. We were shocked beyond words—Steven could hear! God had done the most incredible miracle that I had ever seen in my life. Gary wept as he held Steven close in his arms. And then I noticed something really amazing; I could understand Stephen's words even though his speech patterns were still far from perfect.

Later that evening Gary made a call to the house that Steven was living in, and Steven answered the phone. Before this, he had used the phone for the first time in his life to call home to tell his parents. Their answer to him was, "Yes, we knew the Lord was going to heal you."

Steven's full healing is still in process, but the students believe that by the time he completes his outreach in five months it will be finished. What an awesome incredible God we have! All I could think of to say was, "BIG GOD!"

Gary and I have returned home, and we are committed to prayer and fasting more than ever, because the Lord has told us that we will see the blind see, the deaf hear, and the paralyzed walk out of wheelchairs. We believe that we are all on a threshold of seeing the most amazing miracles as we walk in righteousness through the revelation of the Beatitudes. So if you want to experience the Lord's freedom from the broken and bound up places in your life, stepping into His divine power, then say "yes" to righteousness and make that decision to never stop pursuing the kingdom of God and His righteousness.

Gary:

While this book has ended, the story is continuing, and will be going on until the day of Jesus' return. When we see Him, we will come into the full inheritance that is ours as the children of God, the Bride of Christ. Our prayer is that you have been challenged and provoked to pursue your destiny of power, and that in pursuing the character of Jesus through the study of the Beatitudes, you will reach your power potential, receiving authority on earth as it is in heaven.

Other Resources from Gary Wiens

816-216-7159 • fax 816-216-7159
www.burningheartministries.com

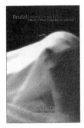

BRIDAL INTERCESSION: A book for such a time as this, approaching the topic of intercessory prayer from the perspective of the Church's place as the Bride of Christ.

COME TO PAPA: Encountering the Father that Jesus Knew. The glory of our Father's infinite goodness.

SONGS OF A BURNING HEART: Text, Poetry, Music & Art (CD included). With passion and artistry, Gary expresses the beauty and emotion of the human heart in the place of longing after the Person of God.

THE FAIREST OF TEN THOUSAND (15-CD album set). A consideration of the attributes of the King spoken by the Shulamite in Song of Solomon 5:10-16.

BRIDAL INTERCESSION CD SET: This 10-CD set is a great way to get the contents of the *Bridal Intercession* book for those who prefer listening to reading, and for those whose lifestyle requires input on the go.

COME TO PAPA CD SET: This 14-CD set is a great way to get the contents of the *Come To Papa* book for those who prefer listening to reading, and for those whose lifestyle requires input on the go.

ORDER FORM
Resources by Gary Wiens

(For complete list of resources, visit www.burningheartministries.com)

	Qty.	Price	Total
BOOKS:			
BRIDAL INTERCESSION	_____	$10.00	_____
COME TO PAPA: *Encountering the Father that Jesus Knew*	_____	$10.00	_____
SONGS OF A BURNING HEART: *Text, Poetry, Music & Art (CD included)*	_____	$20.00	_____
TEACHING CDS:			
THE FAIREST OF TEN THOUSAND (15-CD album set)	_____	$60.00	_____
BRIDAL INTERCESSION (10-CD album set)	_____	$50.00	_____
COME TO PAPA (14-CD album set)	_____	$60.00	_____

Subtotal _____

Shipping Add 10% (Minimum of $2.00) _____

Missouri Residents Add 7.35% Sales Tax _____

Total Enclosed   (U.S. Funds Only) _____

Send payment with order to: BURNING HEART MINISTRIES
P.O. Box 481843
Kansas City, MO 64148

Name _____

Address: Street _____

City _____ State _____

Zip _____ Email _____

For MasterCard/VISA orders and quantity discounts, call 816-216-7159
or order on our website: *www.burningheartministries.com.*